MR. GREGORY'S LETTER-BOX
1813–1835

The Coole Edition
General Editors
T. R. Henn, C.B.E., Litt.D.
Colin Smythe, M.A.

MR. GREGORY'S LETTER-BOX
1813 - 1835
EDITED BY LADY GREGORY

with a foreword by
Jon Stallworthy

NEW YORK
OXFORD UNIVERSITY PRESS
1982

First published 1898
Second edition published in 1981 by Colin Smythe Ltd.
Gerrards Cross, Buckinghamshire as the twentieth volume
of the Coole Edition
Published in the United States by
Oxford University Press, New York
in 1982

Library of Congress Cataloging in Publication Data

Main entry under title:

Mr. Gregory's letter-box, 1813–1835.

(Coole edition; v. 20)
Includes index.
Contents: Mr. Gregory's letter-box – Orangeism
and emancipation – Lord Whitworth, Peel, and the
fear of France – [etc.]
1. Ireland – History – 1800-1837 – Sources.
2. Gregory, William, 1766-1840. I. Gregory, Lady,
1852-1932. II. Gregory, William, 1766-1840.
III, Series: Gregory, Lady, 1852-1932. Coole
edition; v. 20.
DA950.M7 1981   941.5081   81–9436

ISBN 0–19–520281–3   AACR2

Printed in Great Britain

FOREWORD

WHEN Augusta Persse, to everyone's surprise, became Lady Gregory she moved some considerable distance up the social scale but, in the topographical scale, only seven miles to the south-west. Leaving Roxborough – perhaps in the phaeton that was her wedding present from her dashing step-brother, Dudley – she came to a house significantly different from the bustling mansion in which she had been brought up. Although Dudley's namesake, Dean of the diocese of Kilmacduagh, had built his house at Roxborough long before there were Gregorys at Coole, Sir William Gregory's twenty-eight-year-old bride found her own home, unlike her father's house, reverberant with echoes of a proud past. Her love and reverence for her husband's white, eighteenth-century house deepened during the long years of her widowhood to be distilled at last in *Coole,* that lyrical essay printed and published at the Cuala Press in 1931.[1]

This opens with an account of the library, evidently her favourite room, and her meditation on its other occupants throws as much light on her as on the lustrous shelves.

Of the successive generations that have possessed them I think it was to one only they were dumb. Yet, not even one inheritor I believe, could have been so dull of eye as to fail to delight in the mere appearance of these walls of leather and vellum, mellowed by passing centuries, in the sudden illumination of golden ornament and lettering as the sun sinks towards the western hills.[2]

[1] A second edition (incorporating two chapters newly transcribed from the manuscript), edited by Colin Smythe and with a Foreword by Edward Malins, was published by the Dolmen Press in 1971.

[2] Compare with stanza 4 of Yeats's 'Coole Park and Ballylee, 1931'
> *Beloved books that famous hands have bound,*
> Old marble head, old pictures everywhere;
> Great rooms where travelled men and children found
> Content or joy; *a last inheritor . . .*
>   (my italics)
This poem of course was written in the same year as Lady Gregory's *Coole* was published.

5

The riddle of that passage is explained on a later page:

> And as to William, the Under-Secretary, though he had been
> a good latin scholar at Harrow and Cambridge, I find little
> or nothing that he and Lady Anne added to the shelves, nor
> did they I fancy often disturb them, having their converse less
> with print than with people, living as they did chiefly in that
> still brilliant society of Dublin . . . the Viceroys and the Chief
> Secretary, Whitworth, Talbot, Wellesley, Anglesey, Peel,
> Goulburn, Lamb. He and Lady Anne, dining out, giving
> dinners, in the midst of history in the making, what printing
> on a page could compare with the weighty and the witty talk
> to which those ears were used?

Strangely, perhaps in part because of a certain resemblance to
her husband, William the Under-Secretary and least literary of
the Gregorys captured the imagination of his grandson's literary
bride. He may have added nothing to the shelves of the Library,
but he left another legacy – in a large, iron-clamped, leather-
covered box bearing the inscription: "Correspondence of the
Right Honourable William Gregory, 1813–1835".

Augusta and her husband talked of reading through its contents,
but it was not until some years after his death in 1892 that, "being
alone, with patience and long evenings on [her] side, [she] set to
work, and came at last to the bottom of the box". Her decision to
edit the correspondence, prompted perhaps by a wish to tighten
her links with Coole, led her into a reading of history that turned
her, she says in *Our Irish Theatre*, into a Home Ruler. "I defy
anyone to study Irish history without getting a dislike and distrust
of England." The letters themselves yielded no State secrets and
Mr. Gregory's Letter-Box, for all its charm and interest as a
period piece, sheds no new light on the course of history. It does,
however, shed considerable light on its editor in the dawn of her
development as a writer.

Reading the account books that record the expenditure of
Secret Service money, her eye falls delightedly on "a regular
payment of 100 1. per annum to a certain Dr. Parkinson 'for
performance of two odes' on the birthdays of the King and Queen.
That was the golden age for a Court poet". She comments on Mr.
Gregory's personal account book: "I am glad that in spite of his
usual economy of stops he affords a comma between the words
'Frank, washing, Betty, 4 *l.* 0 *s.* 7½ *d.*' " The same pretty wit
turns to good account the most trivial aside in the letters, as
when

Mr. Gregory writes to Peel in 1816: "Lord Norbury has got the whooping cough – do not laugh, the fact is positively so – but he will not give in, and proposes attending the Court to-morrow."

It is to be hoped Mr. Peel did not laugh, for I find by sympathetic allusions in Lord Talbot's letters that about a dozen years later he was himself afflicted with the same malady, which seems in those days to have been ambitious in its choice of victims.

Already she has the dramatist's gift for the arresting phrase, and an ear tuned to the subtleties of Irish speech:

The other day, in a mountain valley I fell into talk with an old peasant, and as usual in Ireland, where politics, like the stones, are always near the surface, we got on to them, and then to the Emancipation time.

"And you have all those letters!" he said; "well now, it's you has the newses! And you so pleasant and so civil to tell them, I wouldn't be tired listening to you.

"O'Connell was a grand man, and whatever cause he took in hand it was as good as won. But what wonder. He was the gift of God."

A modest editor, Lady Gregory keeps herself discreetly in the background, but her choice of material and the manner of its presentation reveal a humanity and good sense equal to Mr. Gregory's own. The horrors of the potato famine of 1822 and the cholera of 1832 grimly counterpoint the comings and goings at the Castle, but the editor's judgement is invariably as generous as her wit is benevolent.

Having read from beginning to end this mass of letters from those engaged in the Government of Ireland, the impression that remains is that they were all, all honourable men, and not only that, but truly anxious for the welfare of the country, looking with kindly, if somewhat prejudiced, eyes through their party-coloured glasses.

The reader, however, can never forget that the editor of *Mr. Gregory's Letter-Box* is a woman. No man would have recorded that the Duchess of Wellington "made all the ladies of the Court live in poplin dresses"; or have set down Lord Manners' melancholy comment to his wife after reading Lady Morgan's *O'Donnell* (and causing it to be burned in the servants' hall): "I wish I had not given her the secret of my salad!" And running like a refrain through the whole book is a loving celebration of the Gregory family.It opens with "my husband and I" and ends:

> So the generations come and go, and the whirligig of time brings in his revenges. A son of Lord Talbot became a Canon of the Church of Rome. The "dear boy at Harrow" broke from the Tory traditions of his grandfather, made friends with Dan O'Connell, and helped to disestablish the Church of Ireland. To-day, it is Mr. Gregory's great-grandson who is a Harrow boy, whose mother hopes he may put into the work he has to do as much good will as she has brought to this self-imposed task of hers.

"Mr. Gregory's great-grandson" became the Major Robert Gregory immortalized in Yeats's elegies. And remembering "the Irish Airman", one's mind goes back to a little boy playing at the feet of his mother and the poet, in that Library where "many of the poems and plays", she wrote, "were dictated to me . . . , I, never a very expert typist, sitting in a window recess, blackening my fingers as I changed the ribbon of my Remington, or forgetting to reverse the carriage so that the ribbon was in holes through standing still; he suggesting changes to the last as he walked up and down the room."

Reading today the *Letter-Box* published in 1898, the centenary of the Rebellion of the United Irishmen, one wonders how much Yeats's vision of history owes to their discussion of Lady Gregory's historical reading as she prepared the Under-Secretary's papers for publication, under the benevolent eye of his marble bust.

JON STALLWORTHY
August 1971

CONTENTS

MR. GREGORY'S LETTER-BOX

"Correspondence of the Right Honourable William Gregory, 1813–1835." A large iron-clamped, leather-covered box at Coole bears this inscription.

We sometimes talked, my husband and I, of reading through its contents. Once we even began to do so, but we happened to strike into a vein of applications for places, and after a few days' work we tired of appeals on behalf of possessors of all the virtues who pined for *any* place, however poor or small, and we gave up the task for the time.

But last winter, being alone, with patience and long evenings on my side, I set to work, and came at last to the bottom of the box.

I have not discovered any grave State secrets. Even the books recording the laying out of the Secret Service money, audited by "Bedford," "Arthur Wellesley," "Richmond," and their successors, reveal no plot against the liberties of the people. It is ostensibly "applied in detecting treasonable conspiracies, &c.," and was also used for the subsidising of newspapers, the protection of threatened witnesses, and small pensions to the victims of political troubles. There is also a regular payment of 100*l.* per annum to a certain Dr. Parkinson "for performance of two odes" on the birthdays of the King and Queen. That was the golden age for a Court poet.

Having read from beginning to end this mass of letters from those engaged in the Government of Ireland, the impression that remains is that they were all, all honourable men, and not only that, but truly anxious for the welfare of the country, looking with kindly, if somewhat prejudiced, eyes through their party-coloured glasses.

One thing to be admired about them all is the beautiful clearness of their handwriting. There have been Viceroys and Chief Secretaries since then whose letters will make more severe demands upon the eyesight and ingenuity of their biographers. Mr. Gregory's writing indeed grows a little shaky as years advance, and his scorn of punctuation and unexpectedness in the use of capitals make his own letters a little puzzling. They are

11

traced in faded ink on thin copying paper, and it is sometimes trying to the patience when a document, pored over and held in various lights and positions, is at last deciphered, to find it relates only to the survey of a road or the Reports of the Board of Health.

But I have striven to write fair what time had blurred, and I have chosen here and there from all the correspondence such letters as seem to throw a light on the history of the time.

But I cannot give anything like a continuous history, for during some months of every year the Viceroy and the Chief Secretary and the Under Secretary were together in Dublin, and, of course, during those months no letters passed between them. The extracts I give, however, seem to me to throw some side lights on Castle government during those years.

I see no need to apologise for their publication, purchase and perusal being non-compulsory, but I may quote a sentence of Lord Rosebery's: "The Irish question has never passed into history, for it has never passed out of politics." And also a word said to me by Mr. Lecky, that far less is known of the early part of this century in Ireland than of the close of the last.

Old Mr. Gregory's bust looks benevolently on my labours. The geniality of his nature beams through its white marble. The bumps of perception are strongly marked, as well they may be after many years of office in Ireland.

My husband says of him in his autobiography: "My grandfather, though not at all a brilliant man, possessed many high qualities—excellent judgment, sound sense, attention to business, great clearness and accuracy in his transaction of it. He had a frank, open manner, and was straightforward, true and just in all his dealings. Few people have been more popular in Ireland during so long a period of great power, and though he was a Tory of the Tories, he was not disliked by those who differed with him in politics.

"My grandfather was originally a man of Liberal opinions, but his connections and the influential persons by whom he was surrounded made him adopt the extreme Tory opinions of that day, though I never recollect hearing a violent expression from his lips as regards Catholics. It is not, however, wonderful that O'Connell was bent on removing all opponents of his views from Dublin Castle, and in several of his letters he lays the strongest stress on clearing out Gregory, though he subsequently acknowledges that 'to do him justice he had some Irish feelings.'

"He had been educated at Harrow and Trinity College, Cambridge. In 1813 he was made Under Secretary for Ireland, a post which he held until 1831. He married Lady Anne Trench, and had three children, two sons and a daughter."

I find among his papers some little note books or almanacs for each year. But unfortunately little is revealed in them save the houses he dined at, the very many guests who dined or stayed with him, and his journeys. There is an indignant entry in 1810 of having been called upon by a Galway squire "to be his second with Mr. A. Martin, a grocer in Henry Street." Very often the arrival is noted of "a hogshead of claret" or "a pipe of port from Sneyd", and the date of bottling is also recorded with due care. His dinner-giving days were nearly over in 1833, when he writes, "My dear old friend Sneyd shot by a madman at half-past two P.M. in Westmoreland Street."

I have also found his account books from 1790, carefully written up all through, though with a coupling of details sometimes rather incongruous—"Print and Pickles, 19s. 6d."; "Play and John, 1l. 6s."; "Stockings Powder Cheese, 1l. 5s. 6d." I am glad that in spite of his usual economy of stops he affords a comma between the words "Frank, washing, Betty, 4l. 0s. 7½d." Lavender water seems to have been a heavy item, and muslin for cravats, which comes to about as much as window tax. Lottery tickets he sometimes invests in, but apparently without success. Before his appointment he borrowed money now and then, but it is honestly paid off afterwards with such expressions as "Creasy, the last of him, 50l." Charity is not neglected. There is more than one entry of "Cloaths for poor Boy." Charity sermons draw an unfailing guinea, 20l. is given in one lump to the poor of Dublin, and even a "Mass-house" receives a small donation. Books appear sometimes—Stockdale's "Shakespeare," "Lord Russell's Letters," "Davis's Tracts." It is curious to look through the accounts for 1798 and see the usual peaceful items "perfumery," "three white waistcoats," "children's" hats, "drawing William's tooth" (11s. 4½d.). But there are some signs of the terrors around in "sword-belt and plate," "barracks" and "trimming regimental hat."

Travelling was in those days a serious expense. In 1805 I see "Dublin to London, 45l. 10s."; "Expenses to Coole (Dublin to Galway), 24l."; "Bath to London (1808), 23l. 19s. 4d." Once in London his sojourn did not cost him much, the houses of Lord Whitworth, Lord Talbot, and others were open to him. He bought presents there, however, and did commissions for friends marked "English money at par," a "hookar for the Duke (of Richmond) is 25l. 8s. 4d." That a prelate should be strait-laced is befitting, but this is perhaps too plainly indicated in "paid for the Bishop of Elphin in London, Kirby, 5l. 1s. 6d. Stay-maker, 2l. 10s."

Mr. Gregory had no lack of work to attend to. He had to show each new Viceroy and Chief Secretary the working of the ropes, and it was not always easy to keep the whole machine from being put out of gear by the sudden changes in the political views of those who from time to time took up the government. An Under Secretary who had worked under Grant and Goulburn, Lord Talbot and Lord Anglesey, may well have echoed the lament of Irenaeus: "This is the common order of them, that who cometh next in the place will not follow the course of government, however good, which his predecessor held, either for disdayne of him, or doubt to have his doings drowned in another man's prayse, but will straight take a way quite contrarye to the former; as iff the former thought (by keeping under the Irish) to reforme them, the next by discountenauncing the English will currye favour with the Irish, and so make his government seeme plausible in viewe, as having all the Irish at his commaunde: but he that comes next after will perhaps follow neither one nor the other, but will dandle the one and the other in such sort as he will suck sweete out of them both, and leave bitterness to the poore lande, which if he that comes after shall seeke to redress, he shall perhaps finde such crosses as he shall be hardly able to beare, or do any goode that might work the disgrace of his predecessors."

He was, as his letters show, strongly against emancipation. He writes to Lord Talbot on hearing some news unfavourable to the Bill: "Your account of the fixed determination to maintain the Protestant religion is very consoling." He adopted the current belief that the savagery and disorder amongst the people should be laid at the door of their religion and not of their misgovernment and misfortune. And no doubt he sincerely believed that the established Church would at last, if given time, lead them to "the blessed comfort of the sweete gospell and Christe's deare passion."

But for the material good of the people he was always ready to work, and he speaks indignantly again and again against absenteeism and the carelessness of the country gentlemen. In 1822 he writes: "The helpless apathy of the gentry of Clare is quite provoking. Because Major Warburton is ill they do not act, and apply with complaints to and against the Government to know what they are to do."

His own father was an energetic landowner, and I see no applications for help from his people. Arthur Young found him in 1776 "engaged in pursuits which if well imitated will improve the face of the country not a little," and "improving his land with

great spirit," having brought over a Norfolk man to teach his
people the management of the newly introduced culture of
turnips. He was a Liberal in politics, and had been chairman of
the East India Company. Edmund Burke, writing to him upon
some Indian subject, said: "I enter fully into everything you feel.
Certainly you must begin with the natives. This was always your
fundamental maxim; and be assured it will be mine. God knows
whether I for one shall have health to get through the business
yours has sunk under. But depend upon it I shall not depart an
inch from your line." This letter he "desired to have carefully
handed down to his posterity, to show how dearly he had the
interests of the natives of the East Indies at heart." And the Under
Secretary instilled these lessons of humanity learned from his
father so well in the minds of his children, that his eldest son
met his death in 1847 through personally attending the fever-
struck victims of famine. Mr. Gregory seldom grumbles over his
work, which had at least the charm of variety. In 1814 he writes
to Mr. Peel: "The news from Paris has made me unfit to think of
Carders, Ribbonmen, Orangemen, Tidewaiters, Magistrates and
all the varied topics of our usual correspondence."

And in 1813: "I have been occupied a great part of the day
in the troublesome part of my duty as Chief of thieftakers. I hear
another gang of Mail Coach Robbers is formed, with a brother in
law of Colliers as their Captain; one of them was closely pursued
last night, but escaped in the usual place of Robbers refuge, the
Demesne of Roger O'Connor. From the information received and
the activity of the Country People who have suffered from these
Depredators I hope we shall disperse them."

And again: "The Negociations between the Paving Board and
the Gas Light Company are very tiresome, and old Taylor, who
is as restive as he is honest, wishes to throw all the Business on
Government. He might as well set me to work on animal
Magnetism as on Gas Light." And finally, in 1819: "I have
never performed a more arduous Task in my varied Official Duty
than the one in which I was engaged for a long time this morning,
no less than attempting to settle the misunderstanding between
the Ranger of the Curragh and the Stewards of the Turf
Club."

He also bore the first brunt of the applications for places, his
good word being eagerly looked for, and his power believed in.

There is a touch of oriental patience and pathos in this appeal
to him from the Countess of G., who begs that 6,000*l.* belonging
to her may be released from a judgment in favour of the Barrack
Board without delay. "Think of me at Cork, and the money only

waiting to be paid to me after waiting for it twenty-eight years. *On my knees* I entreat you to have this done immediately! "

Lady Anne Gregory died in 1833, but his daughter was still his companion. I see by his notebook that she was not an old maid perforce, for there is an entry: "Sept. 10, 1817. Colonel R—— proposed for my Daughter"; then, "19th. My Daughter confined to her bed by Fever, attended by Dr. Perceval." "21st Refused Colonel R's proposal." "24th. Crampton called in to my Daughter."

There is a delightful flavour of Miss Austen about this. Miss Gregory was contemporary with her heroines, and may even have met her suitor at the Bath Pump Room at the end of one of those expensive journeys. One cannot but speculate on an unhappy attachment elsewhere, which combined with remorse for false hopes given plunged her into that "Fever" which we are prone to fancy only seeks its victims amongst the heroines of romance. One can hear her murmur, "My illness has made me think—it has given me leisure for calm and serious reflection. Long before I was enough recovered to talk I was perfectly able to reflect. I saw that my own feelings had prepared my sufferings, and that my want of fortitude under them had almost led me to the grave." But Miss Austen would have brought about a more satisfactory ending, and Colonel R——, like that other Colonel, who, notwithstanding that he "sought the constitutional safeguard of a flannel waistcoat," was made happy by Miss Dashwood, would never have been sent away in enduring despair.

Mr. Gregory's removal had often been threatened as opinions on the Catholic question changed. In October 1827, Lord Lansdowne wrote to Lamb: "Lord Anglesey will be prepared to commence his vice-royalty with the New Year . . . Second, as to Gregory. We are all agreed that it is desirable he should be removed, but in a way that shall be both civil in manner and satisfactory in substance. As, judging from your letter, you are on good terms with him, you can have no difficulty in ascertaining how he is circumstanced, and what provision would best suit him. Goderich thinks there is no harm in granting a pension analogous to that which would exist with respect to an under secretary. But, if no other way can be suggested, he would have no difficulty in submitting the case to Parliament, as he has served much longer than under the law here would entitle him in a parallel case to a pension. Anything you can propose for this purpose will be attended to with a desire to give it immediate effect, as Lord A. is anxious that the arrangement should take effect as soon as he goes, if not before, and C. Grant says that G. must in your case, as he found in his, remain master of the whole machine of government when you are absent."

However, he escaped for that time, and in 1829 we find Mr. Wyse writing: "The petitioner at the Castle did not ask what the Lord-Lieutenant thought, but what the Lord-Lieutenant's Secretary thought, or rather what his Secretary's Secretary thought. It was not Lord Wellesley, nor even Mr. Goulburn, but it was Mr. Gregory who held in his hand the destinies of Ireland."

In 1830 Mr. Gregory notes on September 17: "Not one letter by the English or Irish mail. Such a blank day I have not known for eighteen years."

This was an omen foreshadowing the end, for three months later, on Lord Anglesey's re-appointment, he received from him a letter of dismissal. He writes, December 27: "Removed from the office of Under Secretary for Ireland, which I had held for upwards of eighteen years, having filled other public offices."

It was better, even for his own sake, he should go out with Protestant ascendency. He would have been old wine in new bottles now the new order had begun. He led a quiet and apparently happy life until the end came in 1840. In his last year he writes: "74 years old. How thankless [sic] am I for the mercy that has been shown unto me, living to such an advanced age in the enjoyment of excellent health, the free use of my limbs and my mind unimpaired."

Even after his fall no unkind words seem to have been said of him. Lord Cloncurry, though they had always been in opposite camps, writes in his memoirs: "Notwithstanding the inconsistency of his political opinions with those of Lord Anglesey and with mine, I constantly found the Right Hon. William Gregory a sincere and active friend and promoter of the physical interests of Ireland."

Addresses and letters of sympathy and regret followed him in his retirement. I fancy he kept up his old habit of hospitality even then, for I see in his account book for January, 1831: "Dejeuner to the Lord Mayor and Corporation who presented an Address, 14l. 15s."

ORANGEISM AND EMANCIPATION

The dramatic idea, if one may so call it, of Mr. Gregory's term of office was the emancipation of the Catholics. And so many practical questions of administration turned upon this unsettled question, and so many disorders were caused by the irregular forces of this war of creeds, that it is necessary to know something of the causes and the tendencies of the war when trying to understand the ins and outs of Castle government.

> "They come in the morning, scoffing and scorning,
> Saying, were you harassed, were you sore abused,
> O, Orange haters, ye beat the traitors,
> That betrayed our Saviour to the wicked Jews."

Such songs as the above testify to the depth of religious bitterness that had grown up in Ireland in the early part of this century.

Up to 1795 religious intolerance had seemed to be in abeyance, or to have died away. When the question of the removal of religious disabilities was brought before the Irish House of Commons in that year, "the Protestants of Ireland as a body were perfectly ready to concede what was asked," Mr. Lecky tells us, and he tells us also that "the Protestants of Ireland had many faults, but they were at this time remarkably free from religious bigotry." But the liberty which Irish Protestants were ready to grant was refused by the Protestants of England, and concession having been violently thrown out by the door, rebellion and revolution came in by the window. Before the dawning of the new century two events had taken place which had revived bigotry and drawn a hard line of separation between the two creeds, the birth of Orangeism, and the rebellion of '98.

"No Surrender," "No Popery," the support of the Crown so long as it supported Protestant ascendency, these were the cries of the Orange society. Distrust of the Catholics was its leading motive. William the Third, from whom it took its name, was its hero.

The Protestants were not without provocation in forming this League. The Catholics had already banded together as "Defenders." The "Battle of the Diamond," in which the

18

"Defenders" were the aggressors and the Protestants the victors, was the official birthday of the Orange society, and is still celebrated in its triumphant though unmelodious song:

> "'Twas in the year of '95, September the 21st,
> They rushed from the hills with shouts and with yells,
> The Defenders to do their worst.
> But them to oppose stood Protestant foes,
> Who scattered the murderous crew;
> And ere the sun set the green grass was wet,
> But not with the evening dew."

It was a great misfortune to Ireland that this religious war came into being before the '98 rebellion. A few years earlier, the North had been the headquarters of disaffection. Even in 1796 "the town which showed the worst spirit was undoubtedly Belfast, the capital of the most advanced Irish Protestantism." But by degrees first the gentry and then the Northern democracy drifted away from the national movement, which grew more and more fierce as its channel was narrowed.

If they had held together, sufficient concessions might have been granted to prevent the rebellion taking place. Or had it taken place, and still been put down, the ropes that hanged Protestant and Catholic alike might have acted as "cords of love" in binding different creeds and classes together. We might have escaped that root of bitterness, whose fruit, like the blossom of the furze, is never quite out of season in Ireland.

But when the moment of the rebellion came, its great Protestant leader, Lord Edward Fitzgerald, had already been seized, and lay dying in prison, there was no one competent to take his place, the rising took place spasmodically, its guidance fell into the hands of a few violent priests, and instead of a war for liberty or for justice, it became a war of fanaticism and religious hatred.

I was made to realise this, and the nearness of '98 to 1800, by a talk I had a little time ago with an old lady, born during the Duke of Richmond's vice-royalty, but who is a link with a yet more distant generation.

She had been reading my husband's autobiography, and she put it down and said: "I never knew O'Connell myself, but I have heard him speak from the balcony of his house in Merrion Square, and I have seen him carried about in a chair by the people. I don't think so much of him as your husband did. Yes, he may have believed he was doing good work, but my feelings were not for the Catholics. I was reared in a little chair beside my grandmother, Mrs. B. of I——, and I heard too much of the horrors of '98.

"She was but a young thing when my grandfather first saw her. He had come to buy horses, and she was up in a tree picking nuts, and her sisters were wading in the stream. She was only fifteen, but he fell in love with her that moment, and at dinner time he asked that she might come down, and he married her before many months were over. She had everything she could want, and I remember often when it was a wet day, we children would go and take out the beautiful dresses that were put by, that she used to wear when he took her to Dublin.

"Their home was in Wexford, and all was quiet, and one evening the parish priest had dined with them, and they had no fear of anything more than usual. But in the middle of the night a neighbour, Mr. W., came and knocked at the door and bid them escape for their lives, for the rebels were out. So they flung on what clothes they could, and ran down, and the kitchen was filled with Protestants that had flocked in for safety. So they got carriages and cars and all they could ready, and set out for Dublin. There were parties of rebels along the road, and they stopped the carriage to search it, and tried my grandmother's pocket, but she had left all her money in a cabinet at home, and they found nothing in it but bunches of keys. Lady Courtown was in a carriage behind—they could hear her shrieking—and presently Lord Courtown and my grandfather left their wives and went back to defend their county, but they got safely to Dublin.

"After the rebels were put down they went back home, and the first thing that they saw was the blackened walls of their house, nothing else left standing. The Protestant gardener had refused to come away with them, said he would stay and take his chance. And when they got back there was his body lying across one of his hotbeds, where a pike had been put through him.

"They built the house up again, but there were always cracks to be seen in the walls of the drawing-room. And the kitchen and the offices they built a long way off, as far as the flower beds from the front of this house—my grandmother would never have felt easy to have Roman Catholics sleep near her again.

"Yes, O'Connell may have had some good in him, and once when I was a little girl sitting up on a wall at Kilkenny to see the tinkers sell their wives to each other (yes, they did so, it was their custom, or made an exchange—and the children always went with the woman), his son, Maurice O'Connell, came and said I was sitting in a dangerous place, and took me and lifted me down.

But for all that I wouldn't have given them the Maynooth grant. And as for O'Connell, I had never heard he had any good in him till I read your husband's book."

On the other side, Parnell is said to have been turned into a rebel by the story told him in his childhood by an eye-witness of the very brutal flogging to death by English soldiers of a prisoner who fell into their hands after the rising of '98.

I might have learned this change of class tradition and one at least of its causes by an object lesson at my own old home. My great-grandfather had been active in the Volunteer movement, as an inscription on a bridge built by him shows. As children we were not taught Irish history, and I used to puzzle over the meaning of the words: "This bridge was erected by William Persse Esquire, Col. of the Roxborough Volunteers in the year 1783, in memory of Ireland's Emancipation from Foreign Jurisdiction."

But after '98, National feeling turned to distrust of the people as Catholics, and a colony was formed on the estate of Protestants imported from the North. They were respectable but troublesome tenants, and the experiment was not repeated. A letter from Mr. Gregory to Lord Talbot written in 1820 tells of its results:

"The accounts from Galway continue very bad. The house of Roxborough was attacked on Thursday night. Your friend Persse was absent, but his sons made a gallant Defence and the Ribbon-men were repulsed. The village of Kilchriest (one mile from Roxborough) was plundered of Arms on Monday last, and on the following night a party of Ribbonmen compelled the Protestant Inhabitants (there are several in the Village) to swear on their knees that on the following Sunday they will with their families attend Mass; the penalty of their disobedience, the burning of their houses. Now that confidence has been gained by numbers and the possession of arms, the hatred to Heretics publicly manifests itself, and the extirpation of Protestants is the avowed object of these Miscreants. The completion of such a diabolical wish is in my mind absurd and impracticable, tho' many valuable lives may be lost. But the great and immediate danger I dread is the reaction of the opposite Party. The Protestants find themselves so threatened, and such power gained by their enemies, they will naturally associate and arm in their own defence, and the whole mass of the lower Class of population will be arranged in open hostility against each other. I have seen so many parts of the Kingdom at various times, fully in as bad a state as Galway, and the disturbances suppressed, that I can have no doubt of the restoration of tranquillity, tho' it may be attended with much trouble and the loss of some excellent Men who will not yield to those midnight Legislators. Old Sir George moves with a lock step, when we require double quick time, and General O'Loughlin considers that the danger is much exaggerated. No one dreams of those Rapparees taking the field against the King's troops; but the danger is not the less to the peaceable inhabitants who are attacked by them at night. Large bodies of Military are marching into the Country, there will be this day or to-morrow 2,000 Men in the County of Galway, and before the expiration of the ensuing week 800 more."

We used to hear traditions of this attack on Roxborough in my childhood. My father had been one of its defenders. It was attacked by moonlight, and the garrison could distinguish groups of men, one group surrounding an oak-tree on the lawn. My father took aim at the tree, thinking that in the uncertain light he would thus be sure of hitting one of the party. But his aim was surer than he thought, and next day it was seen that the bullet had gone to the heart of the oak. Other shots, however, were more successful, for trails of blood were to be seen in the morning, where the dead or wounded had been carried away.

The following extracts are from a letter written in 1813 by Baron Smith, in answer to an inquiry of Mr. Gregory's as to the state of religious parties in the North. The letter itself is, as Mr. Gregory says of another by the same writer, "of ponderous and elephantine proportions." Even in Court, the Baron's charges were usually on the same "elephantine" scale, and the vast MS. notes he was wont to arrive with were said to be "the terror of Grand Juries." But he seems to have been painstaking and for those days impartial, and one good deed of his deserves record, that of having learned Irish, that he might not be dependent on an interpreter in the examination of witnesses.

He writes:

"*On state of Catholics and Protestants in the*
North of Ireland

Sept. 4, 1813.
'Perhaps the outline of my opinion will be this, that there does not appear to be a Party Spirit, or rather perhaps that *two* Party Spirits appear to be afloat, and very angrily and troublesomely busy in some of the Counties through which I have passed, that there are faults, animosities, ill-blood and aggression upon both sides, but that the Orange party have not infrequently given the original provocation, to minds ready I am afraid to take fire from a trifling spark, and by contumely and insult and a certain tone and indication easier to understand than to describe, of hostility,

superiority, defiance and contempt, have exasperated feelings which a different conduct might assuage.——I am tempted to add that though I love and warmly share the loyalty of *Gentlemen,* there is a spurious and illiberal loyalty which grows up amongst the vulgar classes, and which is very turbulent, bigoted, riotous and affronting, very saucy, and overbearing, almost proud of transgression, necessarily producing exasperation, and often leading to the effusion of blood. It is a rebellious and insurrectionary propensity gone astray, and running contradictorily in the channel of Allegiance.

"A witness before me at Lifford, being asked why the Corps of Yeomanry to which he had belonged was disbanded, answered (on his oath) smiling and in an exulting way, 'Because it was too loyal.' I am afraid that, with it may be very pure intentions, some of our Country Gentlemen do not always find their fairness seconded by equal coolness, Intelligence or Judgment.

"I do not know, probably you do, whether those Bodies called Ribbon men are or are not of a decidedly political character, and a symptom of rebellious plans and organisation. I have heard the thing asserted and denied; but when I asked for proofs, I was put off with prejudice and empty noise. That they are a Religious Party is beyond question, and if it were not that the gross exaggerations which I have detected make me a little incredulous, I should say that they collect from distant quarters, are bound together by an obligation, appear suddenly in great numbers, act in concert, are very anti-Protestant, or at least violently anti-Orange, and if their present views and prospects are vague and immature and not unequivocally revolutionary, yet that a combination formed for one ill purpose may be equally applied to another equally or more mischievous one, and that objects at first undefined may with the aid that will be given soon settle into something very dangerously certain and precise."

The following, reported by Mr. Gregory to Mr. Peel, is an instance of religious intolerance in Dublin:

May 22, 1813. The Guinnesses "are very extensive porter brewers in Dublin, and a report having been invented that they had signed the petition against the Catholics, the houses of the publicans in which their Beer was sold became unfrequented, or large Parities going into the houses called for Beer, and asking the Landlord whether he bought from Guinness, on receiving an answer in the affirmative, threw the beer about the House, telling the owner if ever he bought any more from the same People, the next visit they paid him should be more expensive."

The Guinnesses, however, had been unjustly accused, as far

as signing the petition went, but were then taxed with having "disseminated the Bible." Mr. Guinness was also said to have helped in the conviction of a '98 rebel, M'Cann. "If Protestants who now only appear racing who shall first elevate the Host, would for one Moment seriously reflect on the proceedings of this Inquisitorial Board, they would be satisfied that concession is vain," is the moral drawn by Mr. Gregory.

He gives another instance in 1820, after a meeting in support of Catholic claims:

"Alderman Manders at the City Assembly voted against the Lord Mayor, calling an aggregate meeting; his son is a brewer in partnership with a Man who is, I understand, a Catholic, but the Alderman has no concern in the house. The day after it appeared in the Newspapers how the Father had voted, the Catholic Customers came to the brewery and closed their accounts; in vain were they assured that the Alderman had no share in the establishment, they were inexorable until the Son signed the Requisition to the Lord Mayor, and they then agreed to deal with the house as usual."

In 1816 Major Willcocks, Chief Magistrate of Tipperary, in answer to questions as to the feeling towards Protestants, the Government and England, put by Mr. Peel, says:

Feeling towards Protestants and towards England

"I don't think in conversation they betray their feelings towards Protestants and towards England, but I think they have a secret dislike to Protestants. I have not known them to express a dislike to English soldiers as being such—in many instances I have known the common people to be very civil to them—but I have also known the Common people to cheer Catholic Irish Regiments because they were such."

The following verses sent to the Castle from Clonmel by Mr. Cuppaige, an active magistrate, in 1816, and docketed by him "Precious Ditty," is of about the same order of merit as "The Battle of the Diamond." Beginning with the usual appeal to the "Sons of brave Milesians" for a hearing, it soon takes a more theological turn:

"Now my boys consider, the time is drawing hither,
    When every branch shall wither, but the bough that wears the
        green,
    When Luther's vile dissension will fall without contention,
    With the curst invention, of the year 17—,
    The Gentry of this place are of curst Cromwell's race:

It's well known by their face, their heart is base and mean.
They are still striving forcibly, to overturn Popery,
By cruel tyranny to elevate their name.

"Now let your hearts be well disposed, and your minds be well
    enclosed,
Until the time affords that, that long expected day,
When Catholics will see the lovely Laurel tree
Displayed for liberty, and the damned Orange cut away."

Mr. Cuppaige, who had taken the song with other papers in
a raid on a Ribbon meeting, found himself thus described:

"There's a Locust in our nation, a Demi-Devil in station,
He surpasses Dioclesian, or Nero's cruelty.
He is daily meditating to vitiate our Nation from every
    consolation—
So superciliously.
Richard Cuppaige is his name, he aspires much to fame;
May his diabolic scheme, be the cause of his downfall.
May perpetual desolation, trace his cursed generation,
Or effectual Damnation the moment death shall befall."

If poor Mr. Cuppaige was a sharer in the old Irish belief that
"a poet's curse could wither the corn in the ground and make
the milk dry in the udders of the cows," he must have trod
delicately when he next disturbed a Ribbon meeting.

An amateur and somewhat officious Informer writes to Lord
Sidmouth, February 19, 1818:

"I am an inhabitant of Ballycastle, where there is a great deal
of Ribbon work carrying on; there is not a night but they are
met on the hills; and as a good and loyal subject of his Majesty,
I warn you that if some measures don't take place soon so as to
quell them, I am afraid they'll murder us all in a short time. They
are talking a great deal about rising all through Ireland before
Easter, so would advise you to take some measures that would
put an end to the work, as I don't think there is 2 Catholics in
Ireland that are not Ribbonmen."

Mr. Hobhouse writes with this to Mr. Gregory.

"I am directed by Lord Sidmouth to transmit to you the
enclosed copy of a letter from a person giving information of an
intended rising of the Ribbon Weavers near Ballincastle, and who
he states hold nightly meetings on the Hills, and I am to desire

that you will submit the same for the information of the Lord-Lieutenant."

Mr. Gregory sends the letters to Mr. Peel, and says, "Pray read these letters, and explain to Mr. Hobhouse that Ribbon Work in Ireland is a very different manufacture from weaving of Ribbons in England."

He writes on May 31, 1813: "A most serious disturbance has taken place in a part of the county of Donegal called Fannet, between the Orangemen and Ribbonmen, in which many lives have been lost."

And a month later he writes of the difficulty of interfering with the Orange and other processions in the North:

"It would be most happy for the country if those religious distinctions of the victors and the vanquished could be done away, but by what authority can this be accomplished? The Orange meetings in the North, consisting of very many thousands, could not be dispersed but by very strong military force. The Catholics assemble constantly in prodigious numbers at funerals, wearing and carrying crosses; they march in the greatest regularity, and are regularly told off by some one commanding in Divisions, but they commit no violence—could they be disturbed?"

This is a question that comes before every succeeding Viceroy, for Orangeism still flourishes, and Orange lilies, here in the West of such harmless tendency that they brilliantly deck the altars of village chapels, still unfold their petals as a declaration of war when the July sunshine falls on Ulster. The feud seems likely to last for many a long year yet, and to give lively occupation to the police and magistrates of the new century. Not long ago, when the Chief Justice of Ireland was transferred to the wider business of the Privy Council in the House of Lords, one of the first cases he had to do with was an appeal from Indian Moham-medans in some religious dispute. "They seem to have sects there too," he said, "the Sunis and the Shiahs they are called. Always fighting they seem to be. I give you my word, I thought I was in Belfast!"

Yet if we look back we see that it was not the bigotry of Protestant Ireland, but of England, that kept its foot for so long on the neck of the "Papist." A record of the whole long struggle would be a record of England's broken promises, beginning with the violated Treaty of Limerick in 1691, and also, more happily, a record of each painful inch gained by wave after wave of agita-tion, until the breaking down of all barriers in 1829.

In 1778 Catholics were granted some liberty of holding their estates. In 1782, Catholic soldiers and sailors were received into the English army and navy, and no longer driven into those of France. "I have had a hundred relatives in the French army," O'Connell says, "but now not one." In 1793 the Irish House of Commons, before it expired, granted the last best gift, the franchise. This once granted, the crash of all systems of intolerance becomes but a matter of time, as the Boers of to-day well know.

With this came admission to the Grand Jury box, to the Magisterial Bench and to the outer Bar.

Then, when the smoke of the Rebellion had cleared away, and the Union was talked of, full emancipation was offered as a bribe. Many good patriots were induced to vote for the silencing of their Parliament by the promise of this, and were bitterly deceived.

Pitt himself was deceived as to his own power to grant the promised boon. Even Lord Castlereagh said in after-years, "his anxiety to see the Catholics emancipated had been one of his inducements to support the Union." Perhaps the King was also deceived, or deceived himself, as to the implied promise, for he boasted that the carrying of the Union had "shut the door for ever against Catholic claims."

So he hardened his heart and would not let his people out of bondage in spite of the voices of warning ringing in the air. Burke had prophesied with luminous foresight the inevitable yielding to agitation on this question, and had pleaded for timely and gracious concession. Fox, "a man who inherited so much of fervour of liberty that it glowed in his heart amidst the chilling scenes of Parliamentary profligacy," set his influence on the side of political freedom in Ireland as well as in France. Grattan, "our best and brightest advocate," had borne the griefs of his Catholic countrymen and carried their sorrows into the new century and the English House of Commons. Emancipation was "backed also by the memories of Sheridan, Dunning, Windham—by the memory of every man who possessed buoyancy enough to float down the stream of time."

But Pitt pleaded promises and prophecies in vain. Thackeray, who has pilloried George the Fourth, has let the third George off far too easily. Liberal measures were brought in again and again, and were dashed to pieces against the dead wall of his obstinacy. He had been brought up by his mother in a German cradle, and he could never stretch his limbs to the length of his English bedstead. The extraordinary patience of England under the

Georges can only be accounted for by dread and dislike of the Stuarts.

At last his failing and diseased mind was so much troubled by any allusion to the question that it had to be abandoned. Pitt resigned, or was dismissed, and went to his grave looking at his great uncrowned, unfinished work, as Stevens afterwards looked on his unfinished masterpiece in St. Paul's, with yearning, disappointed eyes.

Hope came to life again when the Regency was established—Grattan, supported by the Irish Parliament, had held that in case of the King's lunacy, the death of the mind should be looked upon as equivalent to the death of the body, and that the heir to the throne should enter upon the full duties and enjoyments of sovereignty.

Though this opinion was not endorsed by that of England, it was felt that the Regent would cherish a grateful feeling towards the advocates of his absolute power, and would look upon their claims with favour.

In 1812 the Irish Catholics sent him a deputation, bearing a petition for the restoration of their rights, and reminding him of his promised protection eight years earlier. But the Regent bluntly refused to see the deputation, and pigeonholed the petition, it was supposed at the instigation of the reigning favourite, Lady Hertford.

The Catholics, furious at the betrayal of their hopes, called a meeting and passed the "Witchery resolutions." "We learn with deep disappointment and anguish how cruelly the promised boon of Catholic freedom has been interrupted by the fatal *Witchery* of an unworthy secret influence, hostile to our fairest hopes, spurning alike the sanctions of public and private virtue, the demands of personal gratitude and the sacred obligations of plighted honour.

"To this impure source we trace but too distinctly our afflicted hopes and protracted servitude."

The Regent never forgave these insults, nor some remarks of the same nature made by O'Connell. He set his face against emancipation, and even in 1829 made it a rancorous condition of his forced consent that O'Connell should not be allowed to take the seat he had been elected to by Clare.

But others were more faithful. Canning, who had lighted his torch at that which fell from the dying hand of his dear master, Pitt, brought forward in the same year (1813) a resolution to take Catholic disabilities into consideration with a view to remedying them. This was carried by a majority of 129, the largest Canning was ever destined to see. Napoleon was then formidable, Catholic Ireland was looking to him for help and offering sympathy, and England was moved by fear of further exasperating the country. The majority melted after that, with the melting of Napoleon's power.

Thus began the annual bringing in of the Motion for emancipation, or as O'Connell called it "the yearly rattling of our chains in the hearing of the enemy."

Canning pleaded for relief while it could be granted with grace, warning his countrymen that it would become "a thankless favour" when wrung from them by necessity. He proposed safeguards, the most important the "veto" on the appointment of Irish Bishops not considered "peaceful and well disposed subjects." This was a cause of much dispute and wrangling. The Irish Catholics were against it, the English for it. It was said to be already practically in existence, Dr. Curtis, Archbishop of Armagh, having been appointed through the influence of the Duke of Wellington. The Pope himself was won to assent to it, calling forth the exclamation of the old servant of a priest, "Oh, Sir, what shall we do! They say the Pope has turned Orangeman!"

It was something gained that in Lord Liverpool's Cabinet it was agreed that Emancipation should be an open question.

Peel was its strongest and most formidable opponent, a supporter of Canning in all but this. He believed that the Catholics when they had power would attack the Established Church in Ireland. This indeed seems to have been the most solid ground the Anti-Catholics stood on. They could not foresee that when that ill-fated Establishment eventually toppled down, the trumpets that achieved its fall would be sounded by the lips of English Protestants.

Other reasons were more trivial; the fear expressed by Peel himself that Quakers would have to be admitted to the House, the fear of foreign influence, of "the Pope, the Devil and the Pretender" as was tauntingly said, the fear that "there might one day be a Catholic Home Secretary who would advise a Catholic education for the children of the King." Others had a vague dread of evils, they knew not what, issuing from this Pandora's box. An Irish peer exclaimed when the news of Mr. Perceval's assassination arrived in the House of Lords, "You see, my Lords, the consequence of your agitating the question of Catholic emancipation!" Lord Talbot seriously offered Mr. Gregory a refuge at Ingestre, when, the Bill having passed, his further residence in Ireland would of course become impossible.

In Ireland through all this time O'Connell's redundant oratory had kept the country in a state of ferment, and brought the question home to the people. But according to the saying of Napoleon, one bad general is better than two good ones—and Canning, who assured his English supporters that emancipation was meant to complete and consolidate the Union, found the cause damaged by O'Connell's violence and anti-Union speeches. He wished for the discipline of the House of Commons for his unruly ally. "I have never seen a demagogue," he said, "who did not shrink to his proper dimensions after six months of Parliamentary life." Dublin Castle was continually occupied in the struggle with O'Connell and his irrepressible societies. The Catholic Committee was put down but to be succeeded by the Catholic Board, and that again by the Catholic Association. But his power was ever on the increase.

Many say that "the Agitator" is already being forgotten, but I discern signs that his turn will come again, and that he will in some future age appear as a sort of mythical giant.

The other day, in a mountain valley I fell into talk with an old peasant, and as usual in Ireland, where politics, like the stones, are always near the surface, we got on to them, and then to the Emancipation time.

"And you have all those letters!" he said; "well now, it's you has the newses! And you so pleasant and so civil to tell them, I wouldn't be tired listening to you.

"O'Connell was a grand man, and whatever cause he took in hand it was as good as won. But what wonder. He was the gift of God.

"His father was a rich man, and one day he was out walking he took notice of a house that was being built. Well, a week later he passed by the same place, and he saw the walls of the house were no higher than before. So he asked the reason, and he was told it was a priest that was building it, and he hadn't the money to go on with.

"So a few days after, he went to the priest's house, and he asked was this true, and the priest said it was. So, says O'Connell, 'would you pay the money back to the man that 'ud lend it to you?' 'I would,' said the priest. So with that O'Connell gave him the money that was wanting, 500*l.*, for it was a very grand house.

"Well, after some time the priest came to O'Connell's house, and he found only the wife at home. So, says he, 'I have some money that Himself lent me.' But he never had told his wife of what he had done, so as she knew nothing about it; and says she,

'Don't be troubling yourself about it, he'll bestow it on you.'
'Well,' says the priest, 'I'll go away now, and I'll come back
again.'

"So when O'Connell came in, the wife told him all that had
happened, and how a priest had come, saying he owed him money,
and how she said he'd bestow it on him. 'Well,' said O'Connell,
'if you said I'd bestow it, I'll bestow it.' And so he did. Then
the priest said, 'Have you any children?' 'Ne'er a child,' said
O'Connell. 'Well, then, you'll have one,' said he, and that day
nine months their young son was born. So what wonder if he
was inspired, being as he was the gift of God."

In a paper marked "Notes as to Irish Catholics. Private and
very confidential, 1806,' in Mr. Gregory's letter-box, I find a
more prosaic account. "O'Connell, A Barrister. An intimate of
the Master of the Rolls. Talents. Property. Impatient for
emancipation, ambitious, very warm, Uncle rich."

There are still many who remember him, and who, though out
of sympathy with his politics, tell of his charm. One says: "Our
house in Dublin was next his, and there was always some excitement, he was either speaking from his balcony, or walking about
with a train of little boys running after him, or he would order
illuminations for some occasion, and we would have to put
candles in the windows lest they should be broken. One day my
little sister and I were playing in the Square. She was a very
pretty child, and O'Connell stopped and said, 'What is your name,
little one?' 'Jane H——.' 'Are you any relation to J. H—— and
Master H——?' (two members of the Bar). 'One is my grandfather, and the other my father.' 'Then, my children, you may
go home, and thank God for your relations.' "

And another friend tells me: "His voice, when he spoke from
his house on the north side of Merrion Square, could be heard
on the south side.

"I heard him speak for his life at the State Trial—and the
Miss Sugdens, who had seats on the Bench, were crying bitterly
before he had ended.

"I took young L——, an Eton boy, to the Courts when the
trial was going on. He had asked to be pointed out 'the Agitator,'
but when we got into Court, O'Connell was sitting there, and said
in his rather foreign accent, 'Who's that handsome boy?' I said,
'He is the son of Mr. L——, who was in the House of Commons
with you.' 'Oh, I knew him well,' said Dan; 'shake hands, young
man; I knew your father,' and he put out his hand, but the boy
drew his back. 'Shake hands,' Dan said again, and again the boy
drew back. But a third time Dan said 'Shake hands,' and the

Etonian gave his, and even said as we came away, 'Well, I don't believe he's half as bad as I was told.' "

Sheil's oratory helped to keep the country in flames, in spite of an organic defect which made Mr. Gladstone say that his voice was like a "tin kettle battered about from place to place." I hear, from one who was present, of a dinner at his house in Dublin. Some one observed that there were thirteen at table. "Whoever makes that objection," cried Sheil in his high-pitched voice, "has the removal of it in his own power."

George Villiers had been the first to ask him to dine at a Protestant house, when an Irish Commissioner of Customs, and had thereby got into hot water with the Duke of Wellington. But he became the fashion afterwards, and dined with successive Viceroys.

The same friend who tells me of his dinner tells me also of having called at his house to know if he was likely to speak at some meeting next day. "I'm sure that he is," said the servant who opened the door, "for he didn't get up to-day, and it's always in bed that he makes up his speeches."

An old farmer, who attended the Catholic meetings on many a hillside, tells me Sheil was "small, dressed very neat, with knee breeches and a full vest and a long skirted coat. He had a long nose, and was not much to look at till he began to speak, and then you'd see genius coming out from him. His voice was shrill, and that spoiled his speech sometimes, especially when he got excited and raised it at the end. But O'Connell's voice you'd hear a mile off, and it sounded as if it was coming through honey."

He has left more to us than his contemporaries, in his sketches of politics and of the Bar. His fame as an orator had preceded him to the English House of Commons, and there was a rush to hear him speak. But his voice and rapid utterance were against him, and Lord John Russell, asked what he thought of him, said, "It seems to me that he is a man in a very unnecessary hurry."

But in Ireland his name is revered as only second to O'Connell.

LORD WHITWORTH, PEEL, AND THE
FEAR OF FRANCE

When Mr. Gregory became Under Secretary in 1813, the Vice-royalty was held by the Duke of Richmond, but I find but little in the letters in my hands to throw light upon his character or administration. He was considered weak and in the hands of Dr. Duigenan, who in spite of being married to a Catholic and allowing her confessor to live in the house, was of ultra-Orange type. He, however, only consulted him on ecclesiastical matters, giving rise to a sarcastic comparison by O'Connell of the Rev. Doctor to "a tanner's dog, kept chained all day and only let loose at night."

He was "irresistibly convivial," and was somewhat free in conferring knighthood when on tour in the provinces. Saurin was the real Governor in those days, his Excellency leaving him a free hand.

O'Connell in his speeches in the libel case brought by the Viceroy against Magee of the "Weekly Post" sluices him with violent abuse, and accuses him of a "sullen and sulky opposition to the Catholics of Ireland." But we instinctively discount O'Connell's immense and perennial issue of invective.

Mr. Gregory seems to have held him in warm personal regard, and his friendship is said to have been prized because it was personal, not political. But he left but little mark on the country at a time when in the new relations between England and Ireland a greater statesman might have done much to turn the bitter waters to sweet. So at least we in the last decades of the century are inclined to think, looking back regretfully at the first and adapting in a new sense the words "Si jeunesse savait—si vieillesse pouvait!"

He was succeeded by Lord Whitworth, wit, diplomatist, man of the world, and evidently a kindly gracious English gentleman. He was accused of want of energy, though soon in antagonism to O'Connell, putting down the Catholic Board in his first year of office. But he was without bigotry or bitterness. The island government probably seemed a small thing to him who had been the voice of England at the Courts of St. Petersburg and Paris. He had indeed all but measured swords with Napoleon at the Tuileries when he railed at England for not having evacuated Egypt and Malta, accused her of having violated treaties, and ended by flourishing a cane in his hand dangerously near the face of the English Ambassador. Lord Whitworth put his hand on the hilt of his sword. "What would you have done if the Emperor had struck you?" he was afterwards asked. "I would have felled him to the ground," was his reply.

There is a story told also of how at the Russian Court his quick wit disposed of a rival. Fox had sent Adair, whose father was a surgeon, as a sort of Ambassador of his own. "Est-ce un homme très considérable, ce M. d'Adair?" asked the Empress. "Pas trop, Madame," replied Lord Whitworth, "quoique son père fût grand *saigneur*."

After holding his own with the great monarchs of Europe he probably did not take the invective of Dublin orators much to heart. He entertained with great splendour, but perhaps with a little disregard of small distinctions, and there were complaints of people being asked "in and out of their turn." His friends seem to have been devoted to him, and watched his health with critical care. When he talks of going to Naples for sunshine, Lord Talbot writes to Mr. Gregory, "I have had a letter from Verulam, who does not approve of what he calls a frisky fidgety scheme in our friend Lord W. to leave his comforts and his splendours at home."

There was something of splendour about his whole career. When he went to Copenhagen to arrange a treaty for the searching of Danish ships, he was escorted by a squadron of "nine sail of the line, four bombs and five frigates." When he took unto himself a mate she was a Duchess, and his home was at magnificent Knole.

But in Ireland his administration is less remembered as his, than as a part of the administration of his great Chief Secretary.

Of Peel, so much has been written that it would be an impertinence to add to the folios already heaped over his name. Every Harrow boy knows how

> Peel stood, steadily stood
> Under the name in the carven wood,
> Reading rapidly, all at ease,
> Pages out of Demosthenes—
> Where has he got to—tell him not to—
> All the scholars who hear him cry—

> That's the lesson for, lesson for, lesson for—
> That's the lesson for next July!

and how in after-life

> Peel stood up on the famous floor,
> Ruled the people and fed the poor.

This last line might stand for a summary of his work in Ireland. He was able to say in the House of Commons, "My constant object in Ireland was a fair administration of the laws as they exist, and I challenge the country to produce any instance in which, while I held office, an impartial administration of those laws was denied."

The greater number of his letters to Mr. Gregory which contain matter of general interest have already been published. Of those that remain I give one or two, which show him as indeed "a man diligent in his business." One letter in my hands on the subject of seed oats runs to twenty-five closely written pages. And one to which he adds: "Pray show this letter to the Duke of Richmond, or if you doubt his being able to decipher it, for I have written in a great hurry, apprise him of the substance of it," runs to thirty-three. It was in his time that the lean years began, and the feeding of the poor is his chief preoccupation. How to get meal, oats, potatoes to the famine-struck districts, letter after letter refers to this.

There is a later letter of his, written to my husband in 1844, which foreshadows the Landed Estates Act.

He says, "It certainly is a great misfortune that there should be superadded to so many other causes of social disunion and disorganisation as exist in Ireland a state of things in respect to the tenure of landed Property which would without any other cause be a great obstacle to any permanent improvement in the condition of the country.

"I have not much confidence in the efficacy of great works undertaken by the Government, or in any extensive scheme for the reclamation of waste lands excepting through the agency of individual enterprise, and with a good prospect of individual gain, but I do think that the *equitable* commutation of the present complicated interests in and Tenure of Land in Ireland into a fee simple Tenure would lay the foundation of great good. I would not attempt too much at first, for I should fear the introduction of any arbitrary principle in respect to the disposal of landed property in Ireland—but I think with the encouragement of Government, and the cordial co-operation of Equity Lawyers (if that could be had) there might be found with the willing assent of proprietors and mortgagees a gradual improvement in the Tenure of Landed Property.

"If there could be created in each county in Ireland a considerable number of bona fide fee simple Properties or rather Properties without perplexed derivative interests (for I would not limit the Right of entail) there would be new securities for peace, and new temptations to the application of Capital to the improvement of the soil."

His secretaryship is perhaps best kept in mind in Ireland by the "Peelers," who have become a part of every landscape and are a sort of visible emblem of Government throughout the country. Lonely indeed must be the road, deserted the railway station, where two dark figures with short capes and inadequate caps do not sooner or later appear, ostentatiously fingering their rifles and patrolling the Queen's highway. Sober, peaceable, well behaved, they form a happy contrast to the "barony constables" of the pre-Peel period, whose only necessary qualification was a certificate of having received the Sacrament at the parish church, and who were obliged to eke out their scanty pay by a recognised game of "open your hand and shut your eyes." Lord Cloncurry tells us how in swearing in one of these worthies and expounding his official duties he came to that of preventing the straying or grazing of cattle on the public roads, and was interrupted with: "And where am I to keep my own little cow, my Lord?"

In all the letters I have looked through I never find Mr. Peel's name mentioned except with affection and warm regard. Lord Talbot is grieved and saddened by his defection, but still holds him in his heart. In letters to each other he and Mr. Gregory refer with much disturbance to a letter received from Mr. Peel soon after his departure from Ireland, which I have not found, but which seems to have reproached them for having neglected to provide for some old servant of his. They feel the accusation is unjust, no suitable place having become vacant, but are hurt and distressed that he should for a moment think they have neglected a wish of his, whose memory they hold so dear.

Vesey Fitzgerald writes to Mr. Gregory in February 1819:

"Everyone is looking to Peel, and you I know will be gratified to learn that every day adds strength to his reputation. He has already distinguished himself greatly in the Chair of the Bank Committee, and surprised those who did not know him. *We* knew before his extraordinary power of mind, when he applies it to the transaction of business, or the investigation of truth."

And Mr. Goulburn in 1822:

"You will be glad to hear that Peel is very well, and does the business of Secretary of State here as well as he did that of Secretary in Ireland."

His nature may probably have hardened in the years following his Government of Ireland, for he must have suffered keenly, first from having taken up a bad cause, and then in the breaking away from it. But he had already offended Irish Orangeism by not holding its Shibboleths in sufficient reverence, and great must have been the relief of cutting the rope that held him to intolerance. This must have in some part made up to him for the unfriendly and reproachful looks turned on him, when he brought in the Bill of which he said, "If it succeed, the credit will belong to others, if it fail the responsibility will devolve upon me," and when he sat "with folded arms and compressed lips listening to the reproaches hurled at him."

Here in Galway the moist Atlantic air that softens our voices and rounds off our asperities as well as our energies, may have had a mellowing effect upon him, and some pleasant traditions still linger round his name. He came sometimes from his Castle duties to shoot woodcocks with Mr. Daly of Dunsandle, M.P. for the county and his close friend. "Is there anything I can do for you?" he is said to have once asked, when taking leave of his host.

"Oh, you might as well make Denis a peer and Jim a bishop!" was the laughing answer. But in later years, when the Chief Secretary had become Premier, he did both.

And there is still to be seen a ring brought to the west by him as a sort of apple of the Hesperides, and given to the fairest of three fair sisters, and now treasured by her descendants.

Lord Whitworth was the last viceroy in whose time the danger of French influence and French invasion came within the line of practical politics. In England, the danger was from outside, and the people of her seaboard had long shuddered at the fear of invasion. But in Ireland the danger lay deeper, and within her own coasts, and when accounts came of Buonaparte's successes, and the wind blew from the south, hearts beat high, and the "Shan van Voght" was again the song of the moment:

"Oh! the French on the sea,
They'll be here without delay,
And the Orange will decay, says the Shan van Voght!"

A landing of the French seemed a very present hope or danger, as the case might be, to those who had seen French ships off Bantry in 1796, or French troops at Killala in 1798. And there is no doubt that, counting by numbers, hopes were in the majority.

In the home of my childhood there was an old Catholic nurse whose upstair teachings tempered the strict Orangeism of the drawing-room, and whose eye would flash as she told of the triumphant shouting she had heard in 1798 when it was told at a theatre she had been taken to that the French had landed at Killala. She was only a child herself then, but she remembered how all the audience had stood up and cheered and waved their handkerchiefs at the joyful news.

It is striking in these letters of Lord Whitworth's how he takes for granted that the Irish will rejoice at the escape of England's enemy, and only ventures to hope their joy may not take too practical a form. Taking all the affairs of his Government easily, however, he is not seriously alarmed. He had some time before written to Peel, who told him the Catholic Board thought of calling for the intervention of Spain and Portugal in support of Catholic claims, "I do not understand how Spain and Portugal are to assist unless they send a detachment of inquisitors." Accustomed as he was to follow all the movements of Napoleon on the European chessboard, he probably realised how small and insignificant a pawn Ireland was considered in the game.

Yet no one who knew what was going on in the country could be quite free from uneasiness. In March 1813 Mr. Gregory had written to Peel: "I have this day read a letter to Lord Castlemaine from the neighbourhood of Athlone. If the Contents be true, matters are more formed in that county than any of us could have supposed. It represents a system of Organization matured, and Delegates assembled at Athlone from Dublin, Kildare, Wicklow and King's County, various signs of fraternity, with an oath of allegiance to Buonaparte. The writer of the Letter I know well. He is a discreet, active, bold Magistrate."

He gives less heed to the alarm sounded by a noble lord, who had already been dubbed by Mr. Peel "that great alarmist," and says: "Wherever Field Marshall Funck commands, the Enemy is sure of appearing formidable." But no warning was ever quite neglected. In another letter to Mr. Peel in June 1814 he says: "A most absurd report was brought yesterday evening from some of the alarmed magistrates in the town of Naas that a rising was certainly to take place during the night in the county of Kildare. This was sent to Commander of the Forces and Sir E. Littlehales, in consequence of which strong patrols were sent forward and every Precaution used as if the Story had been believed. . . . Tho' I attached no credit to the story, yet I remembered Emmett and the Castle caught napping."

In June of 1813 he had written: "If Buonaparte is successful, the standard of disunion between Ireland and England will soon be raised." In July Mr. Peel, announcing the "glorious and unexpected" news of the battle of Vittoria, orders a Gazette extraordinary to be published—"I am sure the expediency of giving all the publicity possible to good news in Ireland far outweighs every other consideration." And on Oct. 1 he writes: "I am glad to hear that O'Connell and the other itinerant demagogues made little impression in Galway, or if any an unfavourable one. I hear that at Mallow and in that neighbourhood the Gang was more successful. The reverses, however, of their good friend and ally in Germany will damp their efforts in the good old cause of riot and insurrection."

The Government informers were constantly kept at work. A memorandum is sent by Mr. Peel from the Irish Office in 1814.

"*Memorandum.*—June 11, 1814. Information has been for some time received by the Irish Government that a system of organization was forming among the lower orders in the County of Kildare and that frequent meetings of the disaffected took place. The person from whom this information principally came, and who is himself implicated in the proceedings of the disaffected, was desired to give notice of some specific meeting about to take place in order that measures might be taken for the apprehension of the persons and papers of the parties assembled. He stated that there would be a meeting in the town of Kildare on Sunday June 5, and a Magistrate was directed to be in readiness with a party of Military at the time appointed.

"It appears from the report of the Magistrate that on entering the House where it was reported that the meeting of the disaffected was to be held, he immediately went upstairs and found in an upper room several people who were in great confusion on hearing of the entrance of the soldiery, and destroyed several Papers which were on the Table. Seven of the persons present were arrested, and two papers seized, which are considered by the Attorney-General of Ireland to be decidedly of a treasonable nature, and to afford sufficient evidence with the testimony of the informer for the conviction of the persons apprehended, who are committed on a charge of High Treason.

"The papers are written by illiterate persons—they refer to orders given by the *executive Directory* that the Officers should meet once a week until July 5—that no arms should be given out until the Insurrection is to take place—as if they were sent before some parts of the Country would be in a state of Rebellion too soon. They state that the delegates from Dublin, Longford, Louth, Meath, Westmeath, Kildare, Wicklow, Wexford, Carlow, Kilkenny, demand clothing, arms and ammunition immediately.

"It appears from the magistrates of the Queen's County that that County is in a disturbed state. That on Sunday night the 30th May eleven houses were robbed of arms and Money by a party of the disaffected—nine on Monday night and three on Tuesday."

A report docketed 1814, and signed only Q., says. "I went yesterday according to promise to the County Kildare, and remained there until yesterday. I spent the first day in Farrellstown with a weaver named Donelly who works for me, and from whom I received the following information. That there was a system lately introduced in the neighbourhood which he understood to be somewhat similar to the Defenders of '96. That is that none but Catholics were admissible, and that their object was to protect themselves against the Orangemen or to retaliate in case of necessity on either themselves or families, and that they were bound to do this by an oath. Donelly told me that it was a certainty a Mr. Richardson who now lives in Robertstown did belong to a Regiment named the Foxhunters who killed some Rebels in the Curragh in '98, the friends of whom are determined to have revenge (these are his own words). He also mentioned to me that Thos. Beaghan, a Farmer, who formerly lived on the grounds Mr. Richardson lately purchased, with some others similarly circumstanced, were determined to banish him out of the country at the risk of their lives; however, that since the soldiers went into the neighbourhood they were more cautious in committing themselves. From Robertstown I went to Kildare, and immediately repaired to the public house next the post office, as directed. There I found six or seven persons drinking round a kitchen fire, and from their appearance and manner of conversing I immediately suspected them to be friends of the persons arrested. One of them wished that instead of the horse race on the Curragh to-morrow it might be the general Race, and the last Race and big Race; at this kind of nonsense they continually kept laughing. Rankin, the Bricklayer, stated that there was no one concerned in it but the lowest order of Spalpeens whom the sight of a Soldier would frighten to Death's door, and that since their arrival one of them was afraid to raise their voice. He likewise mentioned to me that they took the name of Ribbonmen amongst themselves. I slept at Connell's, a shopkeeper to whom I sold some goods not long since, and he confirmed me in the opinion that the above system was confined to the lowest orders of the people, and appeared to be happy that the soldiers were sent to preserve the peace of the county, stating from what he heard occasionally in his own shop that there was very little to be expected from the Humanity of those concerned. I traversed the town the next day, but could not fasten upon anyone who would commit themselves or that I could get the exact form of their oath from. I went from this to Rathangan, where I saw Locke; he acknowledged that the above system reached the verge of the Town, but that when he came to know it he did all in his power to put it down, that there were no one but farmers' boys and the like in that neighbourhood knew of it until they heard of it through the Magistrates at Rathangan. I went next day to Prosperous. . . . From Prosperous I went to Rathcoffee and found that a man assuming the character of a deserter had passed through Clone about six weeks ago and endeavoured to tamper with some people on the Common. He said he was from the North, and came to warn the people of their danger, that the Orangemen were to rise and murder the Catholics on the same night all through Ireland, but it appears he did not meet with much encouragement there, for he did not stop. This I had from a Schoolmaster named Hogan, who has lately come into Clone. He is a Wexford man and a Rebel; my brother employed him to measure some work he done for Mr. Kenny, the Jesuit in Castlebrown. Old Raddy of Rathcoffee told me that the name of the Irish Legion in France had been changed to the third Foreign Regiment and that a letter had lately been received by the friends of Reilly of Kilcock to that effect, but that as yet they have not heard anything of war."

In September 1814 Lord Whitworth writes in good heart:

"I rejoice to hear that you are so likely to bring your business to a conclusion—good to you as taking a heavy burthen from your mind, and to me as enabling you to return soon to this country.

"I flatter myself, or rather I should say we may flatter ourselves, that it is getting into a state of more perfect tranquillity than it has known for many years. The Bill has operated wonderfully in Middlethird. They, the Farmers, begin to feel the necessity of looking after those in their employ, and are ready to hand up those by whose misconduct they will continue liable to the Imposition. This acts as it should do, and will be a good example to others.

"We passed a most delightful month in the Co. of Wicklow. We were enchanted with its beauties, and the Duchess has laid in such a store of health as will I hope carry her through her winter Campaign.

"I think I have nothing new to tell you. It was not fair to send Lady Anne and your family so far off, depriving us of the pleasure of seeing her, and of paying her all those attentions which from our real regard for her we are both so much inclined to do."

When the moment of danger actually arrived, in 1815, it happened that the Under Secretary was alone in office at the Castle, in consequence of the sad tragedy that had cast a gloom over the Viceregal household.

There is an entry in Mr. Gregory's note-book, dated November 30, 1814. "Dined with the Lord Lieutenant. Duke of Dorset of age."

Three months later, the young Duke was killed by a fall from his horse. He had been staying at Powerscourt, and joined in a hunt near Killiney. His horse fell in jumping a stone wall, and he was thrown, but said he believed he was not much hurt. He was taken to a house near, and his mother and Lord Whitworth sent for, but before they could arrive he said quietly, "I am off," and passed away.

His short life is best remembered through Byron's friendship for him in their Harrow school-days, and the verses he addressed to him.

Moore, on his death, laid aside for the moment his political sarcasms and wrote some lines of sympathy to the Duchess:

"We saw the hope you cherished
For one short hour appear,
And when that hope had perished,
We gave you tear for tear."

The following note seems to have been written on the day of his death.

"My dear Gregory,—Will you have the goodness to put up these letters in a packet to Sir C. Flint, and send it by an Express.

"You will guess the melancholy news they bear and judge of our feelings. I can no more.

"ever yours,
"W.

"There are two which I will beg of you to direct and seal; as were I to do it they might be opened by those to whom it will be necessary to communicate the fatal Intelligence with great caution."

The next letters are on the same subject.

Mr. Gregory to Mr. Peel

February 15, 1815.

"As the Lord Lieutenant writes to you by this Express, I have nothing to add to respecting the most melancholy occurrence of yesterday. The Duke lived upwards of an hour after his fall, but suffered no pain. He was sensible of his approaching death a few minutes before he expired. The horse fell upon him and crushed everything inward. The Lord Lieutenant is quite wretched, she, poor soul, has cried much during the night; but for several hours she could not be brought to believe her son was dead. He was surely a most inimitable young man in every good quality."

February 16, 1815.

"The Lord Lieutenant writes to you by this Post respecting his Intention of applying for Leave to go to England for three months. Although Lord Justices have not yet been resorted to, yet from the peculiar distress of the Duchess and her repugnance to leaving Ireland without her Husband, I think the greatest allowance should be made to the Indulgence of any thing which could alleviate her affliction. She would derive no Benefit from her Departure unaccompanied by Lord Whitworth, deprived of his tender Attention she would derive but half consolation in the society of her surviving Children. Add to all these Considerations which certainly are only private (yet deserving great weight) the present appearances of the Country are tranquil, nothing alarming from the interior, and scarce a smoke from the ashes of the Board portending a Phoenix in the new association. I certainly write under the Influence of strong feeling to promote any object which may tend to alleviate the sufferings of that unhappy Mother, but in so doing I trust I am not wishing for the adoption of a measure which would be likely to produce any evil consequences to the State.

"It was originally intended that the Remains of the Duke should be conveyed privately from the Castle on Board the Yacht. That plan has been altered, first as not suitable to his

Rank, and next to gratify the wishes of all the Gentry of this City who have expressed the most anxious desire to testify their respect to his memory, and his Coffin will lay in state to-morrow in the Castle Chapel, and at 10 o'clock on Saturday morning be removed to the Pigeon House. I have sent a short Notice to the Newspapers apprising such as wish to attend, which I preferred to any circular Letter to Men of Rank. Some would necessarily have been omitted, and Etiquette would have found cause of offence in the solemn Pageantry of Death. . . . There will be very little expense attending the Procession to the Water side, as scarfs and Hat Bands will be given only to the Lord Lieutenant's family. Had the Distribution been extended beyond the Castle it would not have been possible to draw any Line of Distinction. Grievous as is the face of Woe, yet Melancholy is gratified by one sentiment of sorrow which affects the upper Classes of this City—no Dinner Parties etc., all put off, and really no topic of Conversation but the one. . . ."

February 18, 1815.

"The last sad tribute which a pitying Metropolis could pay to youthful virtue, was this day testified by the inhabitants of Dublin in the numerous, decent, sad procession from the Castle to the Yacht; all the shops in the streets through which the Funeral passed were shut, and I believe there was scarce a gentleman's Carriage in the City which did not accompany it; even Scully and O'Connell were in theirs. The Duchess has desired to see me to-morrow after church. From the accounts Lord Whitworth gives of her Composure and Resignation I fear she is making too great an Exertion over herself, but sincerely hope her mind is calmed by the Influence of Religion. They are both gone to your house in the Park, which was equally necessary for both."

Mr. Peel answers:

Mr. Peel to Mr. Gregory

Stanhope Street. February 20, 1815.

"Lord Whitworth's natural wish to accompany the Duchess to England is acceded to without difficulty. I am truly glad of it on his account, and still more on hers. I should have been a strenuous advocate for a compliance with that wish had I foreseen much greater difficulties than I now do from the temporary transfer of the Government into other hands. I am perfectly satisfied with the proposed arrangement, and I need hardly tell you how much my confidence in you contributes to the composure with which I contemplate it. The letter in which you sent me the affecting details of the removal of the Duke's body from the "Castle" has been of the greatest service. You cannot conceive with what interest it has been read by his friends here, and what a melancholy consolation it has afforded them. Poor Lady Delawarr's greatest and only pleasure is in reading every line and word that is written upon her brother's loss.

"I was very much pleased with the anxiety of the Duchess of Rutland; I enclose a note from her which if you think fit you may show to Lord Whitworth. It is one out of a thousand proofs of the deep impression which has been made on the public by this most unfortunate and untimely loss.

"Yours ever, my dear Gregory,

"ROBERT PEEL."

Lord Whitworth to Mr. Gregory

February 20, 1815.

"I have the pleasure to assure you that the Duchess is as well as can be possibly expected, much the better for the change of air and place. We had letters from the Delawarrs and some others yesterday by the express. Poor Lady Delawarr is as well as can be expected. Lady Plymouth was not yet made acquainted with her loss.

"I had a most feeling and amiable letter from Peel. It gave us both great comfort. What an excellent Creature he is! But my dear Gregory he is not the only one. We have met with some here who will be for ever entitled to our warmest and most sincere affection.

"The Duchess desires to be most kindly remembered to Lady Anne and to your daughter.

"I find that our friend the Chancellor has only told the Miss Guns, Lady Rossmore, and about a dozen more, of our intention of going to England. I hope I shall be able to avow it as more than an eventual intention in a day or two."

The desired leave was readily granted, and on March 13 Lord Whitworth writes:

"I return you the papers signed. I wish I could as easily express to you the sincere Esteem and regard I feel for you. We are both very grateful for your kind wishes, and shall be both of us happy to be re-united to you and Lady Anne, to whom the Duchess desires to be most particularly remembered."

His next note is from Holyhead.

Tuesday, 9 a.m.
"Here we are, so you may begin swearing as soon as you please.

"I conclude of course that your Triumvirate will be fairly established this day.

"We got over in Six hours, plenty of wind, plenty of sea, and plenty of miseries of all kinds.

"The Duchess is nevertheless very well, she is now writing to Lady Anne.

"Believe me, my dear Gregory, here as in Dublin and everywhere,

"most truly yours,
"WHITWORTH."

Lord Whitworth was met in England by the tremendous, or as Mr. Peel calls it, the "extraordinary and affecting" news of the escape of Napoleon, and his landing at St. Juan.

His letters which follow, and Mr. Gregory's to him, show the extreme anxiety felt in London and in Ireland.

Lord Whitworth to Mr. Gregory

Hertford Street: March 18, 1815.
"I have the pleasure (if the word pleasure can be used under so many circumstances of distress) to tell you that we arrived here last night after a prosperous journey. The news from France was the first to salute me on getting on shore at Holyhead, and the formidable accounts of the Ruffian's progress has met us at every stage.

"What a Catastrophe, but indeed no more than could be expected from such a wretched want of foresight, or rather such a stupid and fatal forbearance.

"By this time he is, I doubt not, reseated on his throne, where he will remain unless he is torn down by the hand of an assassin, which is supposed not unlikely to happen:

"I expect that our friends on your side will be all alive.

However, I do not fear them. He will never be able to assist them effectually, though it may be his policy to excite them.

"I do not believe that any line of conduct is decided on here. We shall of course be influenced by that of our allies.

"I suppose the Lords Justices, but more particularly the Chancellor, will be in a fine fuss with all these accounts from France. It will be too cruel to avail myself of the whole term for which I meant to be absent. I shall certainly shorten it in consideration of all these events.

"P.S. 6 o'clock. I think I have much more comfortable accounts to give you than I had in the morning. In the first place I have been almost all the morning with Lord Sidmouth, and we have agreed, as Peel will tell you, to keep all the militia, English and Irish, assembled till further orders. Sir G. Hewitt will receive his instructions to suspend the circulation of the orders which he received a few days ago, relative to the partial disembodying of the Irish, and the sending home of the English, provided that they are not actually embarked or in such a state of preparation as to render any change particularly inconvenient. Now for the news from France, which is to-day much better. Letters of the 15th from Paris say that the people of Paris and of the country are recovered from their first consternation, that the population of Paris is arming for the defence of the King, that Bonaparte is still at Lyons, and had got no more than 8,800 men with fifty pieces of artillery very imperfectly equipped. That Massena was advancing from the South upon Lyons in pursuit, and that Ney was coming across from Besançon with 13,000 men, to get if possible between him and Paris should he be disposed to advance to that City. Upon the whole therefore we may consider things as bearing a favourable aspect. The game is not up, and we may hope. I do not venture further.

"This goes by the express, which it was determined to send off at our Conference of this morning."

Hertford St.: March 20, 1815.

"You will of course hear from Peel on business, so that I only write two lines to give you the latest intelligence from France.

"I am this moment come from the Regent, so that it may be depended upon.

"A messenger arrived at 12 with letters stating that Bonaparte had advanced from Lyons on the road to Paris with about 10 or 12,000 men, harassed, ill appointed, and dejected at not finding the Enthusiasm and confidence they expected in Bonaparte's quarters. Marshal Ney is now very close to him with a very superior force, and other Corps are coming against him from all quarters. If numbers are to decide the contest the event cannot be doubtful. It remains to be seen how they will behave when they come into contact with their own Companions in arms. It is thought they may be depended upon. In the meanwhile Paris is perfectly quiet, and every measure of precaution and preparation taken which can ensure its safety. In short the thing looks well, and people are in tolerably good spirits. A very short time must decide whether we have more to hope or fear.

"Peel, who lives very near, calls here every morning after the receipt of the post, so that we talk over your business very comfortably."

Mr. Gregory to Mr. Peel

March 20, 1815.

"Our Rabble are all ears for news of Buonaparte's success, and have already reinstated him on the Throne of France. There has been a scandalous acquittal of two men at Longford on the clearest evidence for attacking the House of a farmer named Goulding, who defended himself gallantly, killed one, wounded another, swore informations and prosecuted the two men acquitted. A Revd. Mr. Moffett gave the prisoners an unimpeachable character, and the Jury believed the probably perjured Divine, and discredited the gallant farmer."

Mr. Gregory to Lord Whitworth

Dublin Castle: March 20, 1815.

"I was made very happy by the receipt of your letter both on private and public grounds, first to hear that you and the Duchess had arrived in London, and next for the cheering Intelligence that Buonaparte had not re-ascended the throne of France. We were in the lowest state of Depression from the accounts of yesterday, but there is now great Life in the Game.

"It will be necessary to keep up a strong military force whether Buonaparte succeeds or not; there was a restless disposition amongst the people before any hope was cherished by them of his Enlargement, the surprize and Joy which that Circumstance has excited naturally has made them more sanguine, and although their hopes and Expectations will, I trust, soon be extinguished so far as Buonaparte is concerned, yet the Country will require a strong force and much vigilance to prevent disturbance.

"Castlemaine writes terrific accounts from Westmeath, but his Insurrections are all in Anticipation of what are to result from Buonaparte's success; however, upon such certain and definite Grounds of alarm, there is to be another memorial from the County for the Insurrection Act.

"I received a letter this day from Enniskillen; he had proposed going to England with his family early in the month, but as he thinks the country may be disturbed, like a good and loyal Paddy, he has deferred his journey and proposes to remain at home.

"How preferable this to the pugnacious Peer who proposes to fight for Ireland in the House of Lords."

Mr. Gregory to Mr. Peel

March 21, 1815.
"None of our County Correspondents gives any account of the apprehended disturbances; yet every one from the country states the general Joy of the lower orders on Buonaparte's Reappearance in France, and their readiness to manifest that disposition on the first favourable opportunity. However, I cannot think they will do more than express their satisfaction by words, unless their Favourite is successful."

Mr. Peel to Mr. Gregory

Irish Office: March 22, 1815.
". . . We must, I fear, make up our mind for the possession of Paris by Buonaparte, at least I think it is the opinion of the best informed that in the calculation of Probabilities the chances are in his favour. I hope that the possession of Paris will not imply the possession of the throne of France. With the present feelings of the French marshals who are faithful to the Bourbons, it is on the whole, I think, prudent in the king to rely on them for his defence, and not to wound their pride by invoking the aid of foreign arms. I think it may be prudent not to allow a foreign army to cross the frontier even until after the surrender to Buonaparte of Paris, then all scruples must be at an end, nor will the most delicate of French honour have a right to take offence, if the king calls in those who gave him his crown, to maintain—perhaps I should say to recover—it."

Lord Whitworth to Mr. Gregory

Hertford St.: March 22, 1815.

"I have just received yours of the 20th by Express, and as Peel was with me, I have also seen what you have written to him.

"I think, all circumstances considered, that you are going on well. We must be prepared for and indeed make allowance for a little Exultation on the return of their friend Buonaparte to power, but I trust their triumph will be of short duration. Should he arrive at Paris and reseat himself on that devoted throne, it is decided that the whole strength of Europe, that is of Russia, Austria and Prussia, with the assistance of what we have in Belgium, shall be exerted to pluck him down. We know that we shall have the hearts of the whole nation with us, and I hope the co-operation of some force in Britany and the Vendée, if not in other parts of France.

"It is supposed by those who are best informed to be about an equal chance whether he gets to Paris or not. Ney, who is in his rear, will not attack until he has the Co-operation of the strong force assembling near Paris, and with which Buonaparte must come in Contact before he gets there. Should Ney be able to fall upon him while he is so engaged, the result can scarcely be doubted. There are, however, fears that Ney's army is not so trustworthy as that which is assembling near the Capital. Upon the whole I see no reason for utter despair. We have yet a chance of checking his progress, and at all events of totally destroying him whenever the armies that have lately triumphed over him can be brought back to action. The Emperor of Russia has declared his determination to exert the whole strength of his Empire for the maintenance of the treaty of Paris, which he considers as his more immediate Act, and for which he is more personally responsible."

Mr. Gregory to Mr. Peel

Dublin Castle: March 23, 1815.

"Had the gloomy Intelligence of yesterday been confirmed, I had intended writing to you this day to put into execution what your Letter received on Saturday suggested. I began to be alarmed that something might have occurred requiring immediate decisive Action, in which your Aid would have been necessary. The Care of Responsibility I do not shrink from, but Authority is always wanting in a moment of Danger. Buonaparte is the

Barometer by which we must judge and Act in this Country, should He (which God Avert) be successful, Disturbance would break out unless kept down by the strong hand of Power. . . . I find several Foreigners arrived in the Yacht from Holyhead. I have sent for Sproule to endeavour to find out who they are, and have directed an official Letter to be written to him to send a Return of Passengers He at any time brings to Dublin. I have directed the Police to watch them closely, also Arthur O'Connor's wife, who I am sorry to find is invited to our best Houses; she dined last week at Lord Castlecoote's . . ."

Lord Whitworth to Mr. Gregory

Hertford St.: March 23, 1815.
"Alas! it is over. We last night received the fatal news of the King's having been obliged to leave Paris, and he is perhaps at this moment at Dover. Buonaparte has allowed him fourteen days to secure his retreat.

"I do not think that this Event creates such a sensation here as might have been expected. The well disposed are of course much depressed, but I see no great exultation amongst those who are otherwise. I hope and trust it will be the same with you. We must expect some triumph, and that some hope will be raised —but I cannot believe that it will go farther. Should it be otherwise, both Peel and myself will be immediately with you. Little did we imagine that the Lords Justices would have such times to encounter. Should the lower orders, contrary to expectation, be inclined to pass the bounds of moderate Joy and triumph, we must immediately apply the Insurrection Act wherever it may be applicable. But Peel will write to you upon this subject more fully."

Mr. Gregory to Mr. Peel

Dublin Castsle. March 25, 1815.
"I communicated your Letter of the 22nd to the Lords Justices, thinking that they ought to be apprised of your opinion of what might probably be the success of Buonaparte's progress to Paris, and also to take such measures as might be thought necessary for protecting this Metropolis from any sudden ebullition of popular Joy at the triumph of the Enemy.
"It has been thought prudent not to make any display of

cautionary measures, but without seeming, to have an increased vigilance. . . . The three Magistrates of the Head Police Office were this day with the Lords Justices, and unanimously agreed that there was no danger to be apprehended from any disturbance in the city; that the rabble would doubtless testify their exultation at the success of their favourite, but they were decidedly of opinion this would not break out into any act of Outrage. However, it happens that these bad accounts arrive at an unlucky Crisis, the eve of Easter, when the lower Orders testify their piety and faith in Drunkenness for two days. . . ."

March 29, 1815.

"Capt. Sproule, in justification of his conduct, says he was requested by Capt. Fellowes to bring over the French Consul and his friends. I have directed a constant watch on the French Consul's house, he has taken up his residence in one of the outlets of the town. What are the strange stories of Lord Kinnaird, I heard some time ago that his Language in Paris was most extraordinary, abusing the Bourbons, and extolling Buonaparte, with whose avowed friends he constantly associated.

"I received an invitation some time since to dine with Lord Castlecoote this day. I last night was told that Mrs. Arthur O'Connor[1] was to be of the party, upon which I called this morning to ascertain the fact from him. He told me she was not. He then wished to know my reason. I immediately answered, if she did, I should not. I then ventured to ask him if she had already dined with him. He answered in the Negative, but said she was to do so. I have perhaps gone out of my way in this communication with Castlecoote, at the same time I should have felt unpleasant in dining in company with a Woman whom I might in a few days receive orders to send out of the kingdom, and who with due deference to my superiors, should never have been admitted into it."

Lord Whitworth to Mr. Gregory

Hertford St.: March 27, 1815.

"Both Peel and myself are very anxious to learn the effect which the news of Buonaparte's success will have in Dublin and

[1] *Note.*—Arthur O'Connor, one of the leaders of the United Irishmen, had gone to France with Lord Edward Fitzgerald in 1796 to try and persuade the authorities to help a rebellion in Ireland with French troops. After the rebellion he was disbarred, and lived in exile in France, becoming a General in the French army. He married a daughter of the Marquis of Condorcet.

the Country, and I think we have partly agreed that Peel shall
go over, if it should be at all likely to lead to anything unpleasant,
and that I should relieve him, so that he may be here to finish
any Irish business in Parliament.

"In a few days I shall expect to hear what the Lords Justices
decide of the offer which I begged of you to make to them in
regard to myself. Unless it should be absolutely necessary I
should wish to remain in this Country a month or six weeks
longer, but I would most cheerfully give up every concern should
it be conceived that my presence at my post at this moment might
be useful. Therefore I am sure you will tell me candidly what you
think.

"We have no further news to-day from France; neither indeed
is it to be wished. I am sure we can have none good. I hope
the Police will keep a good look out after the Emissaries who
may be sent to Ireland. Capt. Sproule deserves to be hanged
at his own yardarm if he suffered any to come over in his yacht."

Mr. Gregory to Lord Whitworth

Dublin Castle: March 29, 1815.
"The reports from the Country and in the Town continue the
same, the expression of Joy which at first declared itself in Dublin
has subsided, tho' I am confident the Joy is the same. The affray
in Cavan would have occurred whether Buonaparte was in Elba
or Paris; in short, nothing has yet occurred to create any alarm.
Do not, however, agree to any reduction of our military forces,
our Country is full of mines which may explode in spite of the
most vigilant care, and although I do not as yet apprehend any
attack from without, still if Buonaparte is seated in power he will
not again overlook Ireland."

Lord Whitworth to Mr. Gregory

Hertford St.: April 1, 1815.
"I am quite satisfied to remain here for some time longer, altho'
perhaps not so long as I originally intended, on your statement.
I quite agree with you in thinking that there can be no present
danger of disturbance, neither do I think that a bare promise
from France will be sufficient to excite any great signs of Commotion. I hope we may always depend upon a good military

force, and that is the best Constitution for Ireland under its present Circumstances. . . .

"We have no particular news from France. The old Women and Children in the street may be imposed upon by the pacific language of the Usurper, but he will impose on no others. I have reason to believe that the most effectual means are in progress against him. No doubt is entertained of the steadiness of either of the allied Powers. His efforts to disunite them will only convince them the more of his present inability to make head against him.

"Peel has been unwell for the last two or three days, but is much better.

"*Our* kindest remembrances to Lady Anne. I know from the best authority that whatever may be the result of the Congress of Vienna, the services and zeal of Lord Clancarty are appreciated. How could Capt. Sproule be such a blockhead as to bring over such fellows? I am quite sure they will be well looked after, but I had rather send them back again. Peel is this moment gone down to Lord Sidmouth to see what can be done."

Mr. Gregory to Lord Whitworth

Dublin Castle: April 6, 1815.
"I was enabled to exhilarate the spirits of the Lords Justices by reading to them your Letter of the 3rd, it gives fairer prospects than We have for some days seen. . . . The friends of Opposition in Ireland anticipate the most happy result to their Party; they have created a serious misunderstanding between Lord Liverpool and his Colleagues in consequence of which a change of administration must follow. Plunkett, who like Mother Carey's chickens never appears but before a storm, is gone over to Parliament. He who so ably advocated the Cause of the Catholics is to fulminate against the unconstitutional Declaration of the Allies in daring to interfere with the free Government of France. . . ."

Lord Whitworth to Mr. Gregory

Hertford St.. April 6, 1815.
"I have to acknowledge yours of the 3rd. I entirely approve of the measure which you have recommended, with a view to give more solemnity and Importance to the Trial of the murderers

of the Sergeant in the Co. of Cavan. It ought and I trust will be productive of a good effect in that disturbed County. . . .

"I hope I have said nothing in the course of my correspondence which could induce a belief that there was the least hesitation on the part of our Government to adopt the most prompt and strenuous measures for the destruction of Buonaparte. All his arts and wiles are duly appreciated, and have no effect whatever, even I hope and believe on the minds of the most vulgar and uninformed. Upon those of a higher description I am perfectly sure they have none. The message from the Regent is to be delivered this day in the two Houses. If I can get it in time I will send it to you from the House of Lords. In the meantime I can assure you that it will be such as you will approve of. Nothing can be better than the state of affairs in France, the South in Insurrection, the nation recovering from its panic and ready to second any attempt from without. I was assured last night from the very best authority that we had already in Belgium quite sufficient to resist and probably to expel any force which Buonaparte can send there, should he be disposed to do so, and others drawing near from all quarters. In short you may depend upon it that it is meant by all parties to act vigorously, and not to relax until the monster is totally destroyed."

Lord Whitworth to Mr. Gregory

Hertford St.: April 7, 1815.

"I hope you got the Prince Regent's message yesterday, both Recket and Flint promised me they would send it by the Express.

"It will be considered to-day in both Houses, and if we may judge from what passed yesterday in the House it is likely to pass with unanimity. We must not however expect the same concurrence when we come to discuss the measures which are to be pursued in furtherance of this preliminary step. Every member of the Administration, and the Prince Regent at their head, are, I thank God, most decidedly for War. Lord Granville is, I believe, of the same opinion, he would be too inconsistent were he to entertain any other. Lord Grey would be equally inconsistent were he not to profess a bias in favour of peace.

"Two days ago these Leaders were decidedly at issue. It is supposed they have compromised the matter; and this night will probably shew in what manner. In the meantime all the accounts from the Allies, and most particularly from Vienna, where it has been very industriously reported that a contrary sentiment prevailed, are as favourable as the most sanguine can expect or desire.

"We are already very strong in Belgium. The Prussians and Austrians will have to the amount of at least 200,000 men in France in a very short time, and the Russian advanced Corps of 50,000 men will be up by the 15th of next month, and a regular succession constantly following."

Mr. Gregory to Lord Whitworth

Dublin Castle: April 10, 1815.

"I received your two letters of the 6th and 7th. . . .

"Nothing but the hearts of Jacobins could have refused obedience to the noble heroism of the Duchess of Angoulême at Bordeaux. The conduct of the troops was worse than treason. . . .

"I received this day a letter from Mr. Buxton, Chairman of the Sessions for the County of Meath, a very sensible discreet man, giving a melancholy account of that part of the County which borders on Cavan and Longford, from whence the Ribbon System has been introduced. They are in great want of troops and Magistrates, the first may with difficulty be supplied, but I do not know how the other can.

"Waterford has continued quiet since the severe Examples at the late assizes, the same Good would no doubt result from the same measures in other Counties, if the Parties injured were not afraid to prosecute. Yet whenever they do, Reward and Protection is always afforded."

Lord Whitworth to Mr. Gregory

Hertford St.: April 13, 1815.

"I have not written to you for some days, as I literally had nothing worth sending you. I mean as to common occurrences, for I am sure you and Lady Anne would have been kind enough to consider a favourable account of the Duchess' health as a matter of sufficient interest.

"I thank God she is as well as I can possibly expect, as are her daughters and grandsons. . . .

"I am happy to tell you that everything is going on well. The Regent told me last night that the Court of Vienna was as determined and as zealous in the Cause as he, or if possible anyone more anxious than himself, can wish or desire. I suppose in the course of the next week we shall hear what is to be done.

'Nothing can be a stronger proof of the zeal of the Court of Vienna than this determination to augment their armies on the Rhine at the expense of that of Italy; no stronger proof can be given of Austrian disinterestedness.

"I am sorry to find from all the letters which Peel receives and which I myself receive, that the bad spirit in Ireland does not improve. As long, however, as we can find employment for their friend Buonaparte at home, and I trust he will soon have much more than he will be able to meet, I do not apprehend anything serious.

"There was an angry discussion last night in the House of Lords on what should have been done to keep Buonaparte in Elba. It put one in mind of the old saying, 'It is too late to shut the stable door when the steed is stolen.' The French call it preparing a *bouillon pour un mort*, and so it is. In fact the Opposition knew well that Government dared not avow the real cause of mischief, which was the stupid magnanimity of Alexander, lest they should indispose him now when it is so important to conciliate him. Such is the liberality and candour of politicians!"

Mr. Gregory to Mr. Peel

Dublin Castle: April 19, 1815.

"The official Letter from the Lords Justices will declare their apprehensions of withdrawing 5,000 troops from Ireland at this critical Period. . . .

"Although it was my Duty to word my official Letter in such manner as the Lord Justices directed, yet I should ill repay the Confidence placed in me by Lord Whitworth and you, if I allowed it to pass as my own opinion. I perefectly agree that the Lower Orders are most dreadfully bent on Mischief, that in many places the Catholic population are united by the most horrible oaths of Association, that there are great numbers of concealed Arms in their possession, and that no Man can foresee when this Madness may break out into open Insurrection. Yet I can never believe there is any formidable State of Organization. The most timid and the most zealous have never been able to discover any Leader beyond the lowest description of Persons—no Depôt of Ammunition or Arms, no Committees, nothing resembling the systematic plans of the Rebellion of 1798, but the Evil Spirit which pervades the Country. If an Insurrection should break out under these

Circumstances it might be fatal to many valuable Members of Society where it appeared, and the greatest care could be taken to prevent its appearance. But I never can suppose it would be of that general tendency as could endanger the Government, unassisted by foreign force. Nothing can be more obvious than the best mode by which the Agents of Buonaparte can serve him, by creating every possible alarm of domestic Insurrection, by which a powerful Diversion will be made in keeping our Troops at home, and preventing our adding to the strength of the alliance abroad. . . ."

Lord Whitworth to Mr. Gregory

Hertford St.: April 17, 1815.

"We are going down to Knole and to Buckhurst for the week, therefore I shall have nothing to trouble you with until my return. I think of setting off on my return to you about the 8th of May, so as to be in Dublin by the 12th or 13th—and I can with great truth assure you that I shall feel very comfortable in living with you. The Duchess is, I thank God, tolerably well, and looks to her return to Ireland without any unpleasant feeling.

"I have great pleasure in assuring you that everything is going on as well and as expeditiously as can possibly be. It is not at all unlikely but I may bring you the news of the opening of the Campaign. Without reckoning the Russians (who will not be on the Rhine before June) we shall have on French ground in the course of the first week in May, at the least 250,000 men—of which upwards of 100,000 will be under the immediate Command of the Duke of Wellington. It is supposed that Buonaparte cannot muster together above 100,000 men fit for service, and that he is in great want of artillery and all belonging to it. We begin therefore under good auspices, and God grant us a favourable issue."

Mr. Gregory to Lord Whitworth

Dublin Castle: April 18, 1815.

"I am sure you would not believe me if I denied being glad that you had shortened the period of your absence from Ireland. Without feeling any immediate Disturbance in the Country, I can easily account for your anxiety to return during this critical time of general uneasiness. I wish it was in my power to give a more favourable Impression of the State of the Country, but I should not be warranted in so doing.

"Our Reports of outrages rather increase than diminish, and the enclosed Copy of a Letter from General Barry represents the County of Limerick to be in a very bad state. . . .

"Should the Insurgents dare to try their strength singly, unaided by their Friend Buonaparte, which I do not think they will, I have no fear of the result, although 5,000 Troops are to be taken from us. We can ill spare them, but it is quite impossible not to approve of their being sent to fight when the Battle is to settle everything."

Mr. Gregory to Mr. Peel

April 20, 1815.

"I have this day had a very long conversation with M. G.[1]; he is fully satisfied that there is not at present any direct agency from Buonaparte in this Country, that if his power is established, or even continued for any time, he has no doubt that Emissaries will be sent. He appears to hold in great contempt any Effort which the low Associations can make against the Government, and gives no credit to their being led or directed by any Description beyond the Rabble. The Ribbon system which is now become so general has, he says, two objects, the first Extirpation of Hereticks, which arises from religious hatred, but the second and more powerful is the possession of Protestant property when the present owners are disposed of. This thirst for the property of others has excited the fever of even the middling classes of Catholics, and prevented them associating with Ribbonmen, as they apprehend that when the poor get possession of Protestant lands, if they are not sufficient to satisfy them they will help themselves without any religious distinction. Under the circumstances he does not think any alarming Insurrection can break out.

"O'Connell, he says, is again becoming very bold, and the new Association is filling fast—150 names are already to it, but no one is admissible who was not a member of the Catholic Board. Young Grattan, because he gave intelligence of Buonaparte's Escape from Elba, is branded with the name of an Informer, and in the Irish phraseology it is added, 'No wonder, it was a kind father for him.' "

---

[1] One of the secret agents of the Government.

Mr. Gregory to Lord Whitworth

Dublin Castle: April 21, 1815.

"The table talk and Garrulity of those who should inspire confidence instead of increasing fear, adds much to the General Consternation which prevails. Although the judicial charges from the Bench to the Grand Juries of Westmeath and Dublin are much admired, and are thought to act as antidotes to Judge Fletcher, I cannot approve of the Wisdom of informing our Enemies foreign and domestic that this whole Kingdom is in that state of prepared Treason that it requires only a spark to make it break out into open Rebellion, this too at a time when the alarmists are ready to believe that the whole Population is not only armed but disciplined, and that Buonaparte has fleets and armies ready to send to their assistance. I trust an early and decisive blow in France will quiet the fears of one Party and destroy the hopes of the other. But should Matters unfortunately prove unsuccessful abroad, still we are not to suppose consequent success must await the malignant efforts of our domestic foes. There is abundance of Power, Strength, and Courage in the Loyalists of Ireland, and if the Battle is again to be fought, I have not the slightest doubt that it will again be won by those who deserve success. . . ."

Lord Whitworth to Mr. Gregory

Hertford St.: April 23, 1815.

"Peel communicated to me all your letters whilst I was at Knole, and I have to thank you for one, and a very interesting one, which I received yesterday by Express.

"I hope, my dear Gregory, that from very kind feeling towards us, or reluctance to bring me, or rather us (for the Duchess is determined not to let me go alone if I was to set out to-morrow), sooner than we intend, you do not disguise the real estate of things, or speak more lightly of the state of the Country than you are warranted to do. I should be inconsolable if anything whatever took place during my absence. My private opinion, and it has hitherto been supported by yours, leads me to think that even the most disaffected will not venture to stir untill (*sic*) they see a little clearer how matters are likely to go on in France. I agree also in opinion with you that although much individual mischief might accrue yet that with the Force we have and the inadequate means which the disaffected can command, nothing very serious could be the consequence of a sudden rising. But notwithstanding all this I shall not be easy until I am with you, and some observations which you make in your letter of yesterday increase my uneasiness. Nothing surely can be more imprudent, but from that quarter we have witnessed the same on every occasion. Our good friend the Attorney should never let him out of his sight.

"Peel and myself have talked over the necessity of calling out some of the best of the Yeomanry, chiefly with a view to enable the regular force to concentrate itself, and to be ready to act in Bodies where it may be wanted. Our present necessity arises from the dispersed state of our regular force. I shall urge this very strongly when I return, and I know Sir George Hewitt will concur with us most heartily.

"You may depend upon it that Peel will be over as soon as it is possible to leave the business here where he is most usefully employed. Had it not been for his diligence and observing eye the Alien Bill would have passed in such a shape as to be, as far as relates to us, a perfect dead letter. He has proposed a Clause which sets the matter right, and I hope that in a few days we shall be able to avail ourselves of it.

"I am much obliged to you for reserving Mr. Lloyd's pension until I return.

"Pray send over Law the messenger, as we find him very useful on the road. On this day fortnight we set out, and on the 11th we shall be at the Head."

Lord Whitworth to Mr. Gregory

Hertford St.: May 4, 1815.

"Everything relating to the War is going on as well as possible. The defeats of Murat are most fortunate. The advance of the Allies, that is of the Duke of Wellington and Blucher, will commence about the 15th. Soon after my arrival we shall, I trust, receive such accounts as will enable us to look forward with confidence to a favourable result. Buonaparte is completely in the hands of the Jacobins, and they furnish him with the means of defending himself with a sparing hand. I do not think the business can last long, and when it is settled, we may have as many troops as we please in Ireland. In the meantime everybody but Sir George agrees in the expediency of employing the Yeomanry, and I shall be prepared immediately on my arrival to give full effect to the measure.

"The Carlton House politicks, which I mentioned to you a few days ago, seem to be all getting right again."

Mr. Gregory to Mr. Peel

June 1815.

"I cannot help feeling much Anxiety for immediately placing a large Yeomanry force on permanent Duty. I know we are to have a very considerable military augmentation, but until that is ready we are nearly defenceless. The Yeomen are quite sufficient to meet their domestic adversaries, tho' despicable in opposition to regular troops. Nothing may occur, and fears of insurrection may be groundless, but in the present fever of disappointment which the Catholic cause has sustained in Parliament, it is impossible to say what mad enterprise may not be undertaken. The distance between a furious Demagogue and a bitter Traitor is very short, and we have never doubted the bad principles of our Irish Leaders to be deterred from anything which could injure England even through their own country. I confess that my anxiety is kept alive by the apprehension of being caught sleeping as in 1803, and to have the first news of the attack on our capital communicated by Sir Stuart Bruce. I think the Lord Lieutenant most desirous for augmenting the Yeomanry force, and I wish facilities, and not difficulties, were presented to meet his views."

June 19, 1815.

"I have received some letters lately from Lord Annesley, with folios of references, of the organised state of his neighbourhood in the County of Down; indeed, if his informer is to be credited, they frequently appear in military array. He has stated that they are to assemble in great force at Milltown on Midsummer Eve. Now that is a most artful day for them to fix upon, as throughout the whole kingdom it is observed with the most general superstitions of bonfires. However to satisfy myself I shall have a person there to ascertain whether the assembly will be more than what will occur in every hamlet of Ireland."

Mr. Gregory to Mr. Peel

Dublin Castle: June 9, 1815.

"I had yesterday a long conversation with M. G. which I now

communicate as briefly and as accurately as I can. Flyn, the Brother in Law of O'Connell, has been for some time in France, and spent some months in Paris since Buonaparte's return. Flyn is now in Dublin, holding forth on the great military strength of Buonaparte. So little is he apprehensive of the allies that instead of keeping his whole force in the interior he has marched 80,000 men to the Coast ready for any foreign expedition. M. G. entertains very little doubt that a Negociation has been opened between some of the Leaders in Dublin and Buonaparte; this he thinks is confined to a very few, nor is it necessary, he says, to divulge it to many, as the Mass of the People require no Organisation, being perfectly ready to join any foreign force which may land. He is confirmed in the opinion of this negociation from the recent cordiality of some of the Catholic Leaders in Dublin, and the original Presbyterian Malcontents of Belfast, between whom no good understanding has subsisted since 1798. Nicholas Mahon said lately sneeringly how confident the Government now felt of the Loyalty of the Catholics, as they had sent all the regular Troops out of the Country, had not embodied the Militia, nor even called out any of the Yeomen on Permanent Duty, consequently they felt secure that no attempt would be made by the Catholics. Whatever is doing he feels satisfied is with the full knowledge of Scully, but from him nothing can be extracted, and he is too cunning to be implicated until success is almost certain. Whether if it shall happen that when Buonaparte finds himself beaten by the allies and unable to keep his power in France, he may be tempted in the wildness of Despair to try his fortune with some troops as desperate as himself to embark for Ireland, is a speculation I shall not attempt to form, the Game is in the Cards, and Buonaparte's adherents would (I have no doubt) induce him to play it."

After Waterloo any fear there had been of a rising in Ireland died away. Foreign stimulus was wanting, and the arms imported and hidden away in bogs and ditches became rusty and useless. But a black thread of crime and disorder is woven into all the records of these years, and however sorrowful a subject to dwell upon, it cannot be left unnoticed.

Whiteboys. Rightboys, Threshers, Whitefeet, Blackfeet, Terry Alts, these are some of the names of the bands that formed this lawless army. Poverty, want of work, the land hunger, or as it was more simply put, "the want of a bit of ground for potatoes," seem to have been the chief causes of or excuses for crime. Where landlords lived at home, gave work to their people and treated them fairly, trouble was less acute. "The whole of that part of the country is destitute of resident gentry, the People are lawless and the middling farmers are afraid to prosecute," Mr. Gregory writes in 1818, and this is a summary of many of his letters.

It is not always easy to distinguish between the various shades of disorder and disaffection. The "Defenders" mentioned in the following report from Monaghan, sent to Mr. Peel, seem still to have thought of a rising; while the Tipperary factions mentioned by Mr. Willcocks had merely local aims.

The report, dated May 4, 1816, gives an account of a meeting of delegates held at a house in Carrickmacross, all the delegates being from the northern Counties. They were all Ribbonmen, but it was proposed at the meeting that they should take the name of Defenders, which was agreed to. The delegates seen by the Informer were gentlemanlike looking men, and rode good horses, but from an alarm of spies, they did not arrive at the meeting. A delegate from Down proposed that there should be an immediate insurrection, and mentioned that a great many of the people of Down were ready to rise, and were well armed with guns, pikes and bayonets and had ammunition in abundance. Other delegates opposed this, and there was a warm debate thereon. It was said that other counties were as well prepared as Down, but that it was useless to rise until the attention of Government should be drawn off.

They then proceeded to change the words and signs by which Defenders should be made known to each other. The meeting dispersed before resolutions could be passed, in consequence of the arrival of a detachment of the 62nd Regiment in the town. All the delegates present were decent respectable-looking men. The object of the league seemed to be the overturn of the Government.

The new signs were: the ring finger of the left hand placed in the left ear; answered by the fore-finger of the right hand placed in the mouth.

Words used by Defenders: —"There is a change in the times."
"Then may I hope for the better."
"Well it never was more wanting."
"If a change does not come, Ireland is destroyed."
"If the Americans would lay off the duty on linen."
"If they would, all would be right, my friend."

Mr. Willcocks writes at the same time, in answer to questions put by Mr. Peel as to the state of the people in Tipperary: —

"With respect to their providing themselves with firearms, it has been a species of crime committing in this county for several years back, and when I was stationed in this county about four or five years ago in a magisterial capacity, their desire for arms was very great, and numbers of persons were forcibly deprived of their arms; but their desire for arms at that period I am fully persuaded sprung from party feeling and faction purposes. At that time the entire of the lower classes, and some of the better sort of farmers, were divided into two parties, one called Shanavest, and the other Caravat. These parties met at almost every fair and public place in this county, and fought with arms in the open day, and in many instances several deaths ensued at both sides. This system of outrage has since been put down, but the greater part of the arms remained in their possession. This late desire for arms which has been so warmly manifested in the county I am fully persuaded rose for very different purposes; for I entertain no doubt upon my mind but that it was the intention of the leaders of those armed Banditties, to regulate both Tythe, Rent, and labour according to their own wishes (and possibly their views went farther), in endeavouring to effect which, many valuable lives would have been lost, had it not been for the timely arrival of those Statutes, the operation of which I trust has met and totally defeated their lawless and diabolical views."[1]

But though the end of the long war had lessened the fear of rebellion, it brought new troubles to Ireland, and Lord Whitworth's last year of office was darkened by the shadow of famine, for the farmers had already begun to suffer from the fall in prices.

We owe to Mr. Peel a picture of the state of the peasantry in this year, which followed the conclusion of peace. Some accounts of distress having reached him, he writes to Mr. Gregory early in 1816: —

"Facts are more valuable than declamation, and therefore I should like to make enquiries with respect to some portion of the Country, and I know none where more impartial sources of information could be found than Tipperary, and I should also select this part of the country on another account, namely that as it is the most disturbed, the presumption is that the Peasantry are as badly off as in most other districts. The sources from which I would propose to collect information are Wilcox, Wills, and Wilson, and it would probably be extracted from them in answer to such questions as the following, as well as in any other words:

[1] Until I read the above I had been puzzled by a passage in a letter of Mr. Peel's, "Young Gee says he has shot a Caravat. Has he done so?" Knowing of Mr. Peel's interest in woodcocks and grouse, I fancied this might be some new species of game or wildfowl.

Are the lower orders of the peasantry generally in possession of a piece of land, and of what extent? What is the usual rent paid by them for land, and if no average can be given let the amount be stated in different individual cases, so much for a half acre here, so much there. What is the price of daily labour, and do the common people support themselves in general by the wages of labour, or the cultivation of their plot of ground. What is their food in addition to potatoes? The more minute the answer to this question the better. How are those of the Poor who are incapable of working from age and infirmity supported?

"What is the tenure on which they hold their land? I presume lease for lives. Are all those who have land, be its amount what it may, registered as 40 shilling freeholders? What description of people does the population of the villages and small towns consist of? Is there a class of people, as there is in England, called Labourers, without any land whatever?

"What is the age at which the Common People usually marry? Is not marriage almost universal, and do not the sons of a common labourer shew the greatest disposition to marry and settle in the place they were born, much more than to enlist or seek employment in England?

"Do the people seek much employment elsewhere, and quit their habitations for a time? Is there not great honesty among the lower orders, and great fidelity in their dealings between each other? Have you known many or any instances of petty theft committed upon each other's property? Are the common people sullen and discontented, or lively and civil to the upper orders in the common intercourse of life? . . .

". . . How are the people as to lodging, and what is the rent of a cabin? How as to fuel, what is the price of it? Have they generally a right to cut turf on some neighbouring bog, and in what mode do they settle for the payment?

"Is the land in Tipperary generally let directly by the Landlord to the cottier, or through the intervention of middlemen? I wish particularly to know to what extent the practice of letting land through the agency of middlemen prevails.

"Other questions may occur to you, and pray add them. This information drawn fresh from the spring will be very valuable to me. . . .

"Have the goodness to write a line to Wilcox &c. &c., explaining to them my object and requesting them to add any other information which they may think valuable, and which they may have acquired in other parts of Ireland. For instance, I should like to know very much whether much difference prevails between the state of the people in Longford and Westmeath and that in Tipperary. To this they would be competent to speak.

"Wills must know a great deal, but unfortunately he thinks himself rather a fine writer. I would give a great deal for his facts, but nothing for his eloquence."

Mr. Gregory, in forwarding the answer, writes:

April 20, 1816.

"I send you the answers to the queries put Willcocks; many of them were answered in the letter to the Att. General sent yesterday. I have received no answer from Wilson or Wills, but I attach more Weight to any opinion of Willcocks on these points than either of the other two."

Cashel: April 17, 1816.

"Sir,—I have had the honour to receive your letter of the 11th instant, requesting that I would, for the information of Mr. Peel, answer certain queries therein mentioned. In reply to which I beg to acquaint you for Mr. Peel's information that I have collected the best authentic information in my power, which together with my own information makes me to answer the queries in the following manner: —

"The Labourers in this Barony, and I believe in general throughout the country, are paid in two ways. Some hold a Cabbin and from half an acre to an acre of ground, for which they pay 2 to 4 guineas a year. The persons who pays two guineas a year for such Cabbin and Ground works the year round with his employer for sixpence a day. He who pays 3 guineas a year gets eightpence a day, and if the labourer pays a higher rent he gets tenpence a day the year round. In general the labourer also gets the grass of a cow from his employer, for which he pays from two to four guineas a year, which is also taken out in labour at the same rate as for the Cabbin and Land. He also gets potato ground at a fair price. These labourers get no lease from their employers.

"The other class of labourers who hold no land, and who are the more numerous, generally get from eightpence to tenpence a day the year round, but at the time of making up the harvest, and the digging of the potatoes, the labourers who come into the county from Limerick and Kerry and those of this county who are not bound by the year, get much higher wages, such as from two and sixpence to two shillings a day. It is my opinion that the labouring classes of this county are fairly dealt with, and taking all circumstances into view, they have no reason to complain of their state or condition, they are in general well clothed, and their food plenty and wholesome.

"As to the poorest and lowest order of farmers, I take their state and condition at present to be very pitiable, particularly those who have taken lands within the last 6 or 8 years. Farmers of this description hold from 10 to 30 or 40 acres of land, for which they pay 40 shillings to four pounds an acre, according to the quality of the land, and from the present prices for the produce of land it is impossible that those rents can be paid. I consider the condition of poor farmers for years back to be bad. In order to pay a high rent, tithe and county charges, and to support a wife and from three to five children, he was obliged to bring every article of produce to market, even the straw that ought to make his manure, all which did not leave him a surplus to lay out or expend on the improvement of his land, and the consequence is that the land has become quite worn out and exhausted, and don't produce half the crop it would, had it been treated as it ought.

"I find that some years back, and before lands became so very valuable as they lately have been, the Leases granted by the Landlords were in general three lives or 21 years, but latterly the general run of leases has been for one life or 21 years. And the rate of Tithes for some years back has been about twelve shillings an acre for wheat, bere, barley and potatoes; oats or meadow land eight shillings an acre, sixpence the ewe, and one shilling the lamb. It does not appear to me that there has been much variation in the rate of tithes latterly.

"There is a difference made in the rent of lands titheable, and those which are not. I have been informed that the lands or the greater part of them in the parish of Holy Cross, part of which is in the Barony of Middlethird, are tithe free, and that those lands have hitherto set from six to eight shillings an acre higher than lands titheable of equal quality in the adjoining parish, and I believe in general this is about the difference in rent in such cases.

"Upon the whole, taking into view the last 6 or 8 years, I think the petty farmer has now a right to complain, for although he got high prices for the last 5 or 6 years, it is well known that lands carried an equal rise in rent, and it is equally well known that the prices of the present day will not pay half the rent which the farmer is bound to pay by the leases granted within the last 8 or 10 years. His exertions to cultivate the land, if bound to this high rent, will cease and his inevitable ruin must follow unless the prices of the produce rise or the Landlords lower their rents.

In my opinion much remains to be done on the part of the Landlord to ameliorate the condition of this class of men. It appears to me that the high rents are by far a much greater grievance than, and infinitely more oppressive than, the Tythes.

"There is an immense population in this part of the Country, and land is the only manufacture in the south of Ireland, so that having no other means of employment, by which they could support their families, the tenants would give any price for land sooner than be without it, for let their ability be what it may to pay the rent by having possession of the land, they were certain of having the means of supporting their families. . . .

"As regards honesty. I think in general there is great honesty among the lower orders from one to the other, and fidelity in their dealings.

"Disposition of the people. I think in general the common people are civil and respectful to the upper classes, except when unlawful combination gets among them. They are in general lively, and fond of rural sports and amusements. . . .

"Lodging and fuel. The habitation is a small, and I am sorry to say in general a filthy Cabbin, which very often contains a cow or a pig in the same appartment with some of the family. Their beds are in general straw, or the chaff of oats in a coarse bed-tick. Their fuel, if convenient to a bog, is plenty, but in many places scarce and dear when at a distance. The lower orders in general have not a right to cut turf, but the farmers when they take land get from the Landlord the right and privilege of cutting turf, and the poorer class purchase from them, and either pay in work or money, but I cannot say at what price.

"Middlemen. The land in Tipperary generally is not let directly by the landlord to the Cottier, but most certainly through the intervention of the middlemen, and in many cases heretofore the middlemen had a greater income out of the land than the head landlord. The middleman will take a piece of land from 100 to 200 acres, and will job this out to Cottiers at more than double the rent which he pays himself, but I think this grievous system of high setting practised by the middlemen is now likely to be crushed or put down, for there is now large arrears of rent due to them by the Cottiers, which I believe they are not able nor do they intend to pay. The Land therefore will fall back upon the middleman, and he must make a new setting at a fair price.

"R. WILLCOCKS.
"Chief Magistrate barony Middlethird."

In 1817 the harvest was a very poor one. Crops failed, and the fall of prices after the war had already impoverished the farmers. The lean years seemed to have begun. Mr. Peel put his hand vigorously to the work of supply. He writes to Mr. Gregory, March 11, 1817:

"I had desired Crofton to write to you the enclosed, fearing I should not have a moment to write.

"There was no time to be lost in deciding upon the purchase of the corn for seed. There was no question between immediate purchase and abandoning the idea altogether, for delay of reference was from the lateness of the season tantamount to abandonment.

"However, from the general tenor of your Letters and Lord Whitworth's; from the statements of the Dean of Raphoe with respect to his own parish, which he says is the best in Donegal, and which statements I conclude you thought to be well founded, from the Plan of Mr. Rawson for granting a bounty on the sowing of oats, from all these circumstances we have inferred that there must be a great deficiency of seed corn, particularly in the North of Ireland, and therefore the Government here have consented to go into the market.

"The only place where we can get any quantity of seed corn is the Eastern Coast.

"The only expeditious way of sending it, is in vessels which can pass the Scotch Canal from Edinbro to Glasgow.

"To Glasgow I propose for the present to direct such corn as is procured to rendezvous, and I must leave it for you in great measure, who are on the spot, to determine on the best mode of applying it to the purposes for which it is intended. . . .

"If the Western parts of Donegal are in *absolute want* of seed corn—and if there be a quantity fit for seed at Sligo, and about to be exported from thence, I really think you might purchase a limited quantity—a thousand barrels or two—on the same principles on which the purchases here are made. You might send this supply to Killybegs under the same regulations that must apply to the corn sent from hence.

"Is Hamilton or Letterkenny a fit place for the landing of corn? But instead of asking individual questions I will ask you to let me know in what way a quantity of corn, suppose 20,000 quarters or thirty being at Glasgow in a fortnight or three weeks at the utmost, and some part much sooner, can be applied to the best advantage as seen in the North of Ireland, and to what places it would best be sent.

"We will sell it at a price which will bring it within the reach of the little farmer."

The vigorous means used, and a better harvest, tided over this year of leanness. Lord Whitworth's viceroyalty was not marked by any further events of note. His health began to give way, and the monotony and ceremony of official life in Dublin must have become a weariness to him.

In February 1817 Mr. Gregory writes to Peel:

"The Lord Lieutenant had yesterday a very crowded Levee, he did not look well, the Room was extremely hot, and he left it soon. He is this day perfectly well, and feels no inconvenience from the fatigue; I was apprehensive of a return to illness. He has determined not to dine out with anyone, of which I am very glad, as it will save him from passing many irksome hours."

And a week later:

". . . I am sorry Lord Whitworth's looking ill at his Levee was conveyed to London, as it really was of no consequence. The room was very crowded and hot, and he was staying too long, but retired certainly before many had arrived. He was oppressed and looked ill, but he had only just before undergone an Essay from Slade of fifty minutes in the Castle chapel. I will say confidentially to you that I am sometimes uneasy at seeing him look so very yellow, but that appearance goes off and his skin is again clear. He eats and sleeps well, and is in excellent spirits, but he does not gain flesh, nor has he by any means improved since he came to the Castle. Every public consideration, every private feeling make Lord Whitworth an object of most anxious solicitude. He has made an excellent rule of not dining with anyone, yet he is more in Representation with his own Dinners, Drawingrooms &c, and last and not least fatiguing, Charity Sermons, than is quite fitting for a Convalescent."

In October of that year Lord Whitworth bade farewell to Dublin, taking with him the "respect and regard" of the people.

The "Dinners, Drawingrooms and Charity sermons" we can hardly expect him to have regretted, but he kept up to the end a warm interest in Ireland, and in the friends he had made there.

His health improved after his retirement, for Lord Talbot writes later:

"I returned to-day from Knole, where you will be glad to hear, I found our amiable friend *as well* in health and spirits as I *ever* saw him. He rides 2 or 3 hours without fatigue, eats a hearty dinner, and sleeps perfectly well. You will scarcely believe that he again weighs 13st. 2lb., his former weight. 'Tis to me the most delightful part of my existence that I pass with him. To know Lord W. is to love him, and to know those *I loved* is a double bond of union to him with me."

How strong was his feeling against Catholic Emancipation may be judged by this letter to Mr. Gregory, written in 1819:

"As matters now stand, I confess I am not without some apprehension as to the event here. You see what a force is mustered under the banners of opposition. If 186 can be got to oppose so trifling a question as whether a few thousand pounds shall be taken from the right or the left hand pocket, what may we not expect when the important and specious question of Catholic Emancipation is brought before them. I rest my hopes on the House of Lords. But even there I dare not look with any great degree of Confidence. The obstinacy of many people with whom I converse on the question, can only be equalled by their Ignorance of its real tendency and of the consequences to which it must ultimately lead in Ireland. Peel will, I am sure, stand in the gap, but I scarcely know what he can add to what he so forcibly said when the subject was last agitated, and opposition is now much stronger.

"I often think of my good and valued friend the Atty. Genl. How vexed he must be at all this. Pray remember me most kindly to him, and tell him that I add my prayers to his and yours and all well wishers to the Cause, 'that all those Evils which the Craft and subtilty of the Devil or Man worketh against us may be confounded and brought to nought.' "...

LORD TALBOT

Dublin Castle: October 9, 1817.

"The Earl Talbot, who embarked at Holyhead at five o'clock on Wednesday, the 8th inst., on board his Majesty's yacht the *William and Mary,* arrived in this harbour at one o'clock this day. . . . His lordship, attended by a squadron of dragoons, proceeded to the Castle, and the Council having attended at four o'clock, was introduced in form to his Excellency Earl Whitworth, who received him sitting under the canopy of state in the Presence Chamber, from whence a procession was made in the usual state to the Council Chamber. The Council sitting, his lordship's commission was read, and the oaths being administered to him, his lordship was invested with the collar of the most illustrious order of St. Patrick, and received the Sword of State from the Earl Whitworth."—*Ann. Register.*

I have read through a great mass of letters from Lord Talbot to Mr. Gregory. Some are too trivial and some too personal for publication, but all radiate kindliness and a sense of duty.

Though he set his face from first to last against the claims of the Catholics, O'Connell gives him the credit of impartiality, and Lord Cloncurry speaks of him as "an honest, high-minded gentleman." The King's visit and the famine of 1821 are the chief landmarks of his administration. His wife's death, and his sudden and ungracious dismissal saddened and, for a time, embittered his memories of the viceroyalty. Had Mr. Peel continued Chief Secretary, Lord Talbot's four years in Ireland would probably have been one long "Amen" to his clear, prompt decisions. But in May, 1818, Mr. Peel resigned.

With the appointment of "the amiable, clever and irresolute Charles Grant," began what I may call the sandwich system of government in Ireland, of which Lord Grenville writes: "What can exceed the ridicule of thus systematically coupling together a friend and an enemy to toleration, like fat and lean rabbits, or the man and his wife in a Dutch toy, or like fifty other absurdities made to be laughed at, but certainly never before introduced into politics as fixed and fundamental systems for the conduct of the most difficult and dangerous crisis of a country."

It was natural that the Orange party should feel aggrieved at his appointment, but he seems also by his unpunctuality, carelessness and neglect of answering letters to have offended his own supporters. Some resolutions against him were even carried at a Catholic meeting at Athenry, "but," writes Mr. Gregory, "though aimed at Grant, they, according to our national Blunders hit the Lords Justices."

Ministers called out that he did not keep them informed of the state of affairs, and complained of his indecision, now blowing hot, now cold, at one moment declaring no troops were wanted, the next, clamouring for them. It must in any case have been uphill work for him. He came over primed with theories of popular government, but found small obstacles in his way at every turn. To understand his position one may imagine how Mr. Morley would have felt when holding office in Ireland, had he been flanked with Lord Londonderry as a Viceroy, and Colonel Saunderson as an Under Secretary.

Groans for "Popish Grant" were given at the decoration of King William's statue, and the correspondence of Lord Talbot and Mr. Gregory shows how little they welcomed this advanced "Catholic" thrust between them. Dublin Castle cannot have been for him a bed of roses.

Mr. Grant was all for turning his theories to practice without loss of time, while Mr. Gregory, fulfilling the usual role of the permanent official, acted as a practical, restraining Sancho Panza to the new Quixote. Mr. Grant, anxious to seize the first opportunity of showing confidence in the Catholics, proposes to make Lord Gormanstown a Commissioner of Fisheries. Mr. Gregory replies that no one could be more respectable, "but I doubt whether he would be gratified by being named as a Commissioner. His habits are very retired, and he has never accustomed himself to publick business. You have already two Commissioners for that immediate neighbourhood."

He proposes what he believes to be a benevolent reform, of sending female convicts to Cork by ship instead of by road. But Mr. Gregory convinces him that the present mode of conveyance "in covered him cars, on springs," is much more comfortable, and much preferred by them.

He had at Cambridge written a prize poem on the restoration of learning in the East, and was anxious to repeat his triumph by devising in prose a system of education that would satisfy all creeds in Ireland. But it did not need a touch from the Under Secretary to make this castle in the air come tumbling down about his ears.

In Parliament, to his dismay, instead of enlightening the world as to Catholic claims, he finds his time occupied in defending details of expenditure of which he knows nothing. He writes (1819): "You have no idea of the temper of the House on the Irish Estimates. If I had not assured them of my intention to examine and reduce, they would have divided and thrown some of them out." And again in 1822: "How I am to defend the expense of 5,300*l.* for our coals and candles I know not."

Extravagance in writing materials can hardly have been his besetting sin, but Mr. Gregory confronts him with an entry in the stationery account for "cutlery, 23*l.* 17*s.* 5*d.,*" and asks if he is to pay it.

Vesey Fitzgerald, in 1819, writes little hits at him from London. "I have not seen Grant except once en passant; and Peel told me to-day he had seen him but once." "Your friend Grant seems to have let the Irish representation slip out of his hands completely." And on the proposed abolition of the still fine system (of which Sir G. Hill writes: "It means the destruction of the revenue, but the Saints and the Squires will have it so") he writes: "Vansittart and Castlereagh had matured a plan with Leslie Foster, in a consultation at which Grant assisted (if I may apply that term to his having been present and dissenting, as I believe, from everything except relinquishment of the whole system)."

Lord Talbot often receives and joins in complaints of his procrastination and carelessness. He writes to Mr. Gregory:

"Sir G. Hill has written a long letter of complaint that his Memorial sent in six weeks ago has not been answered. I told Grant I thought he had fair right to complain. That the protestants were as much entitled to justice at least as the Catholics, and that so far as I could judge this was an atrocious attempt to vilify Sir G. and his Yeomen. We shall see what it will produce."

And again:

"Grant desired me to send the Primate his answer to his Grace's Letter commenting upon his original statement of the Galway troubles. I did so, saying it was at Grant's special request that at so late a date I transmitted the Communication.

"By return of post the Primate returned it to me with this letter.

" 'I return Mr. Grant's Letter dated the 2nd of June, which I received last night, and beg your Excy. to accept my thanks for the Communication.

" 'I have the Honor to be, etc.

" 'W. ARMAGH.'

"His Grace's style is better than mine. I will therefore take the hint and —remain

"most faithfully."

Mr. Gregory writes to Lord Talbot: "Grant was punctual to-day at the Archbishop's Levee, I hope he will continue so."[1]

And to Mr. Grant himself on some appointments under the Law Courts Bill: —

"It would not be right for me to conclude this already long letter, and conceal from you that the Chief Justice is very much annoyed at the manner in which you have treated him.

"He wrote to you two or three weeks since a long Letter on this Bill, and requested to have the earliest Intimation of when it passed into a Law. You answered him that he should. On Monday evening he received a Copy of the Bill, with some marginal manuscript alterations, but without one line from you notifying whether it had received the Royal Assent, nor has he since received the slightest Communication from you on the subject.

"However painful it may be to you to know that you have offended this most excellent man, I feel it my duty not to conceal it from you."

And again: —

"Very great dissatisfaction is expressed by the Judges, and all persons having anything to do with the Courts of Law, as to the manner in which this Bill has passed. It is enacted to take immediate Effect; it is Law before it can reach Ireland, and although the Papers announce it to have received the Royal

---

[1] "They say of the two Grants, Robert and Charles, who are both very careless and unpunctual, that if you ask Charles to dine with you at six on Monday, you are very likely to have Robert at seven on Tuesday."— *Greville Memoirs.*

Assent, it has not been transmitted to Ireland. Great public inconvenience is stated to have incurred, and great Clamour is consequently raised.

"After I had written the above I received yours of Sunday, and also (as I had hoped) the Law Courts Bill, as it had received the Royal Assent. But what you enclosed was only the Bill as ordered to be printed by the House of Commons, on the 2nd of April last."

Croker declared that Ireland was going to the bad in consequenc of Grant's indolence. "He thinks of nothing but devotion, he is a saint, and can and will do no business whatever."

But this is evidently injust; he was filled with zeal, but some fatal want of backbone, or of the belief in himself which is as necessary for current use as the alloy in minted gold, kept him from attainment. And sometimes an element of ill-luck seemed to hang about him.

Sir Robert Peel, in a letter to Croker, gives an account of him at a shooting-party at Drayton: "Grant took the field yesterday, and the moment we left the phaeton and joined the keepers we were attacked by an *infuriated wasp's nest*. . . . Grant's whiskers have been recently dyed black, *possibly* with some redolent mixture, but this will not account for the attack, which was impartially directed against all."

Soon after his arrival in Ireland he went with his sister for a tour in the North, and writes to Mr. Gregory from Donaghadee in great wrath, their trunk having been stolen from the back of the carriage. He suggests strong measures being taken for its recovery, even that a policeman should be sent specially to Belfast for the purpose. But after all has been done, Mr. Gregory writes to him: —"I enclose a note from the Sovereign of Belfast about your Trunk. I am sorry you will not see it or its contents again."

One is irresistibly reminded of Moore's story of Sir——St. George, "who came to a Catholic meeting very drunk—lost his hat and called out 'D—nation, to you all. I have come to emancipate you and you have stolen my hat!' "

I possess a print of him after a portrait by Thompson, in which there is a hint of instability even in his attitude, and in which his hand rests for security on a volume entitled "Ireland," as if he was content to base his reputation upon its contents.

Traditional gossip says that when he came to Dublin his heart was captured by a beauty of the Viceregal Court. But he could not quite make up his mind to irrevocably fix his destiny, so turned his attentions to her equally beautiful married sister. So, wavering between the two, he kept his affections to an even balance; but the sisters were never quite the same to one another again.

O'Connell found him "the mildest, kindest, and best mannered man Ireland has ever yet seen," but I think his letters to Mr. Gregory are a little dry. It is only in 1821 that "my dear Sir" is replaced by "my dear Gregory," and if, rarely, he sends a message of politeness to Lady Anne, he docks her name of its *e*. He more than once, indeed, inquires with interest for Miss Gregory's horse, but I find it had been a present from the Lord Lieutenant, which may have given it a sort of official complexion.

Friction on the Catholic question of course soon arose, and Lord Talbot and Mr. Gregory sadly shake their heads over their restive colleague. "Galway is the most Catholic county in Ireland, and now is in a state of almost open rebellion, yet Grant wants to work through the Priesthood," writes Mr. Gregory. And Lord Talbot, giving an account of the Lord Mayor's dinner of 1819, says : —

"We had a famous protestant dinner yesterday—excellent dinner but *bad* wine. Alderman Archer when half drunk talked some nonsense about the necessity Government was under of supporting the Corporation of Dublin if they meant to subsist as a Govt.—which I thought I had better permit to pass unheeded. The *glorious pious* and *immortal* memory was drunk as it ought to be.

"Peel was given with loud huzzahs. Poor Grant's health passed without notice.

"Duke of Richmond and one Wm. Gregory were not forgotten. . . ."

A meeting called soon after this by the new Lord Mayor at the Rotunda in favour of Emancipation was attributed to the fillip given to the agitation by the new Chief Secretary, and Mr. Gregory indignantly writes to Lord Whitworth : —

Dublin Castle: February 22, 1819.

"We have in this Country little to communicate, and all our political concerns are being confined to one Question, are scarcely considered beyond the Parties who are engaged. In proportion to the High Station you filled here, so must be to you the satisfaction at having withdrawn from it without witnessing those disgusting scenes which have lately disgraced this heretofore Protestant City. The Change appears to me as sudden as the shifting of the scenes in a Harlequin farce; and when in a few Months the Glorious Memory is banished from the Mayoralty house, and the Lord Mayor calls an aggregate Meeting to support the Catholic Claims, is it too much to expect the Elevation of the Host in the streets before the expiration of the year? But I trust the day of triumph is far off. The paltry Prints on the popish side take great pains to impose on the public Mind Lord Talbot's strict neutrality, and almost attempt to mix him up with those who are emancipators, but you require no assurance to be satisfied that such Insinuations are grossly false, though he has a delicate card to play which prevents his shewing his hand, yet everyone here knows his political principles are strictly Protestant. . . . The hopes of the Catholics have been raised by Blandishments which they readily consider overtures for Conciliation, and the Opposition, who only espouse their cause for the Embarrassment it creates, feed their expectations to increase their disappointment."

Lord Whitworth replies sympathetically: —

"I confess, my dear Gregory, I did anticipate all the mischief which I see gathering in Dublin and spreading all over the Country. But how could it be otherwise? It is matter of much Regret, but not of surprise. I confess it did appear to me so long ago as when that in itself nonsensical toast of Glorious Memory was omitted at the Mansion House in the presence of the Lord Lieutenant, that advantage would be taken of it, and inferences drawn from it. Considering the principles of the person with whom Lord T. was obliged to act, I think he should have given ten times more publicity than ever to his own lest he might be supposed to acquiesce in those principles, or at least to be indifferent on so vital a question."

Vesey Fitzgerald writes at the same time from London: —

"You seem to have had a *stormy* meeting in Dublin for the purposes of reconciliation; the Catholics and their friends seem to me to have been madmen in their attempt. Everything was proceeding quietly for them, and they have now awakened what will not be quenched easily. I speak only as I see at a distance, and judging men from their own reports."

Mr. Gregory writes to Mr. Grant: —

February 23, 1819.
"It is very painful, but still my Duty, to communicate to you the great agitation with which this City is troubled from the Effects of that ill-advised Meeting called by the Lord Mayor. That spirit of animosity which had so much subsided has again been called into action, and the greatest party violence now prevails in a City which was lately so quiet, and which animosity will soon diffuse itself through the Country. I did not think it possible that in a few short days such a change could be effected, but the catholic Question now engrosses the attention of all Ranks, and the hopes and fears of the opposite parties interest the highest and lowest orders. All this from a senseless meeting whose opinion could not weigh a feather in the decision of the measure. If the expectations of the Catholics are disappointed (as I trust they will) they of course will be more than usually irritated; but let the Decision be as it may, everything now assumes a very angry and unpromising appearance."

Mr. Grant writes more calmly: —

London: March 1, 1819.
"I am much obliged by your letters. I regret to hear of the agitations excited by the Meetings, and ardently hope they may be somewhat allayed by this time.
"Altho' the Anti-Catholics may say and justly, that all this has been begun by the other side, yet I trust they will also see that it may in some degree depend upon their own moderation and quietness, whether the evil shall continue or subside. It will of course be natural for them to take strong measures when provoked to do so by the example of the other party; and therefore one can hardly expect them to abstain from any other public efforts if the friends of the Catholics continue to resort to such efforts. It is, however, a very distressing event."

Mr. Grant, on his side, was aggrieved by the tone of the Protestant newspapers, and writes to Mr. Gregory in March 1819: —

"I have been for some days wishing to say a few words on the manner in which the Government papers have spoken of the Catholic question and its supporters. The Hibernian Journal, for example, which arrived yesterday or the day before, has some expressions like this: —'On such a day the Catholic Question will be decided in the negative, and we firmly believe there is not a man in the Empire who is not stupefied and blinded by bigotry who will not rejoice at the event.' Opinions like these occur frequently in that paper and in the Correspondent. I need not multiply them. 'We do not think the Church is in danger, because we are aware of the strength opposed to *its enemies,* &c.' I do not of course mind such expressions as relating personally to myself; but I really think such words coming from a Paper notoriously paid by Government when one of the members of that Government is known to be of the opinions thus attacked, are likely, if allowed to continue, to lower in the public view, not only the Respectability of that individual, but also the character of the Government itself. Here are the words in which the Hibernian Journal speaks of the Irish supporters of Grattan's motion. 'The Irish members who are chained down to a promise by the ill-advised measure of enfranchising 40-shilling freeholders, the rotten fragments of mistaken policy and the deadly foes of British Liberty, chiefly engendered under the banners of Roman Catholic Influence.' I think with submission, that this is a sentence which no Government, even if it was completely and in the strongest sense anti-Catholic, should permit to appear in a Paper which goes to the public sanctioned by their support."

Mr. Gregory answers: —

March 25, 1819.
"I have spoken to the Editor of the Hibernian Journal to avoid Personalities, which he has promised to do. I really am not aware of any of the gross terms used by the Correspondent as applied to Members who support the Catholic Claims, except to the opposition Party, who take it up as a political matter, to embarrass a Government so divided on such a vital Question. The Catholic Papers are certainly no models to imitate, but they call those who support the Protestant cause by no other name than Incendiaries."

Mr. Gregory had used stronger language in writing to Mr. Peel in 1813: —

"The Hibernian Journal has made another attack upon the Correspondent, for which he shall get condign to-morrow. He is the most impudent and most useless tributary scribbler that was ever employed."

Mr. Grant, however, carried his point, for Torrens says:—
"The Hibernian had no circulation worth mentioning, and no contributions worth reading. The patronage of the Castle was withdrawn from it by Mr. C. Grant, and the following week it had ceased to appear."

A little storm in a teacup arose in 1821. The Viceroy and Chief Secretary both being in London, the executive power was as usual put in the hands of the Lords Justices. One of the first demands made by them to the Home Secretary seems to have been an extension or renewal of "Coercion" in some parts of the country. Mr. Grant was obliged to forward this letter, but accompanied it with one of his own, intended to neutralise it.

Great was the indignation of Lord Talbot and Mr. Gregory, and very great that of the Lords Justices. Mr. Grant had mentioned as his reason for demurring to the demand of the Lords Justices that "W. Pole expressed his astonishment at the proclaiming of the barony of Upper Ossory, as his account represented that part of the country as perfectly quiet," and Mr. Gregory writes to Lord Talbot, "You will be surprised to hear from whom Pole received his information; I had it yesterday from the Author himself, General Cockburn, who lives near Bray, but who added, 'You were quite right in proclaiming Upper Ossory, as it was not possible for a peaceable inhabitant to reside in it.' Mr. Grant says neither Colonel Trench nor Sir W. Parnell had heard of any disturbances. Very extraordinary; Pole has not been in Ireland since his election, Trench is a decided absentee, and Parnell has been attending Parliament for several months. . . . Mr. Grant wrote to me on the 29th of May, expressing how much he was shocked at the number of Baronies recently proclaimed, and desiring that before any more places are proclaimed the documents on which the Proclamation is to be founded should be sent to him. He never could have reflected on the insult such a proposal would be to the Authority and Judgement of the Lords Justices, and how evidently they would stultify their understandings and humiliate their power by submitting for his decision matters on which they may be presumed to be capable of forming at least as sound an opinion as himself."

Lord Talbot writes at the same time from London: —

June 4, 1821.

"I never was more astonished and confounded than I was on hearing from Grant yesterday that he had regularly protested against the Letter of the Lords Justices to Lord Sidmouth. On cross-questioning him, he had no ground, or at least gave me no reason for this extraordinary opinion, beyond 'its being very odd that they should make such a representation the moment they began to act.' When he takes a dislike to any person or suspects their motives, he has not mind enough to give them credit for correctness of judgment in anything. As soon as he sends me a Copy of this document, unless I have it 'confidentially' I will send it.

"Half past six o'clock P.M.—Since writing the above I have seen Grant and Lord Sidmouth; the former told me he had had a conference with Lord S. and read to him the letters he wrote to you, which communications Lord S. reprobated nearly in the same terms that I did, for I told him most cordially how injudicious and insulting to the Lords Justices I thought his letter was."

But Mr. Grant, who had been ready to flout the Viceroy and snub all Protestant Ireland, had meanwhile climbed down, though in his usual vacillating manner, before the rumoured resentment of the Lords Justices. Such divinity in Scottish eyes doth hedge the law. He writes to Mr. Gregory on June 6: —

"On the whole what I wish to suggest to you is, that if you have not already made the proposal to the Lords Justices the best way perhaps would be not to make it formally as from me, but while dismissing the subject with the Lords Justices you may perhaps be able to throw out that you have heard from me about the Proclamations, and that considering how likely I am to be attacked in the House, it might perhaps be as well to send the papers to me. But I feel this may be more unpleasant to you than a direct proposal from me, and therefore let me beg you to do as you think best. Favor me as much as you can, and as your kindness would lead you to do, in the way of making the Communication; but above all do not put yourself to any inconvenience or awkwardness in order to break the blow on me. If the thing can be done in any way without exciting much irritation, choose that way.

"Should you have already stated my proposal to the Lords Justices you will be so kind as to say that I do not wish to press the thing at all pertinaciously. I am sensible there may be exigencies which will not brook delay. All I wished to say was that where no inconvenience would be incurred by a reference here, it would certainly be more agreeable to me to be a party to proceedings which I am the person that must defend.

"In case you have not yet made the Communication to the Lords Justices and had rather not make it from yourself, will you present to the Lords Justices from me the expression of my utmost respect, and of my earnest request that if any more requisitions be made and it be found necessary to comply with them, (which I ardently hope will not be the case) I may as speedily as possible be put in possession of the grounds of such opinion, and the facts or documents on which it rests, or should the public service admit of the delay of a few days, I should esteem it a great mark of confidence to be allowed a sight of the papers even before the measure is determined upon.

"Let me add that if you have not said anything from me to the Lords Justices, and can substantially without saying anything procure that which I wish, that is to check their rage for proclaiming, and to give me in fact a veto on the proceedings before they are actually in progress, I had much rather not have my name mentioned to their Excellencies, nor appear in any position of personal altercation with them."

The same indecision is seen in more serious cases. On hearing of an increase of disturbance he writes a letter full of flustered suggestions. "That system of Ribbandmen must be checked. Could anything be done in Mayo to meet them? Do you think Sir S. O'Malley is quite to be credited? Would it not be right to recommend all our correspondents to administer the oath of allegiance as Strickland has done? Could not some communication be made to the Catholic Bishops, urging them to swear their people to keep peace?" There is a striking contrast between the above note, and the firm handling by Peel of any matter that came before him.

Lord Talbot's dissatisfaction with his Chief Secretary travels with him across the Channel. He writes from Ingestre, "I will consult with Grant about the police magistrates. Is it not strange that although he must know I am here, as my papers from the Irish Office come here daily, that he has not written me one line?" And from London he writes: —

"Lord L. and I had no conversation respecting G., but with Lord S. I had some confidential discourse. I was on my guard, and said no more than I would say to Grant himself. We both concurred in bearing the amplest testimony to his amiability, talents and honourable policy. But we agreed that the C. Question was a stumbling Block."

And again, "I yesterday saw Lord Sidmouth, to whom I spoke without reserve on the subject of our Chief S. I told him that *we* felt he had no confidence in *us,* and that however well disposed we were to him for his many amiable private qualities, we could not but sensibly feel, that there was no point of union as to the conduct of Public affairs between him and the rest of the Government. But I find that as Lord S. is about to do what I mentioned to you was the case, we have no further hope of redress than that he, Lord S. will mention my complaint of G.'s want of cordiality towards us. I am to see Lord Sid. upon the army reduction to-morrow. *He* is decidedly averse to the measure, but Lord L. is desirous of pursuing reductions wherever practicable— *here* as well as with you. This may be right and even necessary, but I should be more uncompromising! However, I will protest as strongly as I can against the too rapid and extensive withdrawing of troops from Ireland."

Mr. Gregory, though he sadly writes, "Grant, though tired to death of his *unsuccessful* work, has not the least notion of resigning," welcomes signs of conversion, and hopes he may yet return to the fold—"I trust he is sensible of the fatal error with which he undertook the government of this Country, and no longer believes that Protestant Tyranny and Catholic slavery are the causes of Disturbance in this Country. Should he be so convinced and that he returns again to Ireland, I hope the Tide of Popularity may be turned in his favour and that he may receive that Public esteem to which his many excellent qualities entitle him in Private."

But the sandwich experiment does not seem to have been a happy one for any of the parties concerned.

LORD TALBOT, *continued.*

Church patronage was in Lord Talbot's eyes one of the most troublesome duties connected with the Viceroyalty, and 1819 was a busy year in that respect.

In August the Bishopric of Clogher fell vacant, and Mr. Peel writes to Mr. Gregory from Pitmain: —

"Pray let me know what is done or what is intended to be done with respect to Clogher.

"I have a letter from the Bishop of Cork, who wants a translation, and from Magee, who is as anxious for a Bishoprick, and wishing to avoid the possibility of creating any embarrassment by my answer, will postpone a reply to their letters until I hear from you. Pray address to me, Post Office Edinburgh.

"Apsley Yates and I are here shooting by Huntley's permission. The weather is so hot that it is almost impossible to do anything till the evening.

"We have been out seven days, and killed about 720 Grouse.

"Lord Bury killed the other day at Kinrara for a wager of ten guineas 67 brace with one gun and two dogs. Prince Leopold shot at Dalwhinne yesterday, and goes on to Kinrara to-morrow.

"P.S.—The weather is so hot that our birds scarcely reach Edinbro', so I am afraid of inflicting a box full of maggots on you."

(Note by Lord Talbot.—"I wish this had come sooner or that the good Bishop had not applied distinctly for Clogher.").

Lord Talbot to Mr. Gregory

September 10, 1819.

"I regret to say that the melancholy news of the good Archbishop of Tuam's death came to Town this morning. . . .

"I really most unfeignedly lament the loss of this excellent man, in which feeling I am well aware you participate. We must, however, in public Situations check the Tear of Sympathy, and proceed to the filling up of Situations which become vacant by the Death of those whose characters we esteem, and whose loss we regret.

"I shall by this day's post advert to my former letter to Lord Sidmouth, and beg for the opinion of the British Government upon my suggestion as to His Grace's successor.

"The Provost should, I conclude, be named as a candidate for the Bench. Should the Dean of Achonry be named—and Guinness?

"They have the merit of thinking their own pretensions valid.

"*I*, I am sure I do not know why, have a sort of feeling that none of these three are very desirable."

The Archbishopric of Tuam was very well filled after all by the appointment of Dr. Trench, Bishop of Elphin, brother of Lady Anne Gregory. He had known some ups and downs in life, for his education had been begun at Harrow, and was finished at a school at Castlebar, and having begun life as a land agent, he finished as an Archbishop.

He won the affection of the people in both capacities. As agent it was said of him: "He never driv any of the tenants, nor sent a poor man's cow in pound during them three years, nor offended a poor man during that time, but would take him as grand as the best, and any man who paid his rent regular, he would not let him go without a shilling or eighteenpence to refresh himself on the way."

He belonged to the Church militant, and soon after his appointment, hearing that a house some miles from Tuam was to be attacked by Ribbonmen, he put himself at the head of a detachment of the 3rd Light Dragoons, there being no Magistrate at hand, and rode off to the rescue. Nevertheless, when some Ribbonmen he had helped to capture were publicly flogged at Tuam, he would not attend the flogging, but the moment it was over he appeared, gave wine and food to the sufferers, and fed and comforted their wives and children.

His whole heart was in his diocese, and once when on a health trip to Cheltenham he writes: "I pant to be at Tuam."

The Archbishopric of Tuam had hardly been filled when that of Dublin became vacant, and Lord Talbot writes from Marble Hill, Co. Galway, where he was shooting woodcocks: —

December 13, 1819.

"I really fear as much from the having another Bishop to make, as I should do at the intelligence of a *row*.

"Kenny will stand high, and Bagwell will be pressed. Both of them are equally indifferent to me. Pray pursue your enquiries as to Bagwell. Who the Devil is to be raised to the Archiepiscopal Crozier I own I am at a loss to divine.

"Can Fowler be conscientiously recommended? Jocelyn and Warburton are the only two besides that have activity, the first of whom I take to be too soft, the latter too unfit.

"Would it be expedient to ask for an A.B. from England?"

But an English Archbishop could not be found, and after some delay Lord John Beresford received the appointment. Two years later he became Primate of Ireland. He only died in 1862. It is estimated that the amount of Church revenue which he received during his lifetime was not less than 700,000*l*. But he used it generously, and for the good of his various dioceses. He was much looked up to until 1860, when, having recognised the fact that the Church schools in his diocese could not, through want of funds, compete in efficiency with the secular ones established by Government, he advised their being placed under the National Board. He was for this denounced by his clergy as Judas Iscariot.

Lord Talbot had many connections and friends in Ireland, and visited many of their houses. But the following letter shows that in spite of his good Protestant principles the North did not smile upon him: —

Hillsborough: July 22, 1819.

"When a man is made a d——d fool of, the sooner he unfools himself the better. My friend and relation magnified amazingly, may I not add very unfairly, the expectations that existed in this part of the Country for my presence. In good truth there is no person of consequence beyond the Dufferins and the Dean of Downshire. I was dragged to an ordinary Dinner and Ball, without a single soul there beyond a Dam Corporation member, so when I found that the same pleasure awaited me for to-day and to-morrow, Friday and I believe Saturday, I ventured to put in my protest, and said that as Lord Lieutenant I could not think of again attending these seats of Northern festivity.

"The sovereign of Belfast waited upon me yesterday to apologize for not giving me the dinner to which He and the neighbouring gentlemen had invited me. The reason, the melancholy Event that has occurred in the Donegal family.

"I am delighted at the excuse, tho' I am not quite sure it is a valid one for a public body who had invited a public man to an entertainment at which he had notified his intention to assist.

"I am wavering between Dublin and the Giant's Causeway, but I think Dublin will possess.

"TALBOT.

"P.S. Dublin has it—to-morrow."

Mr. Gregory to Mr. Grant

July 24. 1819.

"The Lord Lieutenant returned last Night, he had been invited by the Sovereign to dine at Belfast, but the unfortunate Discovery of the Invalidity of Lord Donegal's Marriage has thrown that Town into the greatest Dismay.

"I understand large sums of Money have been paid for Renewals of Lease in consequence of Lord Belfast having levied fines with his Father."

In Lady Morgan's Autobiography the following passage occurs in a letter from Lady Charleville, dated July 13, 1819: —

"Lord and Lady Westmeath's separation for temper, and the overthrow of Lord Belfast's marriage and fortunes by Lord Shaftesbury having discovered that the Marquis and Marchioness of Donegal were married under age by *licence* and not by banns, which renders it illegal, and bastardizes their children irreparably, is the greatest news of the upper circles at present. The young lady had said she married only for money, therefore, for her no pity is shown; but poor Lord Belfast, to lose rank, fortune and wife at once at twenty years of age, is a strong and painful catastrophe to bear properly. I hear Mr. Chichester (rightful heir) behaves well, but he cannot prevent the entail affecting his heirs, nor the title descending to him from his cousin."

The west, with its woodcocks, proved kinder to the Viceroy later in the year, and he writes from Clonbrock, Co. Galway, on December 7: —

"The Country, Clonbrock says, will not do without a police, and as oppositionists are ever stronger in their memories than ministerialists, He laments that the insurrection Bill was suffered to expire, partially at least.

"He says imprisonment and whipping are not sufficient correctives to the spreading Sedition, and that transportation should be in some Cases the punishment. To this, I believe, little objection would really be made, and I like to hear such sentiments in the Opposition Mouths.

"I have desired him to write to me his opinion, which I would lay before Grant; perhaps this may induce our Secretary to look upon the Peelers as a milder species of force than he seems to do now.

"Lord C. touched upon the expense of the Peelers, and wished to know what Govt. might be inclined to do. I told him Govt. was in all cases disposed to attend to any representation which tended to preserve the public tranquillity, and also to relieve as far as was practicable (a good Bakerism) the pressure upon any class of Society, but that he must be sensible that we could make no promise, nor hold out any encouragement to any District to apply for the Police; this was always left to the unbiassed decision of the Magistracy, but that when the measure *was* decided upon, and the request *was* made, that the Govt. would be disposed to examine into the state of the Case, with every wish to be indulgent, etc. etc. He agreed, but I think expected more.

"I congratulate you and the Country on Peel's brilliant speech. It ranks amongst the best of the day.

"Considering the Wood is in my view, and is, I hear, full of Cocks, I have written at length. Whether you will be able to read it is another thing."

December 12.

"You will *not* have requisition for the peelers here.

"Clonbrock begins to flinch, and the more so as Mr.——, who was strenuous in his wish to have them, has now changed his opinion. Locally speaking he is right, and if all your Galway friends were as stout in heart and body as he seems to be, certainly there would be no necessity for them. He has established a chain of signals by Bonfires, and patroles at the head of forty well-armed followers every other night at least, and on the least symptom of the approach of these rascals a fire is lighted and 300 or 400 fellows are, and have been, in less than an hour, at some specified rendezvous."

He had good shooting at Garbally, Marble Hill, and other Galway places, and seems fully to have enjoyed his days there, the last happy ones he was to know for a long time.

Lady Talbot, whose health had for some time given cause for anxiety, died December 30, 1819. She had given birth to a son in October. There is an entry almost two years later in Mr. Gregory's note-book, "Gerald Talbot christened at the Lodge in the Park. Duke and Duchess of Leinster and the Chancellor sponsors."

A month after her death Lord Talbot writes from Hatfield : —

January 23, 1820.

"It is now very long since I either wrote to or heard from you. I am much as usual, calm at times, wretched at others—such must be my Lot for a long long time. But a truce to my misfortunes, for which no one more sincerely feels than you do. I will proceed to tell you that I went to Town yesterday, where I saw Lords Liverpool and Sidmouth, from both of whom I experienced the kindest reception, and heard that I had had the good fortune to give satisfaction during my stay in Ireland, and

I ascertained what *you* will not dislike to hear, that as far as our friends are concerned, *no* change of opinion has taken place respecting the Catholic Question. Indeed, Lord Sidmouth distinctly said, 'He would not stay in any administration that would concede that vital point.'

"So much for that. This was obtained by my asking distinctly if we were to apprehend a charge of opinion on it, as from Grant's speech we really were a good deal alarmed."

And from Ingestre on February 1 : —

"So our poor dear old King is gone. If this event should make any difference as to my return, *i.e.,* if I ought on account of it to come back directly, *pray* say so.

"I write by this post to Lord Sidmouth, to say I am ready to go if Government wish me to do so."

Ingestre: February 4.

"Well, my dear Gregory, here we are living under the auspices of a new King, who I am sorry to say has been (I believe very) ill at the commencement of His reign.

"By a letter from Bloomfield yesterday, I learn that H. M. is better than even the bulletins report him to be. I called twice at Carlton House, but owing to the Duke of Kent's death I did not ask to see the then Regent.

"I trust our good King will emulate the virtues of his good and moral Father. I hear that he was very much affected on reading His address to the Privy Council.

'. . . Pray also be active about Dr. Lloyd. He, I imagine, would expect to be the provost in the event of Ebrington's moving to the Bench, to which I see less objection than to anybody in our list, and to which our Masters here are inclined. Be careful in ascertaining Lloyd's tenets as to Catholic matters, for Plunkett will be zealous, you know, on that point, and he is in high favor with Government. But I do not think anything is in immediate contemplation for him *here.* Lord Sidmouth distinctly told me *He would not,* were he in my situation, consent to any person being made Provost who was not a *staunch protestant.* Depend upon it we are well backed in that Quarter, as also at Carlton House—at least so said Lord S——.

"I am so much out of the way of hearing news, I can find you none, but from what Lord Harrowby said before the late King's death had occurred I should not wonder if parliament were to be dissolved very soon. It will turn upon what is to be done with the Queen; I believe the people of England are very indifferent upon this question.

"God bless you."

THE KING'S VISIT

Lord Talbot, after a short visit to Ireland, writes again from Ingestre, March 15, 1821 : —

"We had a most delightful passage of fourteen hours and a quarter, and had I been told that I was to be at Dunleary at 7 o'clock one evening, and find myself at home at 11 o'clock on the next, I should not have believed the possibility of such an event.

"Yet such was the fact—under the space of 30 hours I crossed the Channel and travelled 72 miles in England, and 7 in Ireland."

"Pray order me half a pound of Irish Snuff to be sent."

On March 19, Lord Whitworth writes to Mr. Gregory from Grosvenor Square : —

"At present it seems decided that you are to have a visit from Royalty towards the end of May. It will be a Troublesome one for Lord Talbot and for all concerned, but I think it is a good thing, tho' he may not bring the boon of emancipation with him.

"He will not have a Table of his own, altho' he will send his Cooks, &c., &c., but it is to pass for the Lord Lieutenant's table, in order that H. M. may be supposed to be himself a guest, and so not give offence to many who might expect to be invited. Several coach and saddle horses are also to be sent, although his stay in Dublin would not exceed two or three days.

Lord Talbot to Mr. Gregory

London: June, 1821.
"I only came back last night from Hatfield. Hitherto I have not bothered you with the reports of the day, which succeed each other with unabated celerity. One thing I believe is certain, that the Ministers are completely out of favour, and that the favourite's influence, unbounded as it is, is thrown into the scale against them.

"Lady Liverpool's death causes much speculation, but I (from pretty good authority) have been told that Lord L——, much as he loved his wife, he loves *place* better. I will permit myself no observation on this. I *hope* it *is* so for the Country's sake. Sidmouth wishes to go, and if the King would let Canning into the Admiralty, Lord Melville would succeed to the Home Department.

"Last night the King gave a ball to the young Chips of the old Stools of Nobility, to which many of the Whig Lords and Ladies went. To-day H. M. dines with the Duke of Devonshire, no Ministers asked but Lord Melville. What all this forebodes I know not, but I am enjoying my Visit without any observation, which I might not do in quieter moments."

"June 4, 1821. . . . I saw Lord Londonderry yesterday. He has expressed a wish that Downshire should be Governor of the County Down. He is a deep Politician. I told him I had rather speak to D. than write upon the subject. I recommended to him the curtailing of the royal visit to 10 days or 14 at most. On this subject I am persuaded the K. is his sole adviser. The different great Men vary so much in their statements that it is evident he does not speak equally openly to all. Yet what is more probable, he changes his mind every day.

"Bloomfield told me yesterday the preparations for the Coronation would be completed by the 30th inst., that the Ceremony would take place the first week in July, and that the King having held a Levee and Drawing-room naturally consequent on it, would lose no time in setting out. That H. M. was bent upon going by sea, but hoped that if I concurred in the opinion that a Land journey would be better, H. M. would consent to go by Land. I had no difficulty in saying, I thought anything that tended to ensure punctuality would be beneficial, and that if the Westerly Winds we had a right to expect were to set in, that H. M. might be a week at sea.

"The prevailing public opinion is, we shall have *no* Coronation. And again, the Abp. has been told to have his sermon ready by the 16th of July. From these conflicting reports it is hard to draw any certain conclusion. But I think the great Man will be with us currente July.

"There *is* to be an installation. The Dress of the Knights is to be altered, from silk to *Poplin*—at least so said Bloomfield. He brings about 17 Officers of State and 4 or 5 private friends in his suite. He will be at the Park, and means to make his Entrée into Dublin by the Circular road (as I recommended) by Sackville Street, as Grand as possible. He has determined not to sleep out of Dublin. He is to go to the Curragh, and will I believe look at the Boyne! Proh pudor! and the Wicklow mountains. I think I have tried you long enough at this moment, so adieu. The person you and I should wish to see in office does *not* come in, when the Event I named takes place. This is all I have to say at present.

"Ever faithfully yours,
"TALBOT."

"I shall be badgered again about the Attorney, Plunkett, Bushe, Norbury, and Downes, but I shall be stiff and true to my friends.

"5 o'c.—I have seen Lord Liverpool. He has authorised me to give orders for the brushing up the Castle—painting is out of the question; but the walls may be distempered afresh and the hangings in the public apartments replaced by new ones. I told Lord Liverpool that this would cost 600*l.* or 700*l.*, but that I thought it would not be right that old things should appear. You must give general order to every inhabitant of the Castle to provide themselves with Lodgings, as the Officers of State are to be lodged in the places they now occupy. A new Bed, &c., should be provided for the Lodge in the park, where the King will probably be. The Lady Lieutenant's sitting-room had better be appropriated for his Majesty when at the Castle, and fitted up accordingly. I have written an official Letter to you, thinking you would like to have it to show.

"Lord Castlemaine, Monck, O'Neill, Westmeath, Ennismore, Kilmorey, Mount Earl, are to have steps in the peerage. If any other applications have been made, write to me. Young, Shand to be Baronets.

"With regard to Plunkett, *that* you may be satisfied is settled. He *is* to be Attorney General. Say nothing till you hear further from me. They are ready to give Saurin an assurance that Plunkett shall not be put over him as Chancellor. This may soften. Lord L. told me there were two ways of meeting this point, one to have a confidential communication made to him, Saurin, thro' me, the other to write me an official letter stating H. M.'s positive intentions. I made no answer, although I stated what it is obvious I should do, about Norbury, Downes, &c. The fact is, P——tt is necessary *here*."

June 6.
"I had a most satisfactory conversation with Lord Sidmouth yesterday, who has been *commanded* by the K. to remain one of

his Government. This will enable him to come over with the great Man to us. A point of no small interest and comfort.

"I have not time to tell you all I hear, but I am sure *great warm* of concord exists—and some changes would take place if the Successors could be agreed upon. I hope P—l is not so far from office as I thought when I last wrote. Lord S.'s successor was named to me—but by the information I now send, it should seem he was not approved of. More when we meet. . . .

"The reductions in the army will take place; I had a long discussion thereupon with Lord Londonderry, who laments the necessity of diminishing the troops, but says, it is imperative. He *will* come to Dublin.

"Lord S. will be in Grant's apartments, this I am to manage, to be near *you* and *John,* by both of whom he means to be assisted in his Addresses.

"I can *not* see the King. He is in *bed* with the Gout. The *regnante* is in high favour.

"Whatever I *must* do with The Marquess in Ireland—*here* I do not know him. D—n his impertinence.——

"Should there not be a new Throne and new Hangings in the presence Chamber? Things should be handsome and put in execution even for the name of the thing.

"6.30 P.M.—Nothing more was said by Lord S. I am, however, sure much negotiation is going on. I think the Lady thwarts Ministers, and they her. The K—g has not seen me yet, surely there must be ministerial trouble or illness at the bottom of seclusion. He has some Gout, I believe. To-day I dine with the Spanish Minister in this House, to-morrow I go to Epsom, for which the weather is not favourable, it having rained very hard most of the day."

Boodles', Thursday.

"The list of the King's attendants appearing so extravagant I deemed it my duty to submit it to Lord S., who will converse with Lord Liverpool (who resumes his official duties on Tuesday next) on the subject. I hope next week the Ministerial arrangements will be completed by Wednesday, as on Thursday or Friday I shall bid adieu to London, on my way to Ireland, where I shall arrive in nine or ten days after.

"I have just left our friend Lord Whitworth and the Duchess of Dorset. Of the latter I will only say I *never* saw her better. Of the former, he *is well,* but quantum mutatus ab illo. I am happy to think he is perfectly cheerful, with a comfortable flow of spirits, good appetite, and enjoying the comforts of life, the sight of his friends, &c., but he is much reduced, and he seems to want energy, and his usual vigor of body. Yet I do not apprehend any change, and if the summer ever gets like itself, I should hope he will rally sufficiently to make a successful stand against the rude attacks of winter. I thought we did him good—Slade, the Verulams, Drummond and I, the party. Grant looks worn to death."

H. Square: 2 o'c., June 11.

"I am just arrived; if I collect anything you shall have it.

"I understand the Coronation is to precede the Irish Trip, common report says so.

"P.S.—I have seen Lord Sidmouth, but in the turmoil of the House of Lords. I gather from him that H.M. *certainly* comes to us, but not till the end of July or beginning of August, *after* the Coronation. He said he was in a scrape for having allowed me to come over at this Juncture. I answered that I thought it would prove a great convenience, and save volumes of letters. Lord S., 'Yes, on that score alone must I rest my justification, and write you a letter *nunc* to be dated *tunc*.'

"Grant has heard the Irish Government is to defray all the expence on the other side of the Water for the K.

"Unde? . . ."

H. Square: June 27.

"I must write you two lines to say that I think we are *all* in a very uncertain State.

"The Ministers I saw yesterday were terribly out of sorts, Lord Grey and Tierney in apparently high spirits. The K—g has seen and caressed Lord Jersey. Nothing appears of rumoured change in the opposition papers—and I was told yesterday by a friend of Government, but not immediately connected with us, 'our friends are all in a great fright.' Certain it is the K—g was to have seen Lord S. yesterday, who appointed me to hear the result of the conversation, but He was put off.

"The real truth is, the influence of the favourite is unbounded. Ministers set themselves against this (in vain). She rebels and predisposes H.M. against them. Others tell you He is only playing this game to keep the world quiet for the Coronation.

"I *know* he *has* said—'I will shew Liverpool I have two strings to my Bow.'

"I am to see Lord S. to-day, who did see Lord Liverpool last night, and is to see the K. to-day. If I learn anything you shall have it.

"All this for yourself, as at best it is but surmise."

June 27, 1821, 6 o'c.

"I *have* seen Lord S., who has seen the K—. In furtherance of a suggestion of mine, I hope we shall be spared some of the Myrmidons I had a list of. In confidence, I am to be one of the Knights of St. Patrick. You will readily believe I had no wish for honors, but as H.M. has been graciously pleased to honor me with an order connecting me for ever with a Country to whom I am for ever attached, I cannot but prize the distinction.

"The King's horses will move in detachments, the first I believe move Monday—they will come by Liverpool per steam.

"I think Lord L. is in *force since* H.M. has seen him. All difficulties are not got over, but are, he told me, in a way to be so. I hope they are.

"To-morrow I am ordered to Carlton House at 2 o'c. Much will then be settled, I hope."

Ingestre: July 5, 1821.

. . . "The King said nothing to me at all. He kept me two hours before he saw me, and then only expressed his satisfaction at the thought (as he was pleased to say) of meeting me so soon again. I tried to bring him to arrange some points, but was as often foiled by 'You and Bloomfield or Lord Sidmouth will arrange for me.' In fact, things are to fall out as they may. Pray say that the King's horses are at first to occupy the Castle stables. When I leave the Lodge they may occupy those.

"I have returned to all my lone and bitter recollections, which the very perfections of this old place powerfully call into action. Oh, how happy, supremely happy, could I have been! But I will not, dare not murmur. God's will be done."

Haw Lea (?) July 12, 1821.

"I have little to add to what I wrote yesterday. It appears to me, the political horizon is much clouded; how the storms will be dispelled I know not. It appears to me there is a decided disinclination to almost the whole of the Cabinet on the part of a certain great personage, excepting to Lord S. whose retirement annoys all parties, not so much on account of any strong personal attachment towards himself as on account of his being less exceptionable to the different interests than they are to each other.

"I shall not see Lord Sidmouth again till Thursday. I heard that the K—intended to confer honours, either of supernumerary Ribbons, Butlerships or something of this class, on peers. I have therefore submitted to Lord Sidmouth the names of Lord Courtown, Lord Wicklow, Lord Clare, Lord Glengall, Lord Downshire, Lord Meath, Duke of Leinster, Clonbrock—these with a query if H.M. means to conciliate *everybody*—and two or three more whom I do not immediately recollect. If you will tell me of any persons more I will thank you. I have omitted all those who gain promotions in the peerage. Did I name them to you?

"If there is any other person whose services, Character, conduct, or merit, entitle him to Consideration, pray mention him, that I may communicate his name. I think I can obtain almost anything in the way of dignity now, for a man of character. . . . I heard from the K. himself there will be an installation, but I dare not consider this authority sufficient to act upon.

"I go to-day to Hatfield to witness the ceremony of Lord Salisbury's receiving a piece of plate from Hertfordshire, over which he has presided 50 years as Lord Lieutenant. Honourable to both parties! On Tuesday the 19th I go to Knole, and that day week put my horses' heads towards you, whom I shall be very glad to see."

The hopes of the Catholics were raised to their climax in 1821, when George the Fourth came over, it was supposed with the desired gift of Emancipation in his hand.

What hopes were raised by his Majesty's visit! The Catholic Bishops, the Catholic nobility and gentry came from the provinces to hear the message of peace and goodwill. The peasants of Galway and Mayo laid by their pikes and blunderbusses and listened for it. Good Dr. Doyle, called by Sydney Smith "the Pope of Ireland," came to Court in gleeful spirits, chaffing a foolish young sprig of nobility till the company choked with suppressed laughter. He might better have kept in mind the words, "Put not your trust in princes," he had so often heard chanted in his poor cathedral. I see no sign in the glimpse we get of the King's counsels in these letters that such a point was even considered amongst his arrangements. His cooks were to be sent, and his horses "from Liverpool by steam" (more fortunate than their Royal Master when the westerly gales came on). A clerk from the Chamberlain's office, "a vulgarish fellow but accustomed to hunt up upholsterers etc.," is to be attended to and "given every facility," and the inevitable Irish "lick of paint" is to be applied wholesale. Stars and ribbons were to fall and flutter on to the breasts of titled expectancy. But the great question as to whether the promise given by England twenty-one years before was now to be considered as come of age, and kept no longer in abeyance, was, so far as we can see, not even seriously considered.

The incidents of the King's visit are well known.

He arrived after a good passage, during which much goose pie and whisky had been consumed. Word had just come of the death of Napoleon at St. Helena. The story goes that "Sire, your enemy is dead," were the words he was greeted with. "When did she die?" was his response. But the Queen was indeed also dead, and his Majesty was persuaded to wear a piece of crape round his arm during the festivities, which were in no way curtailed.

He had a tremendous ovation from the crowds thronging the roads, though Croker tells us they did not know how to cheer, but shouted; "they have not had much practice in the expression of public joy." The streets, as Lord Norbury observed, if ill paved were well flagged, and his Majesty had to undergo some "oppressive loyalty." At Slane Castle, the only private house where he stayed, he not only captivated Bushe but Saurin, delicately hinting that he bore him no grudge for his resistance to the Union, and "pleasantly asking his legal opinion as to whether he might not stay where he was and send Lord Talbot as Lord Lieutenant to England." He complimented Lady Conyngham on the cookery, comparing it favourably with that of "my cousin, the Duke of Gloucester, who has a talent for giving bad dinners." At the University dinner he bore without flinching an ode composed for the occasion (presumably by Dr. Parkinson), which, though we see Bushe was pleased with it, made some less kindly critic remark that when the Silent Sister opened her mouth, the voice was that of Balaam's ass. With his own royal hand he helped up Lord Norbury, who slipped and fell at the levee, giving occasion to that inveterate punster to say "This is not the first lift your Majesty has given me!" He graciously accepted offerings, the marble chimney-piece hewn from the quarries of Connemara, which still adorns the Carlton Club, the laurel crown presented by O'Connell upon his knees, and still kept up hope as he left by whispering aside to Lord Cloncurry, "I am sure you will be pleased with my letter to-morrow."

When to-morrow came he had faded from the view of the Irish people. "He embarked at Dunleary at seven in the evening," writes Mr. Gregory. "An immense concourse of persons, and it was the most grand and affecting spectacle I ever witnessed."

The Lord Lieutenant and the Chief and Under Secretaries having all been at the Castle during the King's visit, there are naturally no letters from one to the other giving any record of it. But I have been allowed to use the following letter from Chief

Justice Bushe to his wife, by the kindness of his granddaughter, Mrs. Martin of Ross:—

From Chief Justice Bushe to his wife

Dublin: August 28, 1821.

"I have staid at home to-day in the hopes of getting through some study business which has accumulated upon me during the Carnival, for it is nothing else. Our College Dinner to the King yesterday was magnificent, and the singing of the Choir excellent, and delighted him much. The Foxes have gone to St. Patrick's Church to see the Installation. . . . I fear poor Arthur will be drenched by this dreadful rain at the Curragh. When I proposed it as an amusement to him I speculated upon better Weather.

"I wish I had time to gratify the anxiety you will feel about the visit to Slane, but I must postpone particulars till we meet, and only tell you in general terms that there could not have been a pleasanter party. From its nature I feared it would be awful and formal, and it was as much the reverse as if we had been in Kilfane or Kilmany.

"In two minutes after the king came into the room, he thawed the ice and put everyone at ease, and before we were well seated at dinner we were not merely cheerful but joyous, a character which was not lost during the Evening. He is a perfect master of Society as far as it can depend upon Art, but it is plain that his success very much is to be attributed to his nature, which leads him to delight in it. The French word enjoué was never so applicable to any man. Upon serious subjects, he is pointed and even eloquent, but it is the eloquence of conversation and not at all declamatory, and the pleasantry with which he intermixes them is given with all the advantages of great quickness with natural humour, a wonderful memory, the opportunities he has had of hearing, witnessing and collecting all the good anecdotes of every kind, and a talent for mimickry quite surprising. He talks a vast deal, but I think not from natural garrulity, but because his rank makes it necessary for him to originate every subject, and perform a kind of solo to which what others say is little more than an accompaniment. He listens with great good breeding, however, assents in an encouraging manner when he agrees with you, and his contradictions, tho' politely given, are frank and peremptory. He is a perfect story-teller, and has the art which nothing but constant living in good company gives, of keeping out of view all the flat parts of a narrative, and only showing you the points of the picture upon which the light falls. His attentions are very seducing and impartial. He contrives to go round the whole table and bring forward everyone in turn and with the share of notice due, never missing deal by giving a card too much or too little, and letting no one feel that he is forgotten or held cheap. For instance, I was much struck after he had amused us, his subjects, with English and Irish stories, by his turning to the Foreigners, and for a time giving them French ones, which he does admirably, and with the accent of a Parisian, and perfect power over the language. How he manages to get over in a few minutes the space between introduction and familiarity, which it takes some so much more time to leave behind, and which others never can pass, I cannot tell, but I certainly in less than half an hour was as little surprised by his calling me Bushe without any other addition than if I had known him twenty years. I must not, however, conceal that part of his captivating Nostrum is the same secret practised by Sterne's Beggarman on the Pont Neuf, and that in the slyest way possible he insinuates very intoxicating, though almost imperceptible flattery, and with a Grace that would almost make poison irresistible. Think of my poor hot ears and my fry when he began to talk to me across the dinner table of my speeches on the Union, which I had supposed no one now living remembered. You are not to suppose from all this praise of his Convivial powers that his Dignity is for a moment even adjourned, and I cannot conceive how anyone could venture, as they say some have, to take advantage of his condescension and take liberties, which I think of all men I have seen his manners are most calculated to repel.

"The Postman's Bell reminds me that I have been running on in unmerciful scribbling; as to anything he said, either to myself or others, I must reserve them till we meet, when, like the old lady of Tillytudlam, you may expect me to talk for ever of my dinner with his great and Royal Majesty. The company was sixteen in number, Prince and Princess Esterhasy and the Dutch Ambassador, Baron Fagel were the Foreigners, and the Attorney General and myself the strangers. I sat next, at one side, to Sir Andrew Barnard, John Power's great friend, who is a charming fellow, and we talked much of Kilfane people. Adieu, dearest Nan. I fear I am late for Post.

"Ever yours,
"C.B.

"P.S. The Bell man is off, and as I must send this to the office and the Foxes have not come, I shall scribble on. The King thinks

Slane the most beautiful place in the world, and from being only used to flat views about London, says the scenery is bold, a name we would not give it. The house he is justly delighted with, especially one round room, and he praised the good taste (mind Mrs. Bushe and Mrs. Power) of a drawingroom in the Country having no window curtains but white muslin, like the white parts of Anna's at Ballyduff. Oh, but you must know how the king eats and drinks, I suppose. Well he does both very heartily, but nothing like excess, eating a little bit of almost all the made dishes, hobnobbing with everybody, mostly in Sherry, after dinner beginning with hot Potteen Punch and ending with Claret, and breaking up in about an hour after the ladies, who had sat about an hour with us after dinner. From that the Drawingroom scene continued till half past one in the morning. One tray was brought in for supper, which no one touched. Anna and Mrs. Power would never forgive me if I omitted these details tho' I know they have no curiosity to know how Lady Conyngham and her Daughter and Princess Esterhasy were dressed, and therefore I say nothing about them, which I am sure they will thank me for."

LORD TALBOT'S DISMISSAL

The "Annual Register," at the end of its account of the King's visit, says:—"It is melancholy to be obliged to add that the events of October, November, and December destroyed all the splendid anticipations to which His Majesty's visit had given rise in the minds of those who possessed a superficial acquaintance with the character of that people. The gaudy and hollow bubble of conciliation soon burst, and a system of outrage, robbery, murder, and assassination commenced, scarcely to be paralleled in the annals of any civilised country. . . . Notwithtanding every precaution and every remedy that could be devised, the country continued to the end of the year in a very unquiet state."

A letter from Mr. Gregory to Lord Sidmouth, dated November 9, 1821, confirms this account:—

"Mr. Grant having written to you yesterday on the state of the County of Limerick, it is not necessary for me to say anything of that part of the Country except to send you a copy of a notice to which he alluded in his letter, in which you will read that in addition to the rewards offered by the Banditti for the assassination of Magistrates and Policemen, they call to their aid the powerful excitements of religious hatred. I send you a copy of a letter received this day from a Magistrate of the County of Cork, enumerating the many houses deprived of arms, and of Acts of outrage committed in the parts of that County bordering on Limerick. These accounts have been confirmed by letters from several other Magistrates, all stating the rapid progress of the Evil through that County.

". . . I feel no apprehension for the safety of the State, and do not think that the utmost efforts of the present Agitators can shake the Government of the Country. But success creates courage, and from the rapidity of the movements of the Insurgents a country is overrun and sworn before it is possible for the Government to bring any force to meet them—meet them indeed the King's troops seldom can; their Secrecy is wonderful, and Death is the inevitable consequence of even suspected Information. The System of organisation is carried on by powerful Allies, Terror and Inclination, the lower orders are afraid to refuse to be sworn, and when they are sworn they are very ready to obey.

"The disturbances have commenced at an unfavourable period to quell them, the great length of night leaves the Country for so many hours in the possession of these marauders, and as soon as the Potatoes are dug, there will be no employment for the People until Spring. Everything that exertion can effect will, I am confident, continue to be used to put down the evil, but I must express my own opinion that we shall have a very troublesome Winter."

The friction between Lord Talbot and Mr. Grant seems to have unfortunately lasted into these troubled times, when the strength given by unity was especially needed by the executive Government.

On November 19, Lord Talbot writes to Mr. Gregory: —

P. Park: November 19, 1821.

"The accounts from Warburton are not satisfactory which have come this morning. He writes from Ennis.

"Willcocks has been employed in organising and revising his police establishment, which evidently wanted a strong hand over it. Some measures should be adopted in the Castle to ensure the reception of correct returns from the police magistrates, as by Willcocks' statement nothing can have been so irregular as everything relating to the interior of poor Going's establishment.

"An anonymous correspondent gives notice of nightly meetings in Tipperary. This, as it points out a man's house as a place of meeting and refers to any Magistrate who may be appointed to examine into the alleged facts for corroboration after the enquiry shall have been made, has been sent either to Wilson or Willcocks for investigation.

"Grant feels some doubt of the expediency of calling out the Yeomanry lest it should create irritation. 'Where?' said I. 'Among the Catholics,' replied he. But I think this week will hardly elapse ere they will be called upon.

"Sirr, I think, appears to have been a little hasty or alarmed or perhaps jealous of others. Yet attention to all points can do no harm at this critical period.

"There appears to be a design afloat to get a 5th Major General established permanently in this country. But this is mere suspicion.

"We do not want you yet!

"Dennis Brown told Grant Saturday that Mayo was quiet."

And on November 20 : —

"One of the resolutions at the meeting of the Magistrates at Buttevant was this (the first resolution indeed) : —

" 'That a petition be presented to Government requesting, as the only efficient means of preserving the peace of the Country, that the provisions of the Insurrection Act *lately repealed* (bravo!) be immediately acted upon.' Is not this capital.

"These gentlemen abuse the Peace Preservation Bill, in which sentiments I am sorry to observe Lord Aylmer is rather inclined to concur.

"I could not have supposed that our premier would have ventured to have sent his opinions to Government respecting the danger of calling out the Yeomanry, but faith he has done so at no small length.

"In postscript No. 1 he is candid enough to admit that I have differed from him in the view he takes of the subject, and in a subsequent paragraph says the Attorney and Solicitor General both dissent from him, and agree with me in opinion. I saw neither of them.

"In a second postscript he intimates that he believes it will be necessary to run all risks and call upon the Yeomanry.

"When, my good friend, shall we cease to see such vacillation and stupid prejudice in our councils? Truly it is a lamentable circumstance to be bound to such creatures.

"Adieu, I am off to Carlow, where I shall stay to-morrow, and if I do not hear anything to recall me, I believe I may stay over Thursday with Bruen if he presses. I understand that people begin to be alarmed in Dublin.

"But altho' I am not *yet* inclined to think we are in a deuced Scrape, I own I shall do so if no benefit is derived from the strong measures pursued in the South. Lord Aylmer and Willcocks ought to be in activity now, as the former has got his Troops with him and the latter must have reorganised his Police Establishment.

"God bless you."

Mr. Gregory replies: —

Palace, Kilkenny, November 21, 1821.
"Many thanks for the perusal of the different Letters which I herewith return. Mangin sent me a copy of Mr. Grant's Letter to Lord Sidmouth. It is quite disgraceful that after a measure had been maturely considered and finally decided, and orders issued for carrying it into effect, it shall suddenly be suspended from apprehension that it may give offence to the Catholics, who (Mr. Grant says) are already very jealous of the Yeomanry. Their services were not thought of except as a dernier ressort, when the military force was expended, and they were not even intended to be employed against the popish Insurgents of the South. Will he wait until Dr. Woodward has educated the Poor? It is quite impossible for any man with common sense and common Feelings not to see and to bitterly deplore the lamentable poverty of the Irish Peasants, and none but a Brute or an Absentee would refuse his money, his Labour and his time to promote any rational System for their amelioration. But what nonsense is that sympathizing, philosophizing Prancing, when Insurrection of the most sanguinary spirit has manifested itself in so many acts of Outrage and is nightly and rapidly encreasing—an Insurrection into which the Peasants have not been goaded by any immediate pressure of Want, since provisions have not been so cheap for many years as now, but which has been long in its organisation and is conducted with an impenetrable Secrecy and unrelenting Cruelty, how lamentable is it that the efforts of the Government (feeble as they are from the small means at their command) should be paralysed by one whose Duty it is to give Energy and Spirit. But from the suspicions contained in Col. Hodder's Letter, and which are felt by the great Majority of the Protestants, there is no Confidence placed in Mr. Grant."

Lord Talbot to Mr. Gregory

November 24, 1821.

"Mangin sends you a copy of our proclamation offering a reward of 2,000*l*. in certain proportions for the discovery of the murderers of poor Shea.

"I have determined and given out that I shall have an audience every day. Grant does not give satisfaction.

"By a letter from Lord Oriel I learn the meetings, swearing in, &c., have begun at Ardee. He is aware of them and who the people are. The life of Mr. Filgate, the Magistrate who excited himself so much about the Wildgoose business, is threatened, Lord Oriel says. Wills says the evil is peeping out in Roscommon.

"In short, the whole Kingdom is infected, and I doubt we shall have a troublesome winter."

The winter proved troublesome enough, but Lord Talbot was not destined to deal with its troubles in Ireland. The "Annual Register," after the notice of the disorderly state of the country quoted above, adds: — "Among other measures adopted was that of sending the Marquis Wellesley to replace Lord Talbot as Lord Lieutenant."

The letters of recall came December 1, 1821, and were followed so quickly by Lord Wellesley's arrival that there was not even time for the formal honours usually paid to a departing Viceroy. Lord Talbot held an undress Levee at the Castle, which Mr. Gregory notes was "numerously and respectably attended," but withdrew as soon as possible to Carton, the house of his friend and relative the Duke of Leinster.

Lord Talbot had reason to be angry about his political treatment. He had not been ambitious or sought office. He was taken from the pastures of Ingestre, and set on high in the throne room of Dublin Castle, and then suddenly, after all the King's fair speeches and compliments, flung back again into country life. We see from his letters how deeply he took his recall to heart. In an undated note to Mr. Gregory he says: "The accompanying letter I mean to send unless I receive your veto. I have boldly challenged his Majesty's *approval* of my conduct, and have endeavoured to separate myself from all collision with the Beast himself" (Lord Liverpool).

The Government had not, when they recalled him, the intention of giving in on the Catholic question. Lord Talbot had only a year more of office before him. The apparent cause of his recall was his having drunk to the toast of the "pious, glorious, and immortal memory," at the Lord Mayor's dinner. But the toast was proposed by the Lord Mayor himself, and though Lord Cloncurry and other decided "Catholics" turned down theìr glasses, the King's representative may not have felt free to refuse the toast to one of the King's predecessors.

His letters show what a warm spot there was in his heart for Ireland, and how sore he is for a time after his recall, but he "goes to look at flowers," at the wonderful scarlets and crimsons flaming over the grey mud of Holland. Then he takes up the threads of country life aagin, attends the Magistrate's meetings, looks after his property, establishes a sheep show, and does his duty.

The following letters were written in the first soreness of dismissal. He may have found comfort in the fact that Mr. Grant was also recalled, and succeeded by Mr. Goulburn, but he does not allude to it.

Lord Talbot to Mr. Gregory

Ingestre: January 2, 1822.

"I enclose a letter which I have found here, from our dear friend Lord Whitworth. What comfort does it not bring to me. It almost reconciles me to my fate.

"You will be glad also to hear that persons of all parties in this County are indignant at the treatment I have experienced, and I have heard it whispered that a public dinner is in contemplation to me expressive of their regard, and to assure me I hold the same place in their Esteem I ever did. This (if true) is most gratifying. You shall of course hear more when I do. I long to hear the arrangements in all your departments. If Phillimore is right as to the sensation felt in England about our good Attorney, I fear others will soon follow me and him.

"Lord W. told me he meant to lose no time about Saurin's business. I thought Goulburn particularly *cordial* at taking leave. He'll soon go."

[Enclosure] Knole: December 2, 1821.

"I will tell you candidly why I have not written to you. I was so hurt and disgusted at what had occurred, that I could not trust myself to mention it to you until I heard from yourself how you felt about it. I am not surprised at your feelings, and I partake them most sincerely. In all the course of my political life I never knew anything more unjust, more unmerited, more illiberal, or more absurd. I ask of everybody what Lord Wellesley can do, or will do, that Lord Talbot has not done, or would do, if you gave him power to act. If they mean to give him powers which you have been asking for in vain, they will add still to their injustice, for why should not you carry these powers into effect as well as he.

"It is cruel and barbarous usage, but such only as those who engage in politics must expect, and particularly with such people as those with whom we have now to do—whose principle it is to give up everything and everybody rather than give up their places.

"But, my dear Talbot, I will not add to your spleen by venting my own. Come and see us as soon as you can.

"W."

Lord Talbot to Mr. Gregory

Boodles: Jan. 10, 1822.

"Here I am after a semi-conversation with Lord Sidmouth—which was interrupted by the Duke of York's coming into the room. The meeting was most distant on my part, Lord S. saying 'Little did I think, Lord T., that you and I should meet with painful feelings.' 'Most painful indeed, my Lord,' returned I.

" 'Have you heard of the King's gracious intentions towards you?' 'No, my Lord.' 'I wrote to you at Ingestre.' 'I had left home before your Lordship's communication arrived, I suppose.' 'Well,' said Lord S., 'the purport of the letter was to express H.M.'s commands to you to go to Brighton to be *His* Guest at the Pavilion.'

"To which I answered, 'I can set out this moment or to-morrow, whichever day your Lordship may instruct me to go. Am I' (said I coldly) 'to go in Uniform or in frac.' This hit. But after a little Lord S. said, 'We must talk over the matter unreservedly.' 'My Lord, the matter is soon discussed. I have been turned out of office in less time than I should deem it right to turn a servant away, without having been told *Why*— in other words I have been condemned unheard. Had Lord Grey come into power he could not have treated me more unceremoniously. It is for your Lordship to tell me *How* I have deserved this treatment. I thank God I do not feel conscious of meriting it.' I then added that I had been taken out of my County with an unspotted Character, that whatever might be the opinion of the public respecting me, still I was returned to that County with an imputation, if not stigma, cast upon my public conduct. Lord S. then talked of the impossibility that I could seriously entertain such an opinion, the respect, etc., felt for me by the whole Cabinet must satisfy me. I said 'Respect, my Lord, is a cold word, and what we perfectly understand—it is better earned by actions than words.'

"The Duke of York then came in.

"I am to go to Brighton Monday to be humbugged. I think they are ashamed of themselves—as well they may be. I shall get no redress (indeed, what can be offered to me for the outrage put upon my feelings?) but Blarney. They may offer me a Marquisate because they know I will not accept it. I go to Knole to-morrow. As soon as I see Lord S. again I will again trouble you. John has written me word that Saurin is out—pray say everything from me to our excellent friend. The on dits of the day report, too, that you are off the stage, my good friend."

Ingestre: January 16, 1822.

"What a system of H—b-g seems to be the order of the day now.

"I have been to Brighton. The King gracious enough, but tho' he expressed himself sorry my feelings had been wounded, and allowed me to say that I had not been removed on account of any disapprobation of his, still he made no attempt to heal the wound his ministers have inflicted. Indeed, I do not see how reparation is to be obtained, perhaps it cannot be.

"Peel I have seen by chance this morning. He has been to Staffordshire, and finds his father greatly changed, he says. I presume he cannot last long.

"Rely upon it, Peel is as sincerely attached to you as either Lord Whitworth or myself.

"I have received your letter mentioning your conversation with Saurin. He will be satisfied, I hope, that I only consulted His feelings or what I thought his feelings would be, in keeping the business a secret from him. I can have but one feeling, that of respect and attachment, for this most excellent amiable person.

"You can have no idea of how I feel to want the Home I have lost.

"I am lonely, without object, and almost nerveless, and unable to do anything. Had I not these emotions to unman me, I should soon get over this rub; but the coming to what is not a *home* to me is of hard digestion."

Berkeley Square: January 17, 1822.
"This is the last letter from me respecting my dismissal, and this shall be short.

"I am just returned from Lord Liverpool, to whom I expressed myself in strong and indeed indignant terms. If I do not mistake, Lord Liverpool felt (you'll say can *stone* feel) the hardship of my Case, and is either to write to me on the subject, a letter which I am to be at liberty to make public, or say something in his place to remove all suspicion of disapprobation from me. The former will, I think, be what he will do.

"If he does not, questions will be asked in the House of Lords by my friends.

"Now God bless you. I thank you for all the kindness and support you have ever afforded me, and if I know myself I shall not bring any portion of a public man into private life, but always gratefully acknowledge you as one of my best and dearest friends.

"With Peel I am more than satisfied. I told Lord S. that were it not for Peel's being the organ of communication I believe I should resign my Lieutenancy of Staffordshire. But enough of this nefarious sacrifice, I am sick of *them*, and lest you should be of me I will conclude with assuring you of the sincerity with [which] I am, and ever shall be, my dear Gregory. . . ."

Mr. Gregory to Lord Talbot

Jan. 19, 1822.
"I did not answer your former Letters from London and Knole, not knowing where to address you, but yours of the 16th received this day removes any doubts on that account.

"Your reception in London and Brighton was such as might have been anticipated. Civility is cheap, and Flattery is only at the trifling expense of character in the Giver. I do not think you will receive either the Letter or an explanation in the House of Lords from Lord Liverpool, to which Lord Sidmouth thinks you entitled, and what has already been said will be considered quite sufficient Satisfaction for any reasonable man, to which class you will be voted not to belong. But let me beg of you to throw away all care on that account, and seek no more for redress in consequence of the ungracious treatment you have received. It cannot reflect any disgrace on you, you cannot lose the esteem of any honest man in the world, and why should you any longer feel one moment's uneasiness. There were two ways of removing you, one might have equally promoted every object the Government had to gain, and perfectly in accordance with your feelings. The Minister took another line, regardless of your feelings. Attribute it to the awkwardness of Lord Liverpool, who never was taught to dance. . . .

"I like Goulburn very much. Of his Excellency I know nothing, as I have never as yet been honoured by an admittance to an audience. I never met him but once, in a private room, at Dinner at the Chancellor's yesterday. I do not wish this to be mentioned, as it would appear that I was piqued, and which is probably intended. I am so undoubtedly, but there is no necessity for putting it into the orderly Book. I have not touched on the point to Goulburn, nor shall I, but that my removal is intended I have no doubt.

"Everything as unknown about A.D.C.'s Household &c. as when you sailed. The country not improved, on the contrary the evil spreading."

Lord Talbot to Mr. Gregory

Ingestre: January 25, 1822.

"Many thanks, my dear Gregory, for your kind letter and valuable advice, which I will endeavour to follow to the utmost of my power.

"Is it not strange that two such extremes should exist in my mind at once as the perfect oblivion of office, and as perfect a recollection of what my life and habits were here previous to my beginning public life. . . .

"I send you Lord Liverpool's letter, which says little more than that which recalled me. I have thanked him in his own cold words.

"Forbes writes to complain of Lord Granard's not having been included in the recent promotions in the Irish Peerage—and says I had promised to name his wishes. I agree to this, with the addition 'if the subject was first mentioned by the Government in England'—or in other words that I would sanction the advancement if applied to by Lord Liverpool for my opinion.

"I have written to Lord L. and to Lord Forbes stating how I conceive the matter stands, and which I believe I have correctly stated. . . ."

Ingestre: March 28, 1822.

'. . . Lord L.'s answer to my application has not surprised, although it has hurt me in the tenderest point. Why did they select me as a proper person for the distinguished situation they were pleased to appoint me, if they intended to make me sensible by every possible means of my insignificance. But I am humbled!

"By private letters (I *believe* from a sure and wary person) I hear a certain illustrious person is turning Swaddler[1] fast, a sermon of Dr. Pearson's and the preaching of a certain Marchioness have rendered him melancholy, I am afraid. He suffered so much from the violent tossing he got last year on his return home, that he is not to sail again.

"You will be sorry to hear that I have been obliged to reduce my rents full 15 per cent., so that I shall be annually more than 2,500*l*. minus. The Tenants are satisfied, but they express their fears the diminution will not be sufficient. But, however, they also express their hopes that I may soon put them up to their actual rents again. This proves that my land in common times has not been too high let, which I was at one time almost assured was the case. Nothing can be more satisfactory than the manner in which these poor Creatures have received the indulgence. What I cannot understand is the total *cessation of demand*. An abundant harvest, an excessive importation may account for the lowering of price, but why people are to eat less when your population is increased and your manufacturers are flourishing, I cannot comprehend. . . .

"I have had a most friendly letter from our friend Saurin—he is not fond of Humbug—no more am I—but truce to this.

". . . I go to Town the week after Easter, and to Holland after I have shown myself. I cannot *yet bear* to be stared at as an X.X.—or to go into families by myself where I went as a happy husband—so I shall *look at flowers*, and then home again."

Berkeley Square: April 25, 1822.

"I have been to Court twice, having obtained the Entree, and was kindly received. I have also left my name with the Ministers, so that almost all the ceremonious part of my coming to Town has been accomplished.

"Peel I have seen; he was looking harassed when I first saw him, but he has rallied, and is remarkably well. Of Lord Whitworth's health I cannot speak in terms sufficiently strong. He is *wonderfully* well indeed, in spirits and strength equally so. It is quite delightful to see him.

"I presume your friends in the House of Commons send you word what passes there, at least *they used* to do so. They of course have told you how severely handled Master Ellis was by

---

[1] Swaddlers, a term for Methodists.

the Attorney General on Sir J. Newport's motion.[1] I have heard that Sarcasm was never bitterer—he talked of his raising 'a stupendous superstructure of falsehood upon a scanty basis of truth,' and equally strong was he on other points. It was rather supposed possible they might have met the next morning.

"I shall be curious to hear Canning's speech, which I mean if possible to do. No one seems to know whether he will carry his object through the House of Commons or not. Opinions are very much divided upon it, that is to say, some people that wish for the complete emancipation of the Catholics think this a half measure; others say that it is unobjectionable as being purely aristocratical; others, friends of Plunkett's, that it is taking the subject out of his hands—while the protestants inveigh against it as a side-wind mode of carrying the Catholic Question.

"My own Idea is, that it may be considered as a parting blessing from Mr. C., who is determined to set the Cabinet by the Ears, as he does not belong to it, which in some degree it will, I think, effect.

"We are unquiet in Staffordshire, though the last accounts are better. I told Peel I was ready to go there on receiving a hint from him, relying on him alone not to be *superseded*. He laughed. I have been obliged to reduce my rental very seriously indeed, which coming at a moment I had *given up* (like my Sovereign) 30M(?) a year, is inconvenient.

"My best regards to Saurin. Do he and the Chancellor set their horses together tolerably well again?"

May, 1822.

"I hear various rumours, but I believe it is certain that there was a determination expressed at the meeting of Ministers at Fife House on Friday last for their *going out,* if they are beat upon three or four questions now about to be discussed. The truth is they are all at sixes and sevens, and our old friend C——h plays too refined a game, notwithstanding his pliancy, for John Bull now grumbling and groaning under pecuniary embarrass-ments arising from agricultural distress. The country Gentlemen are dissatisfied beyond measure, and if we could peep behind the scenes I doubt not we should see discussion and disunion among the first-rate Actors in the political drama. I believe I told you I surmised Canning meant to leave the poisoned Garment behind him as a legacy, when he made his motion respecting the Catholic peers, and full well has he succeeded. Of Peel I believe I may speak satisfactorily, and I think and hope he will rise. He has

[1] On the renewal of the Insurrection Act.

in no way forfeited the public esteem, he stands up to *his man* like an honourable and decided character, and will, I have no doubt, maintain unsullied his reputation. Certain it is there is a feverish disposition abroad in the world, and if the opposition could make itself respectable, it would soon oust our present Administration. I write to you what I hear, and will not affect to say you may rely on any part of what I have stated, more than as the gleanings of public conversation.

"The Gouty symptoms of the King have left H.M., and he is better I understand, but they say H. M. has not yet quite recovered the effects of his passage from your dear Island last Autumn. La dame is in favour still."

Thursday, May 4, 1822.

"I am ordered off to quell riots in Staffordshire, for as Fanny says, rebellion follows my steps.

"The colliers are up in arms. Unfortunately there has been a man killed, which has excited a great deal of ill will. I hope, however, to put an end to it. 'Tis delightful to have to do with Peel.

"You can have no idea of the powerful speech which Peel made on the Catholic Peers motion. He really surpassed all ideas I ever entertained of close and successful argument. I believe dispassionately speaking that he had the best of the discussion, tho' it must be owned that Canning was very great. I met the latter at dinner yesterday surrounded with his satellites. I am sorry to say they calculate on an addition of *ten* next division—tho' Hobhouse told me this morning that he heard it would have a different result when the question was next argued. God grant it may.

"I was so happy to do business again with Peel, 'twas done à la Gregory, which is to the mind of your affect.

"TALBOT."

"We have been enlivened by a duel this morning. The Duke of Buckingham called the Duke of Bedford out for his observations on the Grenvilles in his speech at Bedford, which his Grace refused to recall. The Duke of B—m fired once, and the Duke of Bedford then fired in the air and exeunt omnes."

London: May 27, 1822.

"We are about to have a splendid Ball for our distressed Countrymen. I hope too much money may not be expended in decoration. The night after the Fête we are to have our Catholic debate. I hope we shall have a fair majority, from 30 to 40. But I learn to my surprise, and, faith, indignation too, if true, that one of our high dignitaries of the Church, the Archbishop of York, has been persuaded to stay away. I cannot conceive it. The new peers are in our favour, I believe 9 out of 11. The City is in great good humour with Vansittart, and so will the whole Country be at the remission of taxes. I do from my heart believe the Country is in a most flourishing state, with the Exception of the landed interest, who will be swept away to make room for others, who coming into the occupation of the farms upon reduced terms and an unimpaired capital, will flourish at the present prices. The cold-blooded politician will not care for the individuals who may be sacrificed, as the general results must be in favour of national prosperity. "General Humbug" is as much in vogue as ever. In Norfolk alone there are 11 Gentlemen's seats to be let. In Cambridgeshire and Sussex I have heard of money being offered to Tenants to farm their Lands. 3s, and even 5s. an acre has been mentioned. I have not had any farm thrown up, but my reductions are great. If they continue, I must shut up and retire, God knows where, notwithstanding the 70,000l. H.R.H. the Duke of Sussex says I realised while in Ireland. Others have said I made 100,000l. with equal truth. The country is in great beauty. I think of going *to fish* to-morrow near Uxbridge, at a famous *trout* stream. I fear I cannot get a Trout like your son Robert's from the Belvidere Lake."

Astley Castle: July 27, 1822.
"I saw Peel *well* I think on my leaving town. He is in good spirits about things in general, and privately may I say it, supposes the present system of *conciliation* will be as prevalent in 1922 as in 1822. He sees through the humbug. The discovery of Saurin's Letter to old N. has occurred since we corresponded. I wish the Letter had never been written—although it may be immaterial, as I hear our friend says it is to him. Still publick Considerations induce me to wish it had not met the Eye of the World. Ingestre had talked of going to see you &c., but I have prevailed upon him *not* to go at present, as my Character might suffer from a Son of mine returning immediately to your hospitable Shores. I fear that my spirits on my return home may flag, therefore I write to you when that is not the case. I mean to occupy myself with my Children. My farm I shall I think diminish, I cannot stand the loss on it; this I regret as it will

diminish the interest and the occupation I used to find at the old Shop. But as all is for the best I shall try to live a harmless and I hope not altogether useless life, though I do not see exactly how the ball is to be kept up."

LORD WELLESLEY AND MR. GOULBURN

It must have been an unpleasant change to Mr. Gregory, after his cordial intimacy with Lord Talbot, to find himself treated *de haut en bas* by the dictatorial and autocratic Lord Wellesley, who had arrived "boasting of his past victories over Indian cabals and anticipating his future ones over Irish," and who, as Sir Walter Scott observed, talked politics like a Roman Emperor.

Mr. Wynn tells of having met Lord Wellesley at Dropmore, with five servants, two of whom were in the habit of making his bed, and is highly pleased at his having, notwithstanding, to carry his own candlestick upstairs.

There is something domineering in his pencil notes on the business letters sent back by him. "Approved—let this be done" has a sort of air of *"Fiat lux*. Even his *W* has an an autocratic flourish compared with the unassuming *W* of Lord Whitworth, the easy man of the world, secure of his position.

"The Irish Government, sir! *I* am the Irish Government," was his exclamation once and his persuasion at all times. Great things were expected of him. He was not only Viceroy of Ireland, but an Irish Viceroy. He had made his state entry with bunches of Shamrock at his horses' heads and in his attendants' buttonholes. He was a prominent champion of Emancipation. He was hailed as a deliverer by the Catholics, and intimated to their Prelates that addresses such as are presented to the King would be acceptable to him. And when the Prelates came, he received them in his private room, with marked attention.

He was expected to call a new world into being and to invert the official pyramid with a nod. But these expectations were not fulfilled. When it came to practical details Lord Wellesley, like all who have had a hand in imperial government, well knew what danger lies in lightly meddling with the delicate and complex working of the machinery of administration.

In Mr. Gregory's little note-book for 1822 I find "Jan 9. Dined with the Lord Mayor. Disgusting speeches of Flattery to Lord Wellesley." He might have made a still more severe entry, for even Sheil laughed at the Viceroy's oratory and self-complacency at this dinner, and tells how he affably assured the company that the Duke of Wellington was not ashamed of his country.

Plunket, however, whose sense of humour sometimes failed, declared he was too much overcome by "the delightful scene he had witnessed that evening" to express his feelings in words.

There are other notes: "Feb. 4. My first meeting with the Lord Lieutenant on Business. A great Talker." "April 23.— King's Birthday not celebrated by the Lord Lieutenant." "Dec. 24th.—Attended the Lord Lieutenant in full Dress to St. Patrick's Ball, where he received a fulsome Address and returned an absurd answer."

But entries of "Dined with the Lord Lieutenant" become more frequent as time goes on. No doubt Lord Wellesley's interest in the little fair-haired "fisherman," the Under-Secretary's grandson, to whom he gave daily lessons in the classics,[1] brought about a more kindly feeling between them. In 1825 I find the entry: "Oct. 29.—Dined with the Lord Lieutenant. His excellency was married in the evening to Mrs. Patterson."

But if Lord Wellesley gained friends in one direction it was not long before he lost them in another. He had not been long in office before a Coercion Act was pressingly needed.

Mr. Gregory writes to Mr. Goulburn: —

April 15, 1822.
"Three baronies in Kilkenny were proclaimed this day, I do not know how many in Tipperary, but all for which applications were made.

"The Council assembled in the Lord Lieutenant's dressing Room, as he is not well enough to leave his bed, and the door of

---

[1] See *Autobiography of Sir William Gregory.*

his Bed Chamber being open, the Proclamation was read so as
to be heard by his Excellency.

   "It was absolutely necessary to pass the proclamations, as very
general and loud Complaints were made by some of the most
respectable Gentlemen of the Country in consequence of the
Delay."

   He would by no means put up with government by disorder.
He receives a complaint that the parish priest of Ballyhooly has
refused the last rites of the Church to his flock, unless they take
their names off an address to Lord Ennismore, and writes
"Enquire into the facts stated" in his peremptory way. Lord
Courtown writes to tell of some veiled threats of "a convulsion"
used by the priest of his parish. The Prelates he had admitted to
his private room would hardly have been pleased with the Viceroy's note on the letter: — "I think the Priest should be required
to make a full explanation of his language, and after the matter is
fully ascertained, he should be punished and exposed."

   At first Mr. Goulburn was blamed, and looked on as the log
attached to him to restrain his free action. But his health was
failing, his energy had evaporated. O'Connell declared the Orange
faction had locked him to their chariot wheels and dragged him
to their Orange Club feasts, that he had only come to Ireland
to enjoy his ease—that he had descended to trail his laurels and
his honours in the dust and mire of that party which insulted
his person and would sully his fame." The Orange Party, on the
other hand, looked on him as little better than a Jesuit. He was
much influenced by Blake, the brilliant sagacious barrister, "the
backstairs Viceroy of Ireland," whose elasticity was shown by his
belonging to two Corporations so far apart as the English Bar and
the Galway Militia, and who was labelled "dangerous" by good
Protestants, though I find that Mr. Gregory could not resist
dining at his house to meet Sir Walter Scott.

   The Viceroy's refusal to allow what was irreverently called
"Old Glorious' to be decked as usual on the anniversary of the
Boyne, led to the celebrated riot in the theatre, where a whisky
bottle, presumably empty, was aimed at his head by an
exasperated Orangeman.

   Lord Talbot writes to Mr. Gregory on this subject from Sand-
well, December 20, 1822: —

   "Although I had purposed keeping the most profound Silence
on the subject of the attack at the Theatre on Lord W. your
Lord Lieutenant, I cannot see the account of Lady Anne's having

been carried out in a state of insensibility without feeling the liveliest interest about her, and wishing to hear that she has not materially suffered from the alarm, and that she has recovered from the shock.

"You are strange people, ye Irish. Is it possible that so much fuss, so much illwill, can be excited by the mere question of whether a few tawdry trappings shall be put on a carved piece of stone, or whether the health of a King who certainly saved you from slavery shall be drunk or not! On their heads be the responsibility who have agitated the question. Far preferable do I hope was the noiseless tenor of our way, to the humbugs and advertizing puffs of the present times.

"What will our gracious Sovereign say when he hears that one of the effects of his beloved conciliation was an insult to his person in the dangerous attack made upon his representative?

"I cannot, however, quit the subject without expressing the strongest regret and indignation at this unworthy treatment of Lord W., much more disgraceful to the perpetrators than to the object against whom the injury was levelled. What inflated language will C. Grant now indulge in! Indeed I regret the occurrence in every account. . . ."

Lord Wellesley's pompous and abortive prosecution of the Bottle Rioters as "murderers in intention" filled all Protestant Ireland with wrath and the English Ministry with inextinguishable laughter. Mr. Wynn writes:—"Wellesley is making too ridiculous a parade even for the taste of Paddy;" and Mr. Fremantle on the same occasion, "There never was such an ass."

He had at least silenced one set of his accusers, who declared that he never promoted a Catholic lawyer unless he had a Protestant wife, by choosing a Catholic bride to share his own throne.

He had found at Calcutta the advantage of governing without close communion with home, and would fain have followed the same course in Dublin, to the great indignation of the Ministry.

In 1824 Wynn writes, on the 24th January, "The silence of Lord Wellesley is really unparalleled. Conceive that since the 20th May, when he wrote that he required nothing but the renewal of the Insurrection Act, and another request (since supplied to him) not one line official or private has been received from him." And in April, "I find the Orange party are loud in their abuse of Lord Wellesley for shutting himself up in the Phoenix Park, seeing nobody, and only communicating with Secretary Gregory by letter. Indeed, I believe that the latter is more than he often favours Secretaries Peel and Goulburn with."

I may give in this context an application from Mr. Goulburn to Mr. Gregory for fuller information for himself and Mr. Peel, and his Excellency's note on it to the effect that they get quite as much as is good for them: —

June 18, 1822.

"You must excuse my anxiety about the state of the country, for I am persecuted nearly to death both in and out of Parliament, and am supposed to be the most inhuman and unfeeling of men because I have not given an assurance that the Government of Ireland can or will feed all the people. Pray send me a return of all Works on which people are employed in any of the distressed Counties, and a guess at least as to the numbers employed. It will be of the greatest use to receive such accounts from time to time."

Lord Wellesley writes on the back of this: —"Mr. Goulburn and Mr. Peel receive regularly by every mail every necessary and practicable information."

Even in 1822, Mr. Gregory writes on April 22, "Saw the Lord Lieutenant for the first time since the 10th inst." And on Jan. 31, 1823, "Saw the Lord Lieutenant for the first time since 31st December."

Wynn writes again in 1824: —

"Plunket arrived Monday night, and we received the next day half of Lord Wellesley's long promised despatch, in which at great length he very eloquently states all the difficulties of the Burial question, but unfortunately breaks off in consequence of an interruption before he proceeds to suggest any remedies." Then in November, "I have seen no letter from Lord Wellesley, and I believe none has arrived, but that a grand epistle is on the anvil."

Lord Wellesley was at the same time, however, able to find leisure to pour forth his griefs to Plunket. "Your generous attachment," he writes in 1823, "is one of my great consolations in this troublesome and thankless station!" And in the following year: — "This country is in the most tremendous condition, and I am left without support or countenance to submit to the kicks of the ass and the dirt of the monkey. The suppression of my despatch on this great question is an ignominy, an insult not to be endured.

It is a sequel to the same plan of extinction which, on the question of the Statue, the Riot, the Orange, the Ribbon confederacies, by concealing my opinions reduced me to the condition of a villain and slave on a mock throne, and rendered me an object of ridicule and contempt to a country which would have hailed me with respect and gratitude if I had not been crushed by pretended candour at Whitehall . . . I am indeed most unhappy here— degraded, vilified, an object of scorn and detestation . . . frustrated, baffled and betrayed by all my own agents; encompassed by traitors even at my own table . . . and in England . . . a contemptuous silence even of my name . . . From such a condition I pant for release."

Plunket was Lord Wellesley's chief guide, counsellor, and friend all through his term of office.

Though Mr. Plunket had nominally taken Grattan's place as representative of the Catholics in the House of Commons, he never quite won their confidence. Perhaps in spite of O'Connell's success, a lawyer is by profession too much inclined to believe there are two sides to every question to make a Heaven-sent leader, inspiring confidence in the infallibility of his cause. Or the expectations from him may have been in the beginning too high to be fulfilled. In Trinity College he had been the close friend of Wolfe Tone and Thomas Addis Emmett. He, like all other eminent Irish lawyers, had "behaved nobly" at the time of the Union. He had even denied the right of the Irish Parliament to vote away its own existence. "As well," he said, "might the frantic suicide hope that the act which destroys his miserable body should extinguish his immortal soul." His popularity came to its height when he defended the Sheares brothers on a charge of high treason.

But in one way or other he gave offence to the Catholics, even while they were trusting their cause to his hands. They were glad of his voice and his vote, but the "authoritative frigidity" of his manner, in a country where manner counts for much, repelled them. Even their dearest foe Saurin won a warmer place in their hearts, with the charm he had brought from his cradle in Languedoc.

It was felt that although Plunket was sincerely in favour of religious freedom, he had as their leader too much of a Moses-like sense of spiritual superiority. He wished to emancipate them first and to Protestantise them afterwards. He was the friend and patron of Archbishop Magee, a bigot among bigots, who would not allow a Catholic priest to read so much as a Latin Psalm over one of his flock, when laid in a Protestant churchyard. He was a keen champion of the "second reformation," the last serious attempt to change the faith of the people. He was known also to cherish the bugbear of "foreign influence," as a danger to throne and constitution. He proposed fresh safeguards which O'Connell indignantly rejected, declaring them to be nothing less than the re-enacting of the penal laws. Brought up a Nonconformist, he had accepted the beliefs of the Church of England, but as if to restore a balance was ready to overturn those of the Church of Rome. Had he been a Catholic, Sheil declared he would have been the chief demagogue of the people.

Croker writes of him: "Plunket is said to be dissatisfied, and when he is sulky no one is so sulky." But among his intimate friends he threw off his reserve, and was as full of quips and puns as Lord Norbury himself.

Blake, whose fascinating humour and practical sagacity there seems to have been no resisting, was said to keep his mind in his breeches pocket. But he must have nodded for a moment when he allowed his two protégés, Plunket and Lord Wellesley, to embark in the bottle prosecution already mentioned. On the other hand, Mr. Plunket began an abortive prosecution of O'Connell and the Catholic Association, and the disorderly element in the country complained of his being as strict in the administration of justice as Saurin himself. The conduct of the Catholic case was taken out of his hands in the House of Commons, and he did not himself lead the people into the promised land. He held to the cause, however, and witnessed its success, and, as a peace-giving measure, one must sorrowfully confess its failure.

His promotion did not come rapidly. In 1827 the King refused to have him made Chancellor, because of his championship of the Catholics, and the English Bar, whose members had so often found a comfortable seat on the Irish woolsack, struck against his being appointed Master of the Rolls because he was an Irishman.

He attained to the Chancellorship at last in 1830. But in 1841 he was thrust out of it by his own party, who wanted the place for another. He never recovered from this wound received in the house of his friends, though his old jesting habits clung to him for a time.

It was during a short period, in which he had been replaced by Sugden, that he met his old friend Nicolas Ball abroad, with a newly grown beard, and shook his head at him in mock warning. "Ah, there's a *shaver* in Ireland will never let you appear before him like this."

Like so many great lawyers, his mind failed at the last, but he never lost the authoritative character that had belonged to him. Once a curate who had incautiously included him in a petition for sinners was obliged to make a precipitate retreat through the window.

An old member of the Irish Bar, to whom I was talking of him, said, "I would not say he had a disagreeable manner, but I saw him very much out of temper twice: once when he gave his farewell charge to the Bench, and was raging against the Government for having turned him out in favour of Campbell—not that he had anything to complain of, for he had feathered his nest well; and once when we dined at Judge ——'s, and after dinner came family prayers. When we knelt down, his chair was next mine—oh, he was very angry indeed! "

The chief feat accomplished by Lord Wellesley in Ireland was the dethroning of Plunket's rival, Saurin, the Attorney-General.

His removal was decided on in 1821, but not carried out until the following year. No one, it is said, had courage to say the word of dismissal until Lord Wellesley arrived. The secret kept itself, and no one, friend or enemy, ventured to hint to him that it was in the air. The following letters show how even the loyal and official mind of Mr. Gregory is moved when Saurin is first threatened, to try and stir up the Viceroy to mutiny on his behalf.

He writes to Lord Talbot June 6, 1821 : —

"Your letter of the 4th has filled me with great alarm, as the Conduct intended to be pursued towards the Attorney-General satisfies me that a new system of Government is to be adopted in Ireland, and that the old and faithful supporters of the Crown must make way for recent Converts."

And on July 7 he writes : —

"I cannot say how much your letter from Sherborne has distressed me, as it discloses an unfeeling Perseverance on the part of Ministers to remove a faithful and invaluable servant of the Crown, from no other than the selfish motive of gaining the parliamentary support of a powerful Advocate, who has for so many years been a powerful Antagonist. In my mind *you* can at once put an end to this disgraceful transaction by declining to be the Channel of Communication, whether official or not, and by declaring that it cannot be made so long as you remain Viceroy of Ireland. I do not think after such a Declaration the measure would be persevered in, nor do I think they would venture on your Removal for the sole Purpose of carrying it into effect. I am aware that this is bold and hazardous Counsel, but you will, I am sure, give me the Credit of its being disinterested."

Lord Talbot writes on November 21 : —

"Saurin's fate is sealed. We (the Chancellor and I) have received a Communication on the subject. But as yet we are only to proceed and obtain Donner's resignation of the C. Justiceship, which is then to be offered to Saurin (in pretty decided language tho'). Bushe is either to have Norbury's situation if he will resign it, or be promised the succession to it. I have written to the Chancellor requesting his assistance. I am very happy in the reflection that I made a stand for Saurin last year."

But Mr. Gregory refuses to be comforted : —

November 22.

". . . Yet when these two very important objects (resignation of the Chief Justice and the Attorney-General) are surmounted, if they can be, what is to be done with Bushe? I shall be surprised if he agree to abide the Disgrace of being superseded by Plunkett, and be satisfied with a promise of dead Norbury's shoes. It is a vile transaction, and will overwhelm the administration with Reproach and shame."

Lord Talbot writes with evident relief on November 24, 1821 : —

"I am *not* to be the Channel of communication with poor Saurin. The Chancellor, who is so much better qualified, has undertaken it. So far I disagree with you, that I do not think Saurin is the first to whom the Business should be communicated. The Chief Justice, in my opinion, and in that of Lord Manners (to whom I read parts of your Letter), is the person with whom he will begin. If the Chief resigns, to whom the *whole* case is to be made known, then there is a something to offer to the Attorney. If the Chief will not resign then the whole thing stops, for a while at least.

"I do *not* think the Attorney will be Chief Justice. What do you say? Then what a business. I enclose to you Lord L.'s Letter to me, by which you will perceive it is a measure of Government.

"However much I deprecate this transaction, and believe me I do so as sincerely as you do yourself, I still think that a Government has a right to expect that an Attorney-General should accept the situation of Chief Justice when offered, and not consider the office he holds a permanent one. What the devil is to be done with Bushe and Norbury I know not."[1]

Of the minor personages, if indeed I may place him among them, mentioned in the letters, Saurin stands out as the most striking. There seems to be a ring of affection in the voice of such different personalities as Peel, Lord Whitworth, Lord Talbot, Mr. Goulburn, when they speak of him.

He was of mixed race. The grandson of a French Huguenot, he had a quick eye for a possible assassin in every Papist, and had St. Bartholomew always in his mind, while some drops of Scottish blood in his veins gave him tenacity.

At the time of the Union he had been its vehement opponent, had scorned bribes of high place, and declared it to be a violation of every moral principle, and even doubted whether it ought not to be resisted by force. He had turned the Irish Bar into a volunteer corps when a French invasion was expected, and may have hankered to lead it into action in one direction or another. A saying of his at this time was often quoted against him afterwards, that "debates might sometimes produce agitation, but that was the price necessarily paid for liberty."

In the Duke of Richmond's time, however, he came into collision with O'Connell, and soon lost, in the eyes of the people, the name of patriot.

He was the Hercules of Orangeism. No sooner did O'Connell re-establish the Catholic Board or Catholic Committee by some new name, than Saurin's quick eye saw the new head rising, and springing upon it destroyed it with the sword of the law.

He and Lord Manners were called the Gog and Magog of the Orange Party, and were often caricatured as they walked arm in arm to the Four Courts as "the brothers in law."

In spite of "a certain sweetness in his glance," his expression struck a stranger as harsh and stern, and his foreign blood was very noticeable. Having walked down Piccadilly one day in his blue coat and buff waistcoat, arm in arm with the Duke of

---

[1] "My belief is that Lord Liverpool will offer you the Home Department, all the formerly existing reasons for which are increased by the alarming state of affairs in Ireland. Grant is certainly to be recalled. And I believe Lord Liverpool will again apply to Goulburn (or has already) to succeed him. . . . I have not heard *distinctly* what Plunket is to have, but I hear Attorney-General Saurin being promoted to be Chief Justice. I learn also that old Norbury has been asked to retire, and that he has declined, I daresay not without a jest."—Croker to Peel, November 1821.

Bedford, a friend said to his Grace when they parted, "I suppose that was *your Jew.*"

This extract from one of Mr. Gregory's letters to Lord Talbot will show his conservatism on matters of religion: —

April 27, 1814.

"The Attorney General was in my room when the Express arrived; I read to him your observations on Insolvent Debtors. I also read to him what you said of assimilating the Law in Ireland to what passed last year in England, for relieving the Persons from Penalties who impugn the Trinity. He shook his head at the Introduction of any religious novelties in Ireland, but will look into the Act. I think the Athanasian Creed will stand in the Statute Book as well as the Liturgy."

However, he agreed to the innovation, for a letter of May 9 says: —

"The Attorney-General says he has written to you on the Insolvent Act. Townsand is preparing the two bills, one respecting the Trinity, and the other for recovering Labourers' Wages."

He had a distaste for criminal business. Bushe tells of the indignation of Admiral Packenham at his not coming in person to lead some prosecution, and his still greater indignation at the reason. "I have no idea," he cried, "of a *sentimental hangman.*"

Those who cared for him would have acted a kinder part if they had given him some warning of his approaching fate. Even his second self, Lord Manners, resisted the usual impulse of a friend to hint at coming misfortune. He was stunned when Lord Wellesley struck the unexpected blow. In his first soreness he refused the Chief Justiceship and the proffered Peerage. They seemed to him a poor consolation for the authority he had seized as Attorney-General in the time of the easy-going Duke of Richmond, and had held unquestioned ever since.

Lord Wellesley told Mr. Lamb afterwards: —"I think it right before leaving Ireland to prepare you for hearing it asserted by Mr. Saurin's friends that he was an ill-treated man. Now I offered him the office of Lord Chief Justice of the King's Bench. That was not ill-treating him. I further offered him a peerage. In truth I had nothing else to offer except the Lord Lieutenancy of Ireland. To that, however, there were two objections—First, *he had already held the office for fifteen years*; and next, I—*I*, was the Viceroy!"

Saurin's imprudent letter to Lord Norbury urging him to use his influence while on circuit for political ends, or rather the discovery of that letter, had given occasion to the enemy to triumph. Lord Norbury, who was of an economical turn, had stuffed this letter with others under the lining of his armchair to make up for some deficiency of horsehair. The chair in process of time being beyond amateur efforts, was sent to an upholsterer, who discovered and published the letter. Such at least was the story, and it may have suggested the famous "black bag" to the mind of the late Mr. Pigott.

But though his friends lamented this indiscretion, they still held him dear, and grieved at his fall. Even the Catholics spoke gently of him. Sheil says: "Whatever were his faults, duplicity was not one of them. I saw him in the height of his power and in his fall. He was meek in his prosperity, and in his adverse fortune he was serene."

And he gives a touching account of him after his deposition: —
"When he was first deprived of office I watched him in the Hall. The public eye was upon him, and the consciousness of general observation in calamity inflicts peculiar pain. The joyous alacrity of Plunket was less a matter of comment than the resigned demeanour of his fallen rival. Richard was as much gazed on as Bolingbroke. It was said by most of those who saw him that he looked as cheerful as ever. In fact he looked more cheerful, and that appeared to me to give evidence of the constraint which he put upon himself. There was a forced hilarity about him, he wore an alertness and vivacity which were not made for his temperament. His genuine smile is flexible and easy, but upon this occasion it lingered with a mechanical procrastination upon the lips, which showed that it did not take its origin at the heart. There was also too ready a proffer of the hand to his old friends, who gave him a warm but a silent squeeze. I thought him a subject for study, and followed him into the Court of Chancery. He discharged his business with more than his accustomed diligence and skill, but when his part was done and he bent his head over a huge brief, the pages of which he seemed to turn without a consciousness of their contents, I have heard him heave at intervals a low sigh. When he returned again to the Hall I have observed him in a moment of professional leisure, while he was busied with his own solitary thoughts, and I would perceive a gradual languor stealing over the melancholy mirth which he had been personating before. His figure too was bent and depressed as he walked back to the Court of Chancery, and before he passed through the green curtains which divide it from the

Hall, I have seen him pause for an instant and throw a look at the King's Bench. It was momentary, but too full of expression to be casual, and seemed to unite in its despondency a deep sense of the wrong which he had sustained from his friends and the more painful injury which he had inflicted upon himself."

Mr. Saurin never held office again. He died in 1839.

In early life he had been ill-treated in love, having been thrown over by a young lady to whom he was attached in favour of a future Earl of Limerick. But with more philosophy than he showed in his other great reverse he did not waste his time in sighs, but married and lived happily with a sister of the Marquis of Thomond.

Lord Wellesley was less successful in dethroning another potentate. An amusing account of a ball at Dublin tells how, seated on his throne, he "shot his fine and indignant eye into the soul of Sir Harcourt Lees, who received it with a grin and showed that a theologian was not to be put down by a frown."

This Sir Harcourt Lees was no doubt a thorn in the side of the Viceroy, being the oracle of the militant Orange party, an excitable man who believed that every "Papist" in Ireland was thirsting for his blood, and was so nervous that he could not sleep in a house where even the striking of a clock was heard. He had great influence in Ulster. There is a story that my grandmother, a sister of Chief Baron O'Grady, her son being quartered in the North, wrote to beg Sir Harcourt "not to let the riots begin till William's regiment had left."

Saurin's companion at arms, the Chancellor, Lord Manners, was an English importation, described as looking like the ghost of Charles the First, and was pelted with descriptive burrs by the Catholics. O'Connell, taking the lead, declared him to have "the natural propensity of a small mind to the practical details of intolerance," and said with some felicity of expression, "He is a bad lawyer, but the most sensible-looking man talking nonsense I ever saw."

Sheil said he made the administration of justice in the Irish Chancery "the subject of Lord Redesdale's laughter and Lord Eldon's tears." Curran said "He is ready for any mischief. In private he is a pleasant dull man." The most congenial side of his character in Irish eyes was his love of woodcock shooting, which he was able to gratify during the Christmas holidays. He was always said to be irritable and fidgety as that time drew near, lest any drawn-out suit should interfere with his anticipated sport. Mr. Plunket used to declare that on the name of Mr. Hitchcock, a member of the Bar, being suddenly called he would start, under the illusion of its being the "Hish! Cock!" of the beaters.

He was said to suffer from "inertness of intellect." Plunket would torture him by subtle reasonings he could not follow. Then he would look appealingly at Saurin, and ask for twenty-four hours to clear his thoughts.

He set his face steadfastly against emancipation. He had given Lady Morgan a lesson in salad making, but afterwards, on reading her book "O'Donnell," he found her sympathies were with the Catholics. Thereupon he ordered the book to be burned in the servants' hall, and said regretfully to his wife, "I wish I had not given her the secret of my salad!"

For all that, he became infected by the natural tendency to rebellion that lurks in Irish air, and he for some time refused to put the great seal to the appointment of Doherty as Solicitor-General.

He was succeeded in 1827 by Sir Anthony Hart, whose short history as Chancellor might be made up of negatives. He had no religious or political sympathies, no wife, gave no dinners, and no one of his decisions was ever reversed. O'Connell said of him and his predecessor that one was law without manners, and the other manners without law.

Lord Norbury was another ingredient of what one must call the upper crust of bigotry. He was indifferently called the hanging, the duelling, and the punning judge. He was the Jeffreys of '98, and the country people say of him even now that "he would hang a man as soon as cut the head off a rush."

I had in my childhood an old nurse who had lived in the family of the pardoned rebel, Hamilton Rowan, and I remember her telling that she had come to the breakfast room one morning with the children, when suddenly Rowan flung away the newspaper he was reading, and seizing a knife dashed it at a picture of Lord Norbury, that hung on the wall, and slashed it across the face. It was probably some harsh judgment or decision of his that had stirred the bile of the old patriot.

He was certainly left upon the Bench too long—Brougham showed that he had fallen asleep in Court during a trial for murder. "I'll resign to demand satisfaction," said Lord Norbury, who had been out with Fighting Fitzgerald in his day. "That Scottish Broom wants to be made acquainted with an Irish stick."

Tradition says that when his dismissal was hinted at, he called on Mr. Gregory and said "I began life with 500*l.* and a case of duelling pistols. Here they are—and if I get a letter from the

Castle that I don't like, whoever writes it will have to deal with *them.*"

Mr. Gregory writes to Peel in 1816: "Lord Norbury has got the whooping cough—do not laugh, the fact is positively so—but he will not give in, and proposes attending the Court to-morrow."

It is to be hoped Mr. Peel did not laugh, for I find by sympathetic allusions in Lord Talbot's letters that about a dozen years later he was himself afflicted with the same malady, which seems in those days to have been ambitious in its choice of victims.

Lord Talbot writes on April 16, 1824: — "I congratulate you upon Lord Norbury's resignation. Really this is a blessing to Ireland! Poor old man, his mind has long been unequal to the arduous duties of a Judge."

Of "the silver-tongued Bushe," nothing but good is to be heard. The letter written by him describing the impression made on him by the king at Slane shows that he possessed a silver pen also. It has been given to me by his granddaughter, who writes, "It affords a curious proof of the effect of manner, for the charm of the finest gentleman in Europe evidently blinded my grandfather to the terrible defects of a character which was 'Charles to his subjects, Henry to his wife.' I suppose two better bred men never met, but the one was a heartless reprobate, the other nearer perfection than any man who in the course of a long life I have ever known." Against him at least no Devil's Advocate has arisen.

Curran says of him "He hands up a point of law with as much grace and pliancy of gesture as if he were presenting a Court lady with a fan." He was one of the great orators before the Union. An old lady, an aunt of my husband's, used to tell of a ball she had been at in Dublin, which was suddenly broken up because word had come that Bushe was going to speak. Even the ladies hurried off in their ball dresses to the House of Parliament to hear him who, as Grattan declared, spoke with the lips of an angel.

Mr. Goulburn was sent as a pendant to Lord Wellesley, to keep even the balance between Protestant and Catholic claims. It would indeed hardly have been possible to have carried on business had Grant and the new Viceroy been left to work together. Their mutual distaste for pen and ink would soon have made Ireland become an unknown country to the Cabinet.

Mr. Goulburn's letters breathe benevolence. He and the Under-Secretary at once became friends. He stayed at Mr. Gregory's house while his own was being made ready, and even extended his amiability so far as to act as escort to the little grandson coming back from school. He was sent to smooth down

the feelings of Protestants, somewhat ruffled by Grant's treatment, and he won golden opinions even from the other side from
his mastery of the routine of business, and attention to detail, as
befitted a future Chancellor of the Exchequer.

O'Connell, however, sneered at his "limited intellect," and
described him as "a hired advocate whose official duty obliged
him to act as protector of abuses in Ireland," and as having been
sent as "a check over the Lord Lieutenant, fearing his Excellency
would be too favourable to liberty."

And more lately he has been written of as "a member of the
Orange Society who will long be remembered with a chill."

He showed more bigotry than one likes to hear of in refusing
naturalisation to the Italian, Bianconi, who by his public car
system had done so much in opening up the country, on account
of his religion. His not being a winebibber was probably looked
on as a more serious cause of offence in the Dublin society of
that day, and Mr. Gregory must have grieved to find so unusual
a lack of appreciation of his carefully bottled hogsheads of claret.

Moore wrote of him in "Captain Rock": —

"A Secretary worthy of the good old Anti-Popery times, and
to whose spirit I would ensure a safe passage over Mahomet's
bridge into Paradise, if *narrowness* (as is probable) be a qualification for the performance of that hairbreadth promenade." Mr.
Goulburn, however, bore no malice, and afterwards amiably hob-
nobbed with the satirist, meeting him one evening at a dinner
party.

In spite of his "narrowness" on the subject of emancipation,
Mr. Goulburn conferred real benefits upon Ireland. He put the
Constabulary system on a more secure basis, and began the
formation of a stipendiary Magistracy, still one of the chief
pillars of law and order. It was not only Mr. Grant who had
complained of the existing Magistracy. Mr. Gregory had written
to Peel so early as 1813: — "Indeed, I am sorry there is a mulish
conduct here which is quite unwarrantable, and only because
everything is not carried on exactly as they wish, whether with
or without law." This letter is docketed "Mulish conduct on the
part of the Magistrates of Westmeath."

And in 1814 he wrote, with reference to threatened disturbance
in Co. Cavan: "The Magistrates, knowing the temper of the
people in those counties, ought of themselves to assemble with
an armed force to preserve the peace of the country, but every
man has discharged his Duty when he has made a Communication
to the Castle. We, or rather I, have grievously offended Colonel
Wolfe for presuming to communicate with any Magistrate but

himself in the Co. of Kildare. He is the most huffy and impracticable man I ever met with—he does not require the King's licence
to change his name to Goose."

To Mr. Goulburn may also be given the credit of the improvement in the gaols. He reformed the Acts relating to them in 1826.
In 1815, Mr. Gregory had written of them : —

"I have this day visited Newgate and the Sheriff's prison; they
are disgraceful to Humanity, nor do I know how they can be
improved, as they are so much too small for the number of
prisoners confined. I am going to make some room in Newgate
by removing many of the Convicts to Kilmainham; but I want
the City Grand Jury to present a sufficient sum to cloath them in
any coarse apparel from this to the time of transportation. It is
scandalous that they have not good clothing. New prisons ought
to be built, instead of presenting for useless Bridges."

And in 1821 Commissioners had been appointed to inspect the
prisons, and found them with very few exceptions "scenes of
filth, fraud, without accommodation, clothing, classification,
employment, inspection, school instruction, order, or cleanliness.
The law totally disregarded, male and female prisoners often not
separated, spirits sold openly in many gaols, and frequently by
the under officers. . . . The families of prisoners were often fed
from the overplus food furnished to each prisoner, who kept little
bags of meal in their rooms to hand over to their relatives on
market days."

The Act of 1826 provided for the necessary reforms, and for
matrons for the female prisoners, whom the Quakers took under
their wing. Hospitals were provided, and discipline was restored.
The local "Black Holes," where prisoners were kept for months
without trial, and only saved from suffocation by being allowed
to sleep out at night on parole, were swept away or reformed. Mr.
Goulburn took great pains with the Act, altering, correcting, and
wording it himself. He also reformed and added to the number
of lunatic asylums.

The most pressing and important work that fell on Mr. Goulburn on his arrival in Ireland was the feeding of the people, and
to this both he and Mr. Gregory set their hand vigorously, not
I think with any ulterior idea of "killing emancipation with kindness," but because of natural goodness of heart, and because it
was the duty that lay straight before them.

A bad harvest and a threatened famine had caused the bubble
of enthusiasm created by the King's visit to burst. The people no
longer believed that the royal touch was to bring a cure for all

their ills, and the scarcity of 1817 proved to have been but an undress rehearsal for the famine of 1822.

It almost seems as if Sir Walter Raleigh, when he butchered in cold blood the garrison of Smerwick, did a less grievous wrong to Ireland than on the day when he planted the first potato in his garden at Youghal.

It was so easy in a good year to scratch up the soil, put in the seed, and then sit down or wander away during the ripening of the crop, that the effect on the industrial habits of the people was disastrous. Mr. Gregory, in a letter to Mr. Peel, gives an account of the usual mode of proceeding: —"A stranger may not know that after planting the potato gardens, the cabins are shut and the male adult population go to England or the vicinity of Dublin for work, and the women and children traverse the country as beggars and return home when the potatoes are ripe." Thus families multiplied, each new generation scratched up another patch of ground, planted more potatoes, and started life with no better outlook than their fathers had done.

The "Lumper" was one of the unlucky gifts brought to Ireland at the birth of this century. It was a large, coarse, innutritious potato, only thought fit for pigs, but so easy to grow even on poor soil, and with little labour, that it largely took the place of better sorts, and encouraged more than ever the setting up of homesteads built on so insecure a foundation.

But in 1822, after many warnings, came a wet season, blight, and failure of the means of existence. The potatoes had rotted in the ground in the preceding autumn, so that there was but a short supply on which to live until the coming in of the new crop. When the spring came, the little stock saved for seed was sacrificed to the calls of hunger. By the middle of April potatoes had risen from a penny to sixpence or even eightpence a stone. Meal grew dear also. The people had no means of earning money to buy it, no work or wages were to be had. Some crowded to the towns, fearing to be left face to face with their gaunt enemy, but only to be seized by fever and scrofula. Some looked to crime and the consequent imprisonment as preferable to immediate death. When meal was sold at a low price by charitable effort, police and yeomanry had to keep the purchasers back by force from a famished rush at the food they were within reach of. The accounts published from the different counties were heart-rending. Sir Edward O'Brien is said, when reading to the House of Commons the accounts he had received from Clare, to have burst into tears and been unable to go on speaking.

And Vesey Fitzgerald writes from London to Mr. Gregory,

"The accounts from Clare make one's heart sick. I should have gone over instantly on my arrival if I could have been liberated here. But I have not yet seen the King, and he is now for a week at Windsor."

This is from a Mr. Colpoys to Sir Edward O'Brien: —

" 'What are we doing in Clare.' I can assure you, My Dear Sir Edward, we are most of us working like horses. I give out oatmeal here to our poor starving parishioners (assisted by Vandeleur and Howitt) on Mondays and Thursdays to a late hour, a third day is devoted to attending the Central Committee in Ennis, and a fourth to the Baronial Committee in Newmarket. This is an exact picture of what is doing throughout the County; but unless you saw them you could not conceive how painful a duty it is to serve the poor creatures. When you come amongst us you will see many a lengthened visage and sallow cheek in place of the round face and ruddy countenance you left behind you. The amount of the local subscriptions is in most Baronies exhausted, and the impoverished gentry of the Country are unable to afford more—not a penny of rent to be had, so that many of our men of moderate fortunes who could and would readily have given their fifties and hundreds last year find it difficult now to pay twenties and thirties. The supplies afforded us by our generous friends in England come in as yet but slowly. We have had, for example, three orders on that fund in this parish hitherto, each received only the day before that of distribtuion, when we had to send to Limerick for the meal, and this keeps us in a constant state of alarm as the numbers in want of relief are increasing every day. Many, many of the poor creatures had pawned or sold their clothes or bedding before they asked for gratuitous relief, and unless *employment* is immediately found for them so as to enable them to buy they will all soon be complete paupers."

The good old Archbishop of Tuam writes from Castlebar to the Chief Secretary: —

June 6, 1822.

"My dear Sir,—I pray you forgive this importunity—the urgency of the case requires it.

"I am just returned from Westport and Newport, and a tour of 24 miles through crowds of half starved miserable men, women and children. I assure you, Sir, hundreds and thousands are depending upon *half a Meal* of oatmeal and water per day, and many have not even that, and are feeding upon *nettles;* this, rely upon it, is no exaggeration.

"Upon you I feel at this moment depend the lives of *multitudes* of our people. *Thousands of pounds alone* will save them, a proportion of 50,000*l.* to each of the distressed counties (if they are all like Mayo and Galway) will *not* answer the purpose. I now leave these unhappy quiet patient sufferers in your hands, and pray God may direct your determination.

"&c. &c. &c.
"Power Tuam."

And again next day: —

"If it were *possible* to strengthen my statement of yesterday, I have now most frightful means. Here I am in the midst of approaching *general* starvation and passed through *large bodies* of *half famished people* seeking a most *scanty meal* from *feeble* but utmost local efforts to relieve them. I again say if *Thousands* are not sent into the County of Mayo and the County of Galway *immediately, Thousands* will die of actual hunger. The 50,000*l.* already voted to afford employment to the distressed counties in Ireland (and how and upon what conditions we as yet know not how to seek for a proportion of it) is *totally inadequate.* Four times that sum would be little enough if I am to judge of what is called the distressed Counties in Ireland by these two unhappy Counties. Instances *already* have occurred of death by actual *starvation,* what must be the event before the end of Ten weeks which we must be prepared to meet. I repeat what I did last night, that all this sad visitation of Providence is suffered with perfect patience by the unhappy sufferers, and all is yet peace and quiet. I visit Westport and Newport tomorrow, where I know I shall find matters worse *if possible* than what I have already seen."

I am glad to be able to give the answer: —

Irish Office: June 10, 1822.

'My dear Gregory,—I enclose another letter from the Archbishop received this morning. Do not, I entreat, let any circumstance prevent a liberal supply to him either of money or of provision or both without delay.

"Henry Goulburn.

(Note.—2,000*l.* to A. B. Tuam without delay.)"

Mr. Peel during the scarcity of 1817 had laid down the principle of finding out to what eexnt the local gentry could or would help the people, and advancing from public funds sums of money in aid of their subscriptions.

Mr. Gregory was strongly in favour of this policy. In 1819, during a partial famine, he had written to Mr. Grant: —

". . . I confess to you that I am adverse to the plan of sending Potatoes to the South in the Manner you propose, not from any doubt of the great partial Distress, but from the principle that the Govt. are not on all occasions to be the first resort when any pressure occurs without the Gentry contributing to the relief of their impoverished Tenantry. Some of the Letters I receive on this subject are very distressing, but they gradually couple the want of Employment with the want of food. The former the Government cannot supply, and without it how can the Poor purchase food even if brought in abundance to their Door. . . ."

And again: —

". . . I send you my answer to the Memorial from certain Baronies in Wexford, requesting Aid from the Government for the purchase of Potatoes. It would be impossible and impolitic to yield to such partial applications. The Gentlemen of the Country should make some Exertions themselves, and not expect only to draw Rents from their Tenantry and lean on the Government to relieve their Wants. . . ."

I see little difference between the above sentence and the famous "Property has its duties as well as its rights," of a successor of Mr. Gregory, which caused so much commotion. The change of ideas on the subject is so complete that to-day the Irish landowner has vainly to proclaim to an unlistening world that property has its rights as well as its duties.

Disaffection, as usual, came in with hunger, but I need only give one or two letters indicating the different quarters in which it was giving cause for anxiety.

Mr. Gregory writes to Mr. Goulburn, March 5, 1822:—

"I regret to communicate to you that the Ribbon system has found its way into the army, and that some soldiers of the 44th Regiment quartered in this City have been sworn.

"The report was made to us by one of the Informers a few

days since, but I delayed writing to you on it till I was satisfied of the Fact, of which there is no longer any doubt. The number sworn is not yet ascertained, but I understand Colonel Morrison the commanding officer thinks it has spread amongst many of them. I fear the Publicity of this matter, as it may produce injurious Consequences—but that it will soon be known there is no doubt—our Cabinet for the Investigation of these matters consists of too many members, and I find there is no State Secret in Dublin. . . . In addition to this information, the same informant has communicated that six men of the 29th regiment, also quartered here, have been sworn. This I will have investigated, and hope it may not be so well corroborated as the account of the 44th."

And on March 6: —

"I am sorry that the accounts from the County of Cork are again assuming an unfavourable appearance. Enclosed is a letter from Mr. Otway, a Roman Catholic Gentleman living in Kanturk, giving accounts of several outrages in that neighbourhood. These are confirmed by a letter from the Revd. Mr. Cope, protestant Clergyman of the same Town, who thinks his representations are entitled to great Authority as he is in no danger from its being known that his sentiments are in favour of the Catholics—a proper Goose.

"From the mode of robbing for provisions and killing the live Cattle and salting them, the taking of Blankets and bedding, it appears that the Malcontents are looking to take the field. Great numbers of Cattle have been taken and disposed of in the same manner in the County of Limerick, and several good houses burned near Newcastle."

And again: —

"July 11.—Sergeant Lefroy returned yesterday from Kilkenny, where he prosecuted in the criminal Court, in consequence of the Chief Justice's illness. He gives an alarming account of the state of that county, and amongst the many bad symptoms he considers the interruption to the administration of Justice the worst. Every Protestant was challenged as a Juror, and none but Catholics left to try the Prisoners, some acquitted of atrocious and already proved murders, and frequently the Jurors became parties in the trials, and examined the Witnesses as if they had been counsels for the Prisoners.

"I do not know whether you are aware that the city of Kilkenny is supposed to contain more disaffection than any part of Ireland. Happy spot!"

By the help of Government and still more of private charity the people struggled at last through this dark year. It is almost forgotten now in the greater horrors of the famine of the forties. Last May, I was looking across Galway Bay to the Connemara Mountains, and an old fisherman, following my thoughts, said, "There's many gardens over there where the pitaties is not sowed at all yet, by cause of the rain. But with the will o' God the harvest might be good yet, and there's no use in giving up. But it's there they had the bad time in the famine! It was bad enough here, an' hardly two families left in some o' the villages that were in it a hundred years ago. But over there in Connemara, it's the dogs that brought the dead bodies out of the houses, and asked no leave."

Mr. Goulburn's letters, being written during his attendance in Parliament, are chiefly occupied with the proceedings there. I give some that bear on the question of Catholic emancipation.

Irish Office: May 27, 1824.

"Nothing can have been more judicious than your whole course of proceeding with the Chancellor.[1] We had to a degree anticipated your suggestion, and the King has personally directed Lord Eldon to state as from him the reason which induced him to insist upon the Chancellor remaining another year in, or until the Catholic Question be one way or other decided in the course of next session. In this feeling the whole Cabinet, Catholic as well as Protestant, concur. All alike deprecate a change now; a discussion whether Lord Gifford should take the office or whether it should be conferred on the Attorney-General could not take place at a more inconvenient moment to all. Many reasons induce me to hope, and I do believe that Lord Manners will remain. Lady Manners wishes it, the King has asked it, there are no more questions of appeal from his decisions until next year, he has no gout, but little business, and a prospect of a better flight of cocks next year than he had the last. As soon as you can set us at ease on this point let me hear from you.

"I have written to-day to the Lord Lieutenant to inform him

---

[1] The King had refused to make Plunket Chancellor because of his Catholic sympathies, and, in spite of Canning, had desired the Archbishop of Canterbury to write and desire Lord Manners to hold the seal for another year.

of the new Peerages which are to take place on the dissolution. Lord Clanricarde of course is to be an English peer, and to keep the Balance even, Lord Thomond is to receive a similar honor. These will not excite any observation. The antiquity of the family of Lord C. makes his elevation not unreasonable, independent of his connection with Mr. Canning, and Lord Thomond is on every account much respected, and has the strongest claim to the distinction. Lord Northland is to be an Earl. This is not quite so happy or so reasonable. Lord Liverpool's only defence of it is that it has been the dying request of Lord Granville to redeem a pledge many years before made by him that the Knox family in addition to all their other honours and advantages should have an Earldom also.

"The King has acquiesced, but not very generously (and for reasons which I will state to you when we meet), in the Irish peerage for Fitzgerald's mother . . .

"We are to be dissolved on 2nd June, Cambridge election is on the 13th, and on the 20th I hope to be with you, if not a successful at least a respectable candidate. Pray send over all Cambridge voters whom you see in Dublin, Blosse excepted, who votes for Palmerston."

Irish Office: May 19, 1825.
"The decision in the Lords will have sufficiently shewn you that there is still a feeling for the Constitution as it stands in that body; and from all I can collect I believe that their feeling is in unison with the feelings of this country. The decision surprised me as much as it has done those who espouse the Roman Catholic cause. The latter had deluded themselves, or at least had deluded others, by the most absurd and exaggerated accounts of conversion, and of Lord Liverpool's change of sentiment. The result has proved that they were deluded. Our Majority would have been 51 but for the unfortunate death of Lord Whitworth and the foolish conduct of the Duke of Northumberland and his brother, who declined giving their proxies in deference to a supposed feeling in favour of the R. Catholics on the part of the French King. At the same time, however, that this majority proves the feeling of a large portion of the Legislature and Country on this question, it has not removed the embarrassments of the situation in which we stand. I might say it has increased them. Had the majority been very small, or but little more than the Bishops, I think it would have been clearly the duty of those who opposed the R. Cath. question on principle to have left an opening for a settlement of the question by withdrawing from

the Government and allowing an experiment to be made by those who thought they could conduct it as to Catholic emancipation with adequate securities. If the Country was inert on the subject, it was fair to calculate that they desired such an experiment, and under those circumstances I should undoubtedly have counselled the resignation of Peel, Lord Liverpool and Lord Eldon. But the propriety of such a course appears to me to be now much altered. I believe that a Government could not make an arrangement of the Question in the face of the decision of the House of Lords and of the growing feeling all over this country against it. The effect, therefore, of any Govt. undertaking it would be to overturn them and to leave the King in the situation of having no materials out of which to form a Govt. to succeed them. Under these circumstances I think it may be a public duty to continue the Government as it is, and although many circumstances which have occurred make it extremely unpleasant personally to those whom I have mentioned to continue in the Government, yet upon the whole I think it may be their duty to do so. What their deciison will be I do not at present know. Peel's situation as the Irish Minister is the most awkward and the more embarrassing as being the *only* Protestant Minister in the House of Commons. But he will not do anything rash, though his feeling is undoubtedly for retirement. Should Lord Liverpool and Peel retire, it is most probable that I shall accompany them. Should Peel alone withdraw I shall be in a most disagreeable difficulty, as his withdrawal would rest upon purely a personal feeling. Should they decide upon continuing in office things will for the present remain as they are, and all these disagreeable contests and divisions will have to be renewed in the ensuing session of Parliament. You shall be the first to know what step is likely to be taken. I have given you very hastily an outline of what is under deliberation. You will of course consider it quite confidential, and say nothing yet to any one whatever."

Irish Office: February 17, 1827.

"I called this morning upon Peel, with a view to the discussion of the course proper to be pursued on the Roman Catholic question, when in the middle of our discussion a message was brought to us that Lord Liverpool had been attacked by Apoplexy. He had as usual received his letters at breakfast, and not having rung his bell as usual afterwards, was found by his Servant senseless on the Floor.[1] Remedies were immediately

---

[1] The letter found in his hand was one from Stapleton, giving an unfavourable account of Canning's health.

applied, and he is partially restored to his senses, but his right side is disabled, and the hopes of his further recovery very slight. As a public man he may be reckoned as dead. He has long been advised by his physicians to give up public business, as likely to produce a seizure of this kind, and whatever reasons he may before have had to neglect their injunction will of course cease to operate now.

"I have lost in him a kind and amiable friend, whose sound principle and practical piety entitled him to every confidence and respect, and the Country has lost an able and successful Minister, whose integrity never was questioned, and whose motives of action were always pure and just.

"It is useless to conceal from you (though, of course, it is to you alone that I make the disclosure) my opinion that this will break up the Government. The embarrassments of the King in making a new Government will be extreme. He cannot find Protestants enough to make a Protestant Government, he will not like a Catholic one, and I think that a mixed one can go on no longer, deprived as it must be of the Lord Chancellor and Lord Liverpool. At the present moment all are too much stunned by the blow to be able to form any rational calculation as to the probable march of events. I will, therefore, hazard no opinion. You may depend upon hearing from me the moment I see even a ray of daylight.

"As far as regards the R. Cath. question, the death or retirement of Lord L. will be a serious blow. It would appear as if God had determined to punish us by depriving us of those best calculated to defend the Church in the danger with which it is threatened. But it is vain to attempt to scrutinise his purpose. Before this event I had reason to believe that we had a majority in the House of Commons. I cannot say what may be the result now.

"Canning still continues ill, but they say he is better. How wonderfully the removal of Lord Londonderry and Lord Liverpool has opened the path to his ambition, and how fearfully it will show the vanity of human objects, if at the moment when everything appears within his Grasp his health should prevent his availing himself of the opening!"

Irish Office: March 9, 1827.

"I write to you for information on a subject on which your knowledge of Ireland may enable you to give me an answer, and on which I think from something which I have heard to-day, that it may be necessary to form an opinion. I have heard it surmised from various quarters that it would be desirable to compromise on the Catholic question by making some concession on an assurance of no further agitation of the question, and I am sure from what I have observed of our opponents in the Government, that many of them would willingly propose such an arrangement. How far it would be possible to agree to such an arrangement must necessarily depend upon its terms, but I should like to know your opinion of what might safely be conceded. My own opinion at present is that the Parliament, Privy Council, and Bench must be exclusively Protestant. But I may possibly over-estimate the danger, and I should be very glad to know what you think of it. If we could secure the points which I have mentioned, and have a truce from further agitation of the question, it would be perhaps worth while to open all other offices to R. Catholics. But I only throw this out for consideration, and should be glad to know what would in your opinion be the effect of doing so. The office of Sheriff is certainly an important one, but if the Bench be Protestant there is less danger in making a R. Cath. eligible to it, as the Protestant Judges would not lightly select a bad Sheriff. Turn the thing, however, in your mind, and let me know your opinion, which I ask merely for my own information."

I.O.: April 12, 1827.

"The Duke of Wellington, Peel, Lord Bathurst, Lord Westmorland, and Lord Melville, have determined to decline to be members of Canning's Government. My own mind was previously made up, but this confirms my determination. I expect, therefore, to be out of office in a few days, but as no communication whatever has been made to me I go on as if I were permanently fixed, and therefore you will not mention the subject of this note to any one. It may be that Canning may give up the attempt to form a Government, but I think not. I can truly say that we have not declined merely with a view to such a result, but merely from a feeling that whatever his wishes might be as to impartiality on the Roman Catholic question, it would be impossible for him to prevent its material advancement by his elevation, and to the material advancement of that question I cannot consent.

"You shall hear again from me to-morrow, or as soon as anything definitive is known."

Irish Office: April 14, 1827.

"Having received no application from Mr. Canning, I to-day requested a common friend to intimate to him that my office was at his disposal whenever it suited his convenience to fill it up. I have written to the Lord Lieutenant to apprise him of the step which I have taken. I therefore consider myself in effect out of office, though I continue to do the duties of it until a successor shall be appointed. The formation of the new Government proceeds rapidly. Lord Granville, Foreign Affairs; Mr. Huskisson, Home Department; Mr. Robinson, Colonies with a Peerage; the Duke of Clarence the Admiralty, as *Lord High Admiral*; Lord Anglesea, the Ordnance. I have desired Bowles to go over to Dublin and collect my private papers. I wish you would put that old Housemaid at the Park, Mary Walsh, on an allowance from office disbursements of 20*l*. a year. She is too old and blind for a successor to maintain, and if removed she will have no subsistence whatever. I wish this to be done because I am myself too poor to make her such an allowance.

"If I were to say that I did not regret my retirement from Office, I should not say the truth. I have formed many friendships in Ireland which I value most highly, none more so than yours and Lady Anne's, and it is a painful feeling to think how rarely it may hereafter be my fortune to meet you. You run no risk, I believe, from the new Government, *because* we all part on friendly terms. . . .

"Let me, my dear Gregory, in conclusion thank you for all your kindness, your assistance and advice, to which I feel more indebted than I can express, and of which I can only say I shall always retain the most grateful recollection."

12 Manchester Square: May 1, 1827.

"On my return from Cambridge I found Mr. W. Lamb in possession of the Irish Office, and I therefore presume that his appointment has either actually taken place or is on the point of being effected. But I have not had a line either from the Lord Lieutenant, Mr. Canning or any other person connected with the Government upon the subject, or indeed since I intimated my determination to quit. The only mark of attention which I have received is the sending down the Solicitor-General to oppose me at Cambridge—which, but for Mr. Canning's orders, I firmly believe he would not have attempted. The consequence is that my prospects of success, which were otherwise most gratifying, are now very much the contrary, and unless Mr. Bankes will consent to withdraw, which I fear is not likely, the probability is that I shall fail. Under these circumstances I shall not attempt to come to the Poll, the expense of a second contest being very ill accommodated to an out of office income. I have opened a negotiation with Bankes, but without much hope of success, he

being extremely obstinate and wrong-headed, and his leading
friends quite as much so as himself.[1]

"To-night will be interesting in the House of Commons. Peel
intends to make a statement on behalf of his Colleagues and
himself which will do away the gross misrepresentations of the
Venal London Press and disabuse the public mind. When he gave
up the seals yesterday the King told him that he was sorry for
his resignation, that he had considered him as a friend as much
as a Minister, and did not expect his withdrawal from office; and
he added that he himself was as firm a Protestant as ever. To
which Peel merely answered that he considered his power of
serving His Majesty depended entirely upon his preserving his
own public character, and regretted that he (as he stated from
the first) considered it incompatible with that Character to form
part of a Government of which Mr. Canning was at the head.
I have been down to take a place at the House. Brougham and
Burdett have taken seats behind the Treasury Bench, a tolerable
indication that nothing but cowardice prevents the introduction
of the Whigs into the Government at the present moment. They
are to come in at the end of the Session. Pray send me the date of
my Successor's appointment whenever it takes place."

12 Manchester Square: June 29, 1827.

". . . I have no news to tell you beyond what you will learn
from the newspapers. Lord Wellesley is permitted to remain for
a few months, and is then to give way to Lord Anglesea. The
Knight of Kerry is to be a Lord of the Treasury, and Whigs are
to be infused into the Government as fast as places can be made
for them. You may conceive the want of places when you hear
that Canning had the folly to offer Lord Palmerston the Government of Jamaica, which considering that he refused last year the

---

[1] Moore wrote some lines on the Cambridge election:—

> "G—lb—n of the Pope afraid is,
>   B—kes as much afraid as he;
> Never yet did two old ladies
>   On this point so well agree.
> Choose between them, Cambridge, pray;
> Which is weakest, Cambridge, say.
>
> Each a different foe doth damn
>   When his own affairs have gone ill:
> B—kes he damneth Buckingham,
>   G—lb—n damneth Dan O'Connell.
> Choose between them, Cambridge, pray;
> Which is weakest, Cambridge, say."

Governor Generalship of India and is now Commander in Chief as well as Secretary at War, is, I should say, an egregious act of folly and not by any means palatable to the noble Lord."[1]

Betchworth, October 3, 1827.

"You are quite right in not supposing my silence to have arisen from any cessation of that affection and regard which I shall always feel for you and your family under any circumstances. I thought it better under all circumstances not to keep up too frequent an intercourse. I was well aware that there was a very strong wish on the part of the Whig portion of the Government to make an attack on you, and I thought that a very active correspondence between us might afford that pretext which your absence seems to have afforded them. I congratulate you upon the foolish choice of topic which your adversaries have made. It is not the only instance in which the folly of a Whig has defeated his wickedness. I ought perhaps to have informed you before that you were an object of present jealousy and intended attack, for Lamb confessed it to me previous to his departure for Ireland, and I was satisfied that feeling was indulged in by members of the Government who were ci-devant Whigs. But I was satisfied from a conversation with Lamb that he was not disposed to encourage such a feeling. I believed that he went away from me determined to resist it, and I therefore thought it better not to excite suspicions in your breast which I was anxious too avert.

"I was quite confident that your conduct unembarrassed could give no cause for just attack. Whether I acted right or not, you must decide.

"I was very glad to hear that you had had an interval of relaxation in the society of your friends. From Peel you must have heard all that you could or would wish to know respecting the late changes and future prospects. I will not trouble you therefore with my speculations. A Chancellor for Ireland has at last been selected. It would have been, I suppose, an insult to Lord Manners to have put it in the power of his successor to have arrived in Ireland, more than a day before the sitting of his Court. Of Sir A. Hart I know nothing either personally or

---

[1] "Some weeks after this Canning sent for me again to say he had a proposition to make to me which he should not himself have thought of, but that the King had said he knew, and was sure that it was just the very thing I should like, and that was to go as Governor to Jamaica. I laughed so heartily that I observed Canning looked quite put out, and I was obliged to grow serious again."—(From Lord Palmerston's *Autobiography*.)

politically. I presume he is a Protestant, but he may be quite the
contrary. Report says that Lord Wellesley will not much prolong
his stay in Ireland. I suppose that he will not wait to surrender
in person to his successor. He will not leave Ireland with the
consolation of having tranquillised Tipperary, even though he has
had the advantage of a Catholic Secretary. I do not think, however, that we shall ever see that object attained. Sure I am it will
not be attained by those who profess to support the R. Catholics
while they do not go the full length of the Priesthood or Demagogue.

"I have seen nobody lately. I was in town yesterday, and only
met Frankland Lewis, but I learnt nothing from him. Lord
Goderich is most happy in the birth of a son. Most sincerely do
I rejoice in his prosperity, for putting public questions out of
view there is not a more amiable person in private life than he is.
We are all very prosperous, and have had a most riotous party
by the union of my Brother's children to mine. That has been
broken up by the commencement of the law term, and we are
now limited to our family party."

Betchworth: January 8, 1828.
"Report gains ground here that Lord Wellesley is to be Prime
Minister. I know not what truth to attach to it. I called on him
the day after his arrival in London, and found him very civil,
in very great force, and evidently anticipating that he was to hold
a very high situation in the Government, though when I saw him
he had neither seen the king nor Lord Goderich. I should not be
surprised if in all the embarrassments which exist as to making
a Government some attempt was not to be made under his
leadership."

Lord Wellesley was not destined to become Prime Minister,
but he had in December, 1827, the happiness of leaving Ireland,
where he had perhaps neither friend nor foe but wished him away.
The Protestant party could not be reconciled to the first
"Catholic" Viceroy of the century, and he had exasperated the
Catholics by his abortive attempts to put down the Association.
Mr. Lamb wrote just before he left: — "Lord Wellesley waxed
more and more impatient to be relieved of his office. His successor
had been some time announced, and men's eyes were turning to
the new Viceroy, Lord Anglesea, whose influence was already
discernible in the horizon. The position of superseded satrap did
not suit the conqueror of Tipu Sahib."

I am glad to think that he and Mr. Gregory parted on friendly terms after all, with the offer, made and refused, of a baronetcy.

I see in the note-book for 1833, "October 4.—Had an interview with Lord Wellesley at his audience. He was very gracious."

And I find a note written from London: —

"I shall be happy to hear of the health of yourself and your family in this "Annus Mirabilis" (see Dryden's verses). I am particularly anxious to know how 'The Fisherman' *progresses*. Whenever he is in London I should be happy to see him.

"Always, my dear Sir, with true regard and esteem,

"Yours most faithfully,

"WELLESLEY."

LORD ANGLESEY AND MR. LAMB

Lord Anglesey came over with the good militant principles that had been usually held by Lords Lieutenant in days when their temporary subjects devoutly prayed on Sundays that they might "use the sword committed to their charge for the protection of the true religion established amongst us."

He had said in the House of Lords that if the Irish wished for war, the sooner they drew the sword the better, and the King had given him his parting blessing as "a true Protestant."

But even in crossing the Channel he seems to have drunk of that mystic love-compelling draught, of which Ireland since the days of Iseult has held the secret. Like many a previous invader, the gallant soldier who had left his leg under a willow tree at Waterloo became *Hibernis ipsis Hibernior,* and his lips breathed blessings where curses had been looked for.

He tried nevertheless to act impartially at first, and boasted to Croker in 1828 of being "not only well with both parties but in their confidence," and of having persuaded both the Catholic Association and Sir Harcourt Lees to moderation. But it was well known that at his little dinners a sort of inner Cabinet met, Lord Cloncurry, George Villiers, Anthony Blake, W. H. Curran, all of whose names stank in the nostrils of good Protestants, and that many weighty matters were there decided.

He fascinated Sheil among others by his frank manner and sunny smile, and made him a regular attendant at the Viceregal parties. Sheil indeed was one of the few who held staunchly to him to the end, laying the mistakes of his second administration at Stanley's door, and declaring him to be the most chivalrous and high-minded nobleman he had ever come across.

Lord Talbot writes to Mr. Gregory after his installation: —

"Your letter received to-day has been very satisfactory indeed. I do augur well from your beginning. Lord Anglesey is so straightforward that I am sure, however strongly he may express his feelings, he never will condescend to assume what he does not really feel."

O'Connell hoped great things from him, and afterwards, at the news of his recall, was "so low that C. Villiers and Shiel had to go and dine with him to calm him down."

G. Ensor, however, wrote with some bitterness of him as "the satrap of England," and sneers at seeing "the surprised Irish rush into his arms and sob their unalterable gratitude in his bosom." His attempts at impartiality were not always graciously expressed. He writes to Mr. Gregory August 4, 1828: —

"A Cus. Rot. of Mayo must be appointed. . . . He must be a resident, influential and of good character, and then I care not whether he be Whig, Tory, Catholic or Protestant in principle. Only I would avoid a *violent* Orangeman, or a *furious* Liberal, as being two mischievous animals. I am actuated by a similar feeling in regard to the Colonelcy of the Militia."

The Tories did not bear snubbing well after their long ascendency, and a Liberal deputation from Cork fared no better, for Lord Anglesey, having lost his temper with them, threatened in his high-handed way to seal up the Irish ports, and cried, "I will put you both down."

"For myself," he says later, "I am suffering martydom between the parties."

What he intended to make a well balanced administration was criticised as one of see-saw, and Moore sarcastically compared him to a circus rider at Astley's on two horses: —

"So rides along, with canter smooth and pleasant,
    That horseman bold, Lord Anglesea, at present;
    Papist and Protestant the coursers twain
    That lend their necks to his impartial rein,
    And round the ring, each honoured as they go
    With equal pressure from his gracious toe,
    To the old medley tune, half 'Patrick's Day'
    And half 'Boyne Water,' take their cantering way;
    While Peel, the showman in the middle, cracks
    His long-lashed whip to cheer the doubtful hacks.

"If once my lord his graceful balance loses,
    Or fails to keep each foot where each horse chooses,
    If Peel but gives one extra touch of whip
    To Papist's tail or Protestant's ear-tip,
    That instant ends their glorious horsemanship—

Off bolt the severed steeds, for mischief free,
And down between them plumps Lord Anglesea."

But, as is the way with new converts, his zeal was too fervid to
be quite judicious, and he showed himself ere long to be wholly
on the Catholic side, as an ardent partisan. The Duke of
Wellington grew seriously angry. It was perhaps not a very happy
experiment to have one soldier as head of the English and one
of the Irish Government. Each expected to be absolute in his
own camp. Lord Anglesey complained of getting only official
letters from England, and the Duke on his side complains of the
insolence of his replies. The Duke complained, probably with
reason, of his private letters being shown to members of the
Catholic party, and Lord Anglesey of not being made acquainted
with the intentions of the Government. The King had his own
grievance, declaring that his Viceroy acted at if he were King
of Ireland. Smaller causes of friction arose, such as his refusal
to remove O'Gorman Mahon from the magistracy, or to grant
Lady Westmeath's pension. His imprudence and unreserve were
crowned by his letter to Dr. Curtis, advising the Catholics to
renew their agitation. Mr. Gregory notes on December 30, 1828,
"I dined with the L.L. He received a letter from the Duke of
Wellington of his recall."

And he writes to Mr. Goulburn: —

"I cannot write to you upon such a trifling matter as is contained in my note to you of this day and leave unnoticed all the
important concerns that have lately occurred here. As soon as I
was informed of the answer Lord Anglesea had written to a letter
from the Duke of Wellington previous to my return from England,
I was satisfied of the impractibility of those two Persons continuing together in their relative situations, and under the impression that a change must unavoidably be made here, I refrained
from writing either to Peel or to you until the matter was decided.
No considerate or impartial Person but must be satisfied, not only
of the propriety but of the necessity of the course adopted by the
Duke.
"There has been such a persevering perverseness which has
of late actuated the conduct of Lord Anglesea, he had not one
who could dissuade him from committing any of the rash acts
into which he had plunged himself and from which he never can
be extricated. The failure of the attempt to excite the regret and
sympathy of the Country on his departure must have been very

mortifying, but I fear he has greater trials of mortification before him. Personally I feel very sorry for his degradation, but it is quite impossible for me not to be glad that he has been removed from the Administration of this Country. The imprudence of his expressions (which were faithfully repeated) on public matters would shake the stability of any Government."

Lord Talbot writes to Mr. Gregory: —

January 6, 1829.

"Astonishment cannot be deemed a sufficient expression to signify my surprise at the Letter I have seen in the papers from the L.L. to D. of W. Had I taxed my imagination to have devised an impolitic composition I think I could not have equalled this. I say this, for upon my Honor, had it been upon our side of the Question I should deprecate it with equal sincerity.

"Whether this arose from the circumstances of his Excellency's recall or whether he was recalled in consequence of it, Dates do not authorise us on this side of the Water to judge. Of course we have our opinions.

"Personally I admire Lord Anglesey's Character as a Nobleman, as a Gentleman, as a Soldier, as a Friend, I believe he is ἐνὶ πρώτοισι, but as a counciliator or a *politician* I cannot say so much. Who will succeed him will not be known till it is declared. Our Chief is a man who does not permit his measures to transpire till they are perfected.

"Lord Melville, I conclude, from what I once heard Peel say (some years ago), is not unlikely to be the man—this, I should say, was only an expression that he thought Lord Melville (though a Catholic) would make a good L.L.—this was to shew that he should not object to any person on the score of his Cat. Eman. principles, if in other respects he deemed him to possess the requisites of the situation.

"I have had a fall from *Nancy* since I wrote, blackened my Eyes and cut my nose, but no worse. I have been dancing too to-night with Lamb, and I fear my old sinews have given way. Vive l'Allegresse! "

And on February 1, 1829: —

"My dear G,—I anticipate much sparring between Lord Anglesea and the Duke. Yesterday I was told by a soi-disant friend of the former that there had been a serious misunderstanding relative to Lady Westmeath's pension,[1] which Lord A. had refused to place upon the list, but which had been effected by an order of an illustrious person, whose sign manual had been sent to Lord A. commanding it. I am too old to believe half I hear, but have been also told by another person, a friend of the Duke's, that he (my informant) was afraid the Duke was in a scrape. From all I have seen and observed, I must say that the Duke appears to me to be too wise a man, and too experienced a politician to commit himself beyond the power of satisfactory explanation. That that little Cousin of mine would embroil a Universe I doubt not, but fortunately she has not the power.

"Adieu."

Lord Francis Leveson had found Lord Anglesey after his dismissal "very smiling and glorious, but angry, and deciding that he would do just the same again if he had to choose his line of conduct."

It would have been better for his happiness if, having left Ireland with that "smiling and glorious" halo of martyrdom round him, he had never set foot on her fickle shore again.

The removal of Mr. Gregory, for which he stipulated on his return in 1830, does not seem to have helped him much. He quarrelled with O'Connell, who threatened Repeal, Lord Anglesey bringing out his old threat of force, and they parted, O'Connell travelling as an *avant-coureur* to raise Irish feeling against him.

He who had boasted that he could lead the Irish with a silken rein, had to re-enter Dublin in a "jog-trot carriage," and was even advised by friends to make his entry a secret one. The Protestant papers pelted him with abuse, the Catholic population with stones. Only his beautiful horsemanship, so much admired by Sir Walter Scott at the Coronation, saved him from being thrown over Carlisle Bridge. There is no need to speak of the measures of his second viceroyalty, or what O'Connell, with his usual overloading of epithet, called "Lord Anglesey's ludicrous yet ensanguined career."

There is a glimpse of him later on in Mr. Gregory's note-book.

---

[1] "Lady Westmeath was the woman meant in the article in the *Times*, from Ireland, about the pension to which Ld. Anglesey would not agree. There was 700*l.* disposable on the Pension fund, and the D. of W. desired 400*l.* might be given to Lady Westmeath, which Ld. A. and the Secretary both protested against, and were resolved to resign rather than agree to it. The Duke gave in, but it caused an alienation."—*Greville Memoirs*, January 16. "This pension of Lady Westmeath's makes a great noise, and it is generally believed that when Ld. Anglesey refused to grant it, the Duke got the K.'s sign manual for it, and the job was done."—*Ib.* January 25, 1829.

"June 21, 1833. I went to Dublin and returned. The Lord Lieutenant, who lives in a small house within a few yards of the hotel, sent for me. I had not seen him for upwards of two years, and was greatly shocked at his altered appearance. His manner was very cordial, and he seemed fully sensible of the perilous state of the country, but not that it was owing to his misgovernment. He said to me: 'You see a poor Devil broken in body and mind.' "

Lamb had seen the old year out with Lord Wellesley, and the new year in with Lord Anglesey, as Chief Secretary.

"William Lamb, William Lamb, put him anywhere you like," said the King when Canning proposed him for Ireland. So he was put in Ireland, but only for six months, leaving in January 1828. He had already shown interest in Irish character, having written a sketch of Sheridan's political life, which he afterwards handed over to Moore.

He is one of the happy officials who had no history there, earning no anathemas, nor even a nickname. Hyde Villiers reported him to Greville as being "popular beyond all precedent." He was a Liberal as far as Emancipation went, but of Repeal he spoke as "d——d nonsense." He proposed withdrawing subsidies from the Press altogether, but even Plunket, when he heard this, burst out laughing, and said "Oh, this is Utopian! "

Lady Caroline, of course, did not come with him to Ireland. There is a glimpse of her in a letter of Vesey FitzGerald's to Mr. Gregory in 1819.

March 4.

"The Whigs are exulting in their Westminster triumph, one enjoys the defeat of the Anarchists without participating in the boasts of Brookes's. I am consoled for a great deal in its being shown what the disposition of the populace is towards these popular leaders. Yesterday they were cruelly assailed *inter primos*. Domk. Browne fell, and it was no immaterial hand that subverted him and Lord Sefton. For near five hours Lamb was imprisoned in Henrietta Street. Had they known that *he* was there his fate had been inevitable. He was at length rescued and escorted to Whitehall by the lifeguards. I do not suppose that Lord Essex or Folkestone will complain now of military intervention. When the *popular Candidate* was thus brought home, he found Lord Sidmouth sustaining and administering eau de luce to Lady Caroline! What a picture! But Gillray is no more. . . ."

On his appointment he wrote to Mr. Gregory: —

May 2, 1827.

". . . I cannot close this, the first communication which I feel myself called upon to make to you, without expressing my satisfaction that the Country is to continue to have the benefit of your abilities and experience, and I beg leave to subscribe myself,

"with great respect,
"your faithful servant,
"WM. LAMB."

He was at home to all who came to his door, "Show him in" being ever on his lips, for he wanted to see and learn everything for himself.

Torrens says "Old Mr. Gregory groaned, melancholy Mr. Mangin sighed," over this new order of things. But I hear no hint of a groan in the tone in which Mr. Gregory invariably speaks of Lamb. They had probably many a good laugh together, and in spite of Lord Lansdowne's letter, and Mr. Canning's advice as to the re-making of the pack, he apparently took no step towards displacing the old secretary, who for his part was won over by "his frankness and love of honour" and good looks.

Mr. Goulburn writes of him to Mr. Gregory, May 26, 1828 : —

"The newspapers will probably inform you of all that I am about to tell you, but I nevertheless have been so long in the habit of intimate communication with you that I cannot but state to you how the Government now stands. Huskisson has resigned his office most foolishly in my opinion, and I believe in his own also; but having resigned he would not recall his resignation, and the Duke would not solicit him to remain, and I think could not consistently with his own character do so. He is therefore out. Palmerston has done the same, so has Lamb, which is more interesting to you and to me, a subject of sincere regret; he is a man of perfect honour and frankness, and you will not find another who in these times will so impartially administer the difficult office of Chief Secretary."

And Mr. Gregory answers : —

"Amidst your Political anxiety I feel very much obliged by your finding time to write to me, and most sorry I am at one part of your communication, which is the resignation of Lamb. He is, I think, a serious loss to this Government, not from his aptitude or inclination to business, but from his open manly and honourable Character, and possessing an excellent understanding he was daily gaining unprejudiced knowledge of this Country, and the leading Men in it."

It was not the first or second, but the third time in the first three decades of the century, that through the Chief Secretary's lodge had lain the path to glory, to the Premiership of England. And among Premiers, Lord Melbourne's position as keeper of the young Queen's conscience was "the most despotic the world has ever seen."

THE CARRYING OF EMANCIPATION AND
THE DUKE OF NORTHUMBERLAND

The Duke of Northumberland's short viceroyalty did not give him much chance of working out a policy. But we must not speak ill of the bridge that carried us over the water, and his term of office arched the agitated year that brought Emancipation in. It is necessary to look back and note the steps that finally led to the acceptance of the measure, both in Ireland and in England.

The King's visit having led to no good result, O'Connell again became the mouthpiece of the people's wrongs and not of their adulation. Lord Talbot's sudden dismissal was but a flash in the pan, and Lord Wellesley's apathy was a sore disappointment. O'Connell and Sheil formed the Catholic Association, an open club, protesting against landlord and magisterial as well as religious injustice. It used its influence against violence and agrarian crime, the truth being perceived that every man who broke the law gave an advantage to the enemy.

Then in 1826 came the revolt of the forty-shilling freeholders against the landlords. Estates had been stocked with them for the sake of their vote since the granting of the franchise. Now the force the landowners had brought into being was turned against their own body. The first blow was struck in Waterford, the stronghold of the Beresfords. An Emancipator was elected against a member of the dominant family by a majority even of their own tenantry, and Louth, Monaghan, Westmeath followed suit. The landlords resisted in vain. Eviction was tried, but the Catholic Association supported the houseless tenants. Agitation was renewed when the Duke of Wellington came into power. Canning's appeals for moderation had to some extent kept it in check. The power of peace and war was in the hands of O'Connell—he blew hot or blew cold, and the people followed his lightest hint.

His power reached its climax in 1828 at the Clare election, where he stood against Vesey Fitzgerald, some extracts from whose letters are given in this book, a member of the Government, the great friend of Peel, a popular man, with great charm of manner. He had been Chancellor of the Irish Exchequer until its amalgamation with that of England in 1816, and had protested

157

against the preposterous over-taxation of Ireland since the Union. But both then and later, when he spent three years at the Swedish Court trying to recover the money advanced to Bernadotte for the war with Napoleon, he experienced the truth of the homely proverb, "It is hard to get butter out of a dog's mouth." He was a Christ Church man and a trustee of the British Museum. Not only did O'Connell, though disqualified for taking his seat in the House, head the poll, but the vivid glimpse given on the day of the election of his power and the unity of the people on the Emancipation question startled all those in England who had eyes to discern the signs of the times. Lord Palmerston says in his journal, "The Clare election began a new era, and *was an epoch in the history of Ireland.* . . . There were 30,000 Irish peasants in and about Ennis in sultry July, and not a drunken man among them save O'Connell's own coachman, and not a blackthorn." And again he writes:—"I speak of the election for Clare which led to Catholic Emancipation, which led by a new defection in the Tory party to the Reform Bill, which led to a complete social and political revolution in our country." The fire had indeed begun to burn the stick, and the stick to beat the dog, and the dog to bite the pig, if we may so term the long-obstructed bill for Catholic Emancipation.

O'Connell had done his share of the work, but he was not without helpers. A petition in favour of the Bill was now presented by the Protestant landowners of Ireland, representing more than three fourths of its landed property. Peel's own brother-in-law, Dawson, speaking at Londonderry, avowed himself a convert to Emancipation. The stars in their courses fought for it. Of the Archbishops, Magee was too old and Beresford too gentle to direct the canons of the Church against the enemy. Rank, talent, property, all had come round to the Liberal side.

Those who still held out, the members of the Brunswick clubs in Ireland, held a meeting, to raise their voices for the last time against relief, but their thinned ranks proclaimed that the hour of dissolution was near.

Moore, who had been singing down anti-Catholic feeling in London drawing-rooms, sharply satirised the gathering in his Letter from Beelzebub—

> "Who the devil, he humbly begs to know,
> Are Lord Glendine and Lord Dunlo?
> Or who with a grain of sense would go
> To sit and be bored by Lord Mayo?
> What living creature—except his nurse—

> For Lord Mountcashel cares a curse?
> Or thinks 'twould matter if Lord Muskerry
> Were t'other side of the Stygian ferry?"

Not names, one must confess, that have had "buoyancy to float down the stream of time."

In England the Bill had been brought forward again and again with varying fortunes. Grattan had for the last time introduced it in 1819. In March of that year Vesey Fitzgerald writes to Mr. Gregory: —

"Grattan has just given his Catholic notice for the 22nd of April. They rumour here that they are to make the greatest division that they have ever made. I believe it not. Nor do I portend anything but angry exasperating discussions. I do not envy you your situation in Dublin, or in truth just now your responsibility."

And Mr. Gregory writes to him in May: —

"After all the vaunted Expectations of a great Majority against the Catholic Claims I cannot by any means attribute to accident or trick that they were rejected only by two. I much fear the apathy of the Protestants, and that the present House of Commons is more Popish than the last. Here all is quiet, though the Protestants are much dismayed, they have no democratic Leaders to inflame the Minds of the People as their adversaries practice."

At Grattan's death, Plunket succeeded him as the Irish advocate of the measure in the House of Commons. The Catholic leaders, however, became dissatisfied with him after a time, and chose Sir Francis Burdett as their representative.

In 1821 it was lost on the second reading by a majority of 39, giving rise to a fashionable toast of "the thirty-nine who saved the thirty-nine articles."

In 1825 it passed the Commons, but was rejected in the Lords through the effect of the Duke of York's violent speech against it, concluding with the words: "These are the principles to which I will adhere and which I will maintain and act up to, to the latest moment of my existence, *whatever may be my situation in life.* So help me God!"

This was the speech that was printed in gold and distributed widely by the Protestant party. Canning, pointing to a copy of it, said "This is a sign of the times which augurs ill for future peace." It was a grievous disappointment, for new converts in the Upper House had been rapidly coming over to the Catholic side, and many felt what Lord Lurgan with a pardonable bull expressed, that "this was the golden moment, when the voice of party is quiet, and nothing is heard but the stillness of suspense."

These Irish debates, as may be imagined, were not without their humour. Mr. Battley pointed out the danger of a Protestant king being *surrounded by* a Catholic Lord Treasurer. Sir C. Wetherell spoke with such violence that Mr. Manners Sutton said "The only lucid interval in the speech was the interval between the orator's waistcoat and breeches." Colonel Wilson ended a vehement speech with the lines, presumably original: —

"While I can handle stick or stone
I will support the Church and Throne;"

and finally Sir J. Yorke expressed his hope that "the sister Kingdoms might be united, and live hereafter like two brothers."

In 1828 the Test and Corporation Acts were repealed, another step in the path of religious freedom. The next year fresh converts declared themselves on its side, and Peel confessed in private that further resistance was impossible, and offered to retire until the question was set at rest.

In May 1828 Mr. Shawe writes to Mr. Gregory: —

"The Lords will save you this time—but, as Sir J. Shelly says, 'they are sure to be emancipated or damned next year, and he cares not which.' "

Canning had at last brought the expectant people almost within sight of the promised land when his summons came . It was at last by the reluctant hands of its old enemies, Peel and the Duke of Wellington, that the boon was granted, and that too late to awaken gratitude or to give peace; now the cry for Emancipation was already almost lost in the cry for Repeal.

In the first days of 1829 the King was formally asked to assent to the measure. He refused, and the Duke offered to resign. Then he cried, stormed, and at last was brought to yield, it was said by a new effort of "witchery" this time, that of Lady Conyngham. His speech at the opening of Parliament recommended the removal of the civil disabilities of His Majesty's subjects.

Thenceforth, like Giant Pope, he had to content himself with sitting in his cave's mouth, grinning at the Emancipationists and biting his nails because he could not get at them, while Croker writes "The thing is well over, and will make Windsor as Popish as Downing Street."

It was too late for debate to be of much use, but the arguments for and against were roughly put by the Dukes of Cumberland and Clarence, and form a fairly good summing up of the case, as it presented itself to conscientious minds.

The former (echoing the King's real sentiments) said: — "I will put it to your Lordships, for that of course is the question, whether this country is to be a Protestant country with a Protestant Government or a Roman Catholic country with a Roman Catholic Government. This is the question and none other. The moment that there are Roman Catholics admitted into this or the other House of Parliament, this House must cease to be a Protestant House of Peers, and the House of Commons must cease to be a Protestant House of Commons."

The Duke of Clarence said: — "I wish to God that his Majesty's Ministers had been unanimous on the question in 1825 —or rather I wish that a united administration could have been formed in 1804 for the purpose of carrying this measure, for from that hour to the present my opinion has invariably been, that what is falsely called Catholic concession ought to be restored to—I say *falsely called concession,* because I maintain that that which is asked for is not concession but Justice. It is merely an act of Justice to raise the Roman Catholics from their present state of degradation. And when an Act is passed for that purpose, I will pledge my life that it will have the effect of uniting and quieting eight millions of His Majesty's subjects."

On April 10th, 1829, the Bill passed the House of Lords by a majority of 104.

And so ended the long struggle.

The following letter shows that Peel was not unmindful of his old friends in Dublin, who were doubtless mourning over him as a Lost Leader. It was to have appeared in the promised volumes of Sir R. Peel's correspondence, but his son, Lord Peel, has added to other helpful acts in the editing of this book the very kind one of allowing me to use it here.

Most Private.   Whitehall, February 1, 1829.[1]

"My dear Gregory,—When I have more leisure than at this moment I have, I will send you all the details which have passed respecting my Position in the Government, and respecting the

[1] In the 1898 edition, Lady Gregory incorrectly dated this letter as July 1, 1829, but later noted her error on an Errata slip.

discussions which have preceded the important notice of Ireland which was made in the King's speech.

"But overwhelmed as I am with Business I must write you a few lines.

"Nothing should have induced me to return to the King's service but the peculiar circumstances under which the Country was placed on the breaking up of Lord Goderich's administration on the eve of the meeting of Parliament. I mean nothing could have induced me to return to it, the Catholic Question remaining in the state in which it was. However, I had no option under those circumstances, and did not hesitate to return.

"I was left in a minority on the Catholic question in the course of the Session.

"When all the business of Parliament was over I expressed to the Duke of Wellington an opinion, in which he entirely concurred, that matters could not remain as they were—that it was discreditable to the Government and dangerous to the Protestant Interest—and prejudicial in every way to the country—with a divided Government on the Catholic question, with a divided Legislature with a majority in the House of Commons voting for the Roman Catholics year after year.

"I intimated to him that the time was come for me to retire— that to form an exclusive Protestant Government out of such material as the House of Commons afforded—and in the face of 272 members opposed to the Principle of such a Government would fail—and would deliver up the Government at once into the hands of those who would settle the Catholic question under circumstances most disadvantageous to the Protestant Interest and to the Country.

"That to dissolve Parliament—and to permit the R. Catholic association to send fifty or sixty Radicals from Ireland—ousting the gentry of the Country—would be a fatal measure.

"I told the Duke that I was so sensible of the present evils arising out of a divided administration, that I would in a private capacity support any course with respect to Ireland which a Government headed by him could suggest.

"As the meeting of Parliament drew near we were compelled to decide on the course which should be pursued.

"My opinion was, that to meet Parliament saying nothing about Ireland—professing entire contentment with the state of things—having nothing to propose—would be discreditable to us, and would ensure the speedy downfall of the Government.

"That to propose measures of restriction—the Government being divided, it remaining neutral on the Catholic Question, could not succeed in the face of an absolute majority of the House of Commons which had last Session voted for another course of proceeding.

"That to propose such measures and to fail would be a serious injury to the best interests of the Country.

"The Protestant ministers of the Crown, the Duke, the Chancellor, Goulburn, Herries, Lord Bathurst and myself came to the same conclusions—that things could not remain as they are, and that the formation of a Government united on permanent grounds against further concession, was totally impracticable.

"There was but one alternative—to advise the King to permit His Government to consider the whole state of Ireland, and to attempt to make some safe and satisfactory settlement with regard to that Country, excluding nothing from this view.

"In the course of the discussions my own Position in the Government occupied a prominent place.

"The King called upon us for our advice—and he had a right to call upon us.

"The question at last resolved itself into this—the question which I had to decide for myself.

"I cannot let things remain as they are, that is I mean let a disunited Government—having neither Concession nor restraint to propose, meet Parliament. I cannot advise the dissolution of the present Government and the attempt to form an exclusive Protestant Government, from the perfect conviction it will fail.

"Will I advise *the King* to take the only remaining course—I myself shrinking from the sacrifices and the Responsibility that it entials—or will I remain in my Post—setting the example of sacrifice to others—and abiding for myself the issue, be what it may? I have chosen the last alternative—painful as it is to me. I may be wrong, but at any rate I am prepared to make sacrifices which will prove that I think I am right.

"I have felt it my duty to tender my immediate resignation of my seat to the University of Oxford, if they shall think fit to accept it.

"This letter is written in the strictest confidence to yourself, but I beg you will communicate it, under injunctions of entire secrecy, to Saurin.

"I doubt whether we shall not find a very prevalent impression among Protestants that anything whatever is preferable to continued *disunion* and *neutrality*.

"Ever yours most affectionately, My dear Gregory,

"R. PEEL."

There is an entry in the Greville Memoirs dated January 21, 1829: —"The Duke had never told F. Leveson about the Duke of Northumberland till Sunday, when he wrote to announce the appointment. His Grace seems mightily pleased with it, and fancies that his figure and his fortune are more than enough to make him a very good L. L. He says he was obliged to coax him a little to get him to accept it. January 25.—Everybody thinks the appointment of the D. of N. a very good one, and that the Duke is in great luck to get him. It is surprising that he should have consented to go, but he probably likes to do something and display his magnificence. He is a very good sort of man with a very narrow understanding, an eternal talker and prodigious bore. The duchess is a more sensible woman, and amiable and good-natured. He is supposed to be ruled in all things by her advice; he has no political opinions, and though he has hitherto voted against the Catholics, he is one of the people who pin their faith on the Duke, and who are made to vote in any way and upon anything he may be pleased to desire them."

Lord F. Leveson-Gower writes thus to Mr. Gregory of the coming Viceroy: —

London.

"I think you may reckon on the Duke's arriving in about a fortnight; I have only had one hour's conversation with him, and I think it will be useful to you, and consequently to the public service, to learn in *strict confidence* what I think you will find him. I trust you will have no difficulty in inducing him to take your opinion on all matters of business, but the great difficulty you will find is to *give* it, for it is necessary previously to hear him out, and *on this point* I Tremble for you and myself. In the few matters I have had to present to him, nothing can have been more obliging than he shewed himself. He has lived a life of state and seclusion, and is, of course, totally ignorant of Ireland. I should therefore entertain grave apprehensions for him at starting if he were to fall into the hands of such an adviser as the Cr. with his posse comitatus notions. I do not, however, think the latter inclined to meddle more than he is compelled to do. There seems to be no different opinion as to the Duchess, who is pronounced to be a delightful person by common consent. I meet them at the D. of W.'s to-day,[1] and if I obtain any new lights which I think may be useful to you I will write further."

---

[1] Croker was at this dinner, sat between Peel and Archdeacon Singleton, and says: "For so great a dinner it was tolerably pleasant."

He was a conscientious Viceroy, and tried to develop Irish industries, and the Duchess made all the ladies of the Court live in poplin dresses, yet Greville writes in August (1829): —

"Melbourne thinks the Government will have to adopt strong coercive measures in Ireland. The D. of N. is an absolute nullity, a bore beyond all bores, and in spite of his desire to spend money and be affable, was unpopular. The Duchess complains of it, and can't imagine why, for they do all they can to be liked, but all in vain."

There seems to have been some gift lacking at the birth of this excellent well-meaning man. Things went wrong with him. He was anxious to make a figure in politics, but when sent as Special Ambassador to Paris, he was made a butt for absurd stories. In Ireland his good will and anxiety to please went for nought, perhaps because of that very anxiety. There is a story told, I know not with what truth, that a Viceroy of more recent years failed in the same way, and was criticised by an attendant at the Levee with a sigh of regret for his predecessor. "Give me——, scowling at you over his *berd* as if you were dirt."

He kept great state. The dazzling effect of his blue and silver liveries is still remembered in Dublin. Mr. Gregory writes soon after his arrival "Anne and I dined with the L. L. and Duchess of Northumberland, 48 at dinner, the most splendid I ever saw. Gold service of plate."

In spite of his well-known munificence there was a standing joke against him of having as an answer to a deputation of distressed weavers given an order for a waistcoat.

Lady Morgan says: "Lord Cloncurry made me die by the simple way he told me that when the D. of N. was coming to stay a few days at Maretimo he said to Lord C.: 'Do not put yourself to any inconvenience for my people' (his servants)?; 'they never drink either port or claret.' 'Upon my word,' said Lord C., 'I am very glad to hear it, for with me they will only get very small beer.' "

But he did not disdain to do small acts of graciousness, and a young lady who stayed at the Under-Secretary's lodge in his time, owed her first ball, before she had "come out," to his kind insistence. And at the ball he found time to look after his shy young friend, offered to find her a partner, and told her an interminable story about a ball in Paris, at which, in spite of dancing not being in his line, he had been ordered to lead out the Duchesse de Berri.

The late Lord Houghton having asked a friend's opinion as to an official he had been brought into contact with, listened to a string of estimable qualities, but said at the end "Yes—that's all very well—but has he got *imagination*?" And I am inclined to think that this was the touch of Divine fire needed by the ducal Viceroy to make the dry bones of good intention live.

Sir Walter Scott had visited him at Alnwick a year or two before his appointment, and speaks warmly of his efforts to improve his estates and the welfare of his people. His woods had been ill planted and neglected, and renovating an old wood is a far more discouraging task than planting a new one, and may account for some depression of mind, but cheery Sir Walter says, "He seems to despond more than a young man ought to do." Of the Duchess, he, like every one else, says all that is charming.

He was sorry to leave Ireland in the end. Sheil dined at the Castle on the November day in 1830 when the news of the defeat of the Tories arrived in Dublin. "It was an exceedingly dismal festivity. A profound depression was spread over the countenances of almost all the functionaries, who were to meet no more in their official gatherings. The Duke himself did not appear to consider his liberation from the Irish royalty of the Castle as a fortunate incident in his life; and so lugubrious was the feeling which diffused itself over their final conviviality that, with all his fine wit, his admirable humour and mirthful narrative, Sir Philip Crampton, who was there, failed to produce the ordinary results with which his delightful hilarity is attended."

On the 7th December, the day before the viceregal departure, Mr. Gregory writes: "Received from the Lord Lieutenant two splendid silver vases." Of all the Under-Secretary's high friendships, these "splendid vases" are the only visible token that remain to his young great-grandson. So here at least we must hold his memory in esteem. I trust that on his return to Alnwick he found his plantations growing strong and green after his absence on what must have been to him after all uncongenial soil.

Lord Francis Leveson-Gower

Lord Francis Leveson-Gower came to Ireland while Lord Anglesey was still in office, and served both under him and the Duke of Northumberland. Coming after Lamb, he was considered "cold and cautious" in manner. But his arrival was hailed with delight by Mr. Gregory, who held Frankland Lewis, who had been expected to take the office, in horror. Lord Francis redeemed the Chief Secretaryship from the slur cast upon it by the refusal of Lewis and of Horton, and in doing so earned the gratitude of the Irish Government, though O'Connell contemptuously described him as the barber's apprentice or "Shave beggar" of the ministry.

He had been perhaps best known as a poet, the translator of "Faust" and of Schiller's "Casting of the Bell." Sir Walter Scott spoke well of these, and also of an original poem, "A Tale of the Mill," and says "He has certainly a true taste for poetry."

Lord Francis in Ireland was indeed Pegasus in harness. His poetic mind cannot have found stimulating food in the subjects I find treated of in his daily routine—"Survey of the Antrim Road", "State of Provisions, Ennis," "Stipendiary Magistrates, Roscommon," "Jury Bill," "Police of Dublin," "Coal Yards," "Levying of Cess"—I take these at random from the dockets on his courteous clearly written letters.

He did his work well, however, and gave no sign of finding it uncongenial, and it was he who originated the project of paying the Catholic priests by means of a *regium donum*.

Mr. Gregory writes of him to Lord Talbot: —

"The conduct of Lord Francis Gower has been manly, discreet, and worthy of a faithful servant of the Crown. I am very glad he remains in his present situation, as I have no doubt he will discharge the duties of his office free from all party feelings, and reserve the expression of his opinion on the R. C. claims to the House of Commons."

The Catholics, a little disappointed at the benefits of the long-desired Emancipation Bill not becoming at once visible, were inclined to blame a sympathetic Chief Secretary for not instantly causing their pint of prosperity to hold a quart. But it would have been hard indeed to satisfy the vague expectations that had been raised. An old farmer has told me of the enthusiasm of that time. "When the bill passed, there were bonfires lit all about the village, and on the top of the hill, and the greatest excitement that ever was. The people didn't know exactly what it was about. They thought O'Connell and Sheil would stream gold into their pockets, and I know some that wouldn't sow a crop in those years because they had been told the millennium was coming."

Lord Francis never took very high rank in politics any more than in poetry, but he was held in esteem by both parties, made no enemies, and as Lord Ellesmere, ended a useful and blameless career in the Nirvana of the House of Lords.

THE PLACE-HUNTERS

Swift once prophesied, "Employment will be in the hands of Englishmen, nothing left for Irishmen but vicarages and tide-waiters' places," and in looking through these letters one must give him the credit of prescience. A tide-waiter, according to Johnson, is "an officer who watches the landing of goods at the Custom House." The duties of a land-waiter seem to have been hardly distinguishable. A lady now living remembers that when a friend of hers applied for a tide-waiter's place, he was told it was not a gentleman's office. "Then I will make it one," he said. And apparently he did so with but too much success, so frequent and eager are the applications for the post.

The candidates for Church preferment were yet more ravenous. Mr. Arthur French "intrudes upon Lord Talbot's private hours" to seek preferment for his son. Dr. Bernard and Dr. Mansell want to exchange livings, and the former applies to Lord Wellesley and offers "to supply him with any more information about their families and circumstances he may wish to have," but is silenced by the peremptory Marquis, who absolutely refuses to sanction the change *sede vacante*.

"I have scarce time to write, my room has been besieged by clergy fighting their bye battles for the inferior Livings. I hope the Duke will have them settled to-morrow," writes Mr. Gregory in 1813.

The disestablishment of the Church must have considerably lightened the burden of government at Dublin Castle.

It was impossible to satisfy a tithe of the applicants, but they were thrown a bit now and then. "It might not be amiss to get rid of old Castlecoote by making him a Viscount," Lord Talbot writes. "Martin is very pressing to have Martin French appointed Inspector of Stamps in an expected vacancy. Of course I shall give no promise or expectation, but we must do something for Martin soon. Think of his tide-waiter," writes Mr. Gregory. "Lord Waterford is refused some unreasonable demand, but the refusal requires sixteen pages of apology. Mr. Lynch wants an appointment in 1822 on the ground of having in 1799 procured an address in favour of the Union from the Catholics of Galway.

Captain B——, who has done a service in reporting police irregularities, wants a place. 'His previous conduct is not such as to warrant our giving him employment here, but we might send him to our Colonial possessions.' Another applicant 'can hardly be appointed to any position of trust, being an uncertified bankrupt.' The sister of a Recorder writes to beg for 'any place whatever.' Such a sentence as this is not infrequent—'——is dead —and his place vacant.' "

Miss Edgeworth herself, who writes a whole novel on the evils of patronage, cannot even in its pages resist providing for her hero, Mr. Temple, by a Government situation procured by his patron directly from the King. Patronage was in the air, and it will be long indeed before the Irish mind will be convinced that it is now dead.

No doubt Mr. Gregory inflicted disappointments as courteously as was possible, and I suspect from his note-book that his refusal was sometimes softened by a pleasant dinner.

I have chosen a few extracts from the mass of letters bearing on the subject.

Mr. Gregory to Mr. Peel

May 21, 1813.
"You may expect an angry expostulation from Hans Hamilton in consequence of the County of Dublin Militia being given to Luke White's son. One of his Brothers has this day been pouring out the feelings of the family on the occasion."

June 29, 1815.
"Since the Publication of your Speech on the proposed Police Bill, the applications for Magisterial appointments with salaries have been innumerable, and every applicant represents his part of the Country as the most disturbed, and requiring the aid of paid Magistrates. Without the Salary the Country might have slept in peace or been burnt to Cinders. I trust great care will be taken in the choice of Persons to be selected when occasion may require the appointment of Magistrates under the New Act. You may be assured that County Members will attempt to grasp them as part of their parliamentary opima, in which case the best fitted Person for the magistracy will be according to his number of registered Freeholders. However, it is, I know, needless to dwell upon a point of which your residence in Ireland must have fully satisfied you."

May 7, 1814.

"Mr. Lynch called upon me. He then asked me to consider the promise binding as to the Chairman's place of Galway whenever it should become vacant. I informed him that the Lord Lieutenant and you were perfectly ignorant of any such Engagement, that should any such vacancy occur his Excellency would feel himself at full liberty to appoint to it any eligible Barrister he should think proper. I reminded him of his Expressions 'that should a vacancy occur he should demand it as a right, and not take it as a favour!' He seemed to regret having used, but did not deny his words, saying the construction put on them by me was not his meaning, which was only to convey that he did not come without pretensions to the situation from the Documents in his possession, but that he should feel equally obliged to the Lord Lieutenant as if such promise had been made—the Bully failed and he tried the Coax. However, finding the Engagement not considered binding on the present Viceroy, he began loading his Castlereagh, which he will certainly fire at you."

May 21, 1816.

"Sir George Hewitt was yesterday overturned in a Jaunting car with his Daughter Mrs. Carey; he is much bruised, but no danger apprehended. However, any severe hurt to such an old man may have dangerous consequences. Perhaps you had better not mention this, as it will only set Candidates starting for his place."

Decr. 1813.

"Lady Clare is in town, frantic that the nomination of the Sheriff for Co. Limerick should be given to the Chief Baron. She showed me what is called by her your very impertinent Letter to Odell. Unless she gains her point her son is to go into opposition. She is to have an interview with the Duke of Richmond as soon as he returns from Castletown."

On the other hand the Chief Baron (O'Grady) writes on a later occasion: —

"I am told that Mr. Henry Baylee, one of the Limerick Psalm singers and Independants, has been recommended to Mr. Grant by Mr. F. L. Price for the office of Inspector of Prisons. Have the kindness to give me a line to say if it be true. To you I need not express my Surprize and Indignation and from others I will not conceal it when I can speak with effect.

"I am not sure that Lord Gort won't have a word to say for himself."

Mr. Gregory to Mr. Peel

"February 24, 1815.—James Daly called upon me to apply for the Barrack Master's place at Portumna, value 7s. 6d. per day, and did not seem well pleased when I informed him that the Lord Lieutenant had appointed to it. In the first place Barrack Masters were always kept free from the Gripe of the County Members; in the next, Lord Whitworth felt great anxiety to give some situation to the Gentleman to whose house the poor Duke was taken after his fall, and in which he died. He received from the whole family the most assiduous attention during the short period he lived, and the Lord Lieutenant was anxious to bestow an early mark of his Gratitude. The Gentleman (Mr. Farrell) has seen happier days, and now farms part of those lands of which he was formerly the owner."

Mr. Croker to Mr. Gregory

Admy, August 31, 1818.
"Can you advise me as to the probability of success in the following matters, which I have much at heart? Old Dr. Bond, the father of Dean Bond, my brother-in-law, has a living in the Diocese of Elphin (Sligo) which he would gladly resign to his Son, if the Bishop's consent could be procured. If the Bishop were likely to continue long at Elphin and so to have the free disposal of the living on the old Gentleman's death, I have no kind of pretence for asking him for the favour of giving my brother-in-law this piece of preferment: but if, as I cannot but think likely, the Bishop looks higher, he will probably never have the disposal of this living, and by now consenting to the transfer he would confer a very great obligation on me.

"Even if Peel were still in Ireland I should have consulted you on this subject first; now that we have lost him, I have no other friend in the Irish Government than yourself."

Lord Talbot to Mr. Gregory

"I have told Lord Waterpark the rule of the Irish Govt.,

namely that it never listens to negotiations in Church preferment, unless the parties are about the same age, and unless a positive and solemn assurance be given that neither of the parties receives or gives any consideration for the exchange. This will settle him I think."

Mr. Gregory to Mr. Goulburn

Dublin: 1826.
". . . Do not let it be known that this appointment is at your disposal until you have made arrangements for filling it. There is a powerful Personage here whose Claims you well know are irresistible. He has many Sons yet unprovided for, and their qualifications are indisputable, as they depend not upon themselves but upon the value of the place to be disposed of."

The following is worth giving as having roused Lord Wellesley to a compliment.

Mr. Goulburn to Mr. Gregory

Irish Office: April 2, 1824.
"I have just received the enclosed from the new Member for Westmeath; considering that he has not yet taken his seat, it promises well; at least it shows a very perfect idea of that part of his duty which consists in his obtaining offices for his constituents. I enclose also a copy of my answer. Pray show them both to the Lord Lieutenant."

[Enclosure.]
"Sir,—I have had the honour of receiving your letter of the 29th ultimo making an application in favour of five Gentlemen for whom you are desirous of procuring the appointment of Chief Constable whenever the Lord Lieutenant shall determine upon extending to the Co. Westmeath the Constable Act.
"I will not fail to submit your request to his Excellency's consideration, but I should be wanting in Candour if I did not at the same time apprize you that I do not see much prospect of his Excellency's acquiescence in your wishes, His Excellency having laid it down as an invariable rule that he will not in the appointment of Chief Constables attend to any local recommendation.
"If, however, among the Gentlemen whom you have recom-

mended for the Co. Westmeath there should be any willing to serve in other parts of Ireland, I am sure the Lord Lieutenant will not be indisposed to give a fair consideration to their pretensions, in common with those of other prior Candidates for the Office. I ought, however, to add that the appointments of this nature at the disposal of the Lord Lieut. are extremely limited, and the number of Candidates beyond all proportion great.

"I have the honour to be, &c.

"HENRY GOULBURN."

(Note by the Lord Lieutenant.) "This is indeed a perfect model. Mr. Goulburn's letter is very proper.

W."

A letter of 15 pages from a Mr. Boyse to Mr. Grant begins with such a flourish that the Chief Secretary must have been relieved to find that the request which is at length arrived at is only for the admission of a friend to the magistracy: —

"Sir,—The wise facility of access, which I know that you are disposed to afford to every Irishman who approaches you in the sacred garb of a Lover of his country, has emboldened me to address you, and in doing so I am anxious to guard myself from the imputation of speaking the language of adulation when I say that I am deeply impressed with the conviction that your administration of the affairs of our unhappy Island is conducted on principles of the strictest Public probity, and has been distinguished throughout by the conscientious exertion of Talents as splendid as they are useful."

Mr. Gregory to Lady Glengall

Dublin Castle, 1819.

". . . Admitting the claims of your family on the Government, I am sure you cannot be aware of the many pressing claims from meritorious officers who have distinguished themselves in the Army and Navy, but who from the late Reductions are seeking for and gladly accepting the most inferior Situations, to which very small salaries are annexed."

Mr. Gregory to Mr. Grant

"The Lord Lieutenant desired me to say in answer to the

Duke of Kent's application in favor of the Rev. Mr. Miller, that during the last 12 months there has been but one ecclesiastical Preferment vacant in Ireland in the Gift of the Crown, and that amounted to 140*l.* per Annum. With the numerous list of Claims left by his predecessors and the many strong applications made during his own Administration, he cannot expect to satisfy one fourth of the present Claimants.

"W. GREGORY."

May 25, 1819.

". . . I do not know where Martin obtains his information respecting vacant Tidewaiters' places. The Board of Customs report only two Vacancies, one at Limerick, the other at Derry. I do not understand how it happens that so few Vacancies occur in Dublin, as it is the only place in which the Lord Lieutenant's Patronage is not questioned. . . . Lord Kingston called upon me, and among 100 other points mentioned the supposed sale of Mr. M'Carthy's place to Drinan. . . ."

To Mr. Grant

June 7, 1819.

". . . If Colthurst cannot recommend a Person duly qualified to discharge the Duties of the Office, I should advise your giving the place to Lord ——. I make no comparison between the Men, as Colthurst has always been a steady supporter, Lord —— not to be relied upon longer than suits his convenience and Caprice, but as he has been allowed to return to the Government Ranks, it may be right occasionally to gratify him, but to satisfy him will be impossible."

Mr. Grant to Mr. Gregory

July 28, 1819.

". . . I will write to the D. of Kent, as the Lord Lieutenant wishes. Besides what the Lord Lieutenant says, it seems that after a clergyman has made a bad bargain for himself, it is no unusual thing for him to try to baulk his parishioners, and get a better living. This motive should be resisted. . . .

"I see there is a tide-waitership at Cork. What is the amount? Would it do for Canning's friend Tisdale? . . .

"Owen Wynne has applied thro' Peel, for a land-waitership in

Sligo. I send his letter . . . but surely he has no sort of claim, and how can we refuse the local member?"

Mr. Gregory to Mr. Grant

July 30, 1819.

"The Bishop of Clogher dead, the Lord Lieutenant writes by this Post to Lord Liverpool and you. How fortunate you are being absent from Dublin during the First hungry Importunities for the division of the Spoils. . . ."

Lord Talbot to Mr. Gregory

August 31, 1819.

"Henry D——'s Letter, I must freely confess, disgusted and annoyed me. I am really not aware what his Brother's *Claims* are, but as far as I am a competent judge of them, they have not been ill attended to, as they have procured 1,100*l.* a year in the Church for his Brother. . . .

"Did Grant tell you that Lord Liverpool still wished 600*l.* pension to be given to Lord Brandon. I answered this by saying it was impossible without Lord L. would allow me to give away 1,500*l.* this year instead of the customary 1,200*l.* Lord L. should not make positive promises without communicating with us. . . ."

November 15, 1819.

"Lord Glerawly presents his compts. to Mr. Grant. . . .

"Lord G. has for a long time been soliciting a living for his Brother in-law, the Revd. Mr. Johnston, contiguous to Lord Annesley's estates . . . but the Irish Government have not hitherto paid that attention to his request which Lord Glerawly would naturally have expected, especially as Lord G. (tho' not having the honour of being personally acquainted with Mr. Grant) begs leave to inform him that he has for a length of time supported the present administration and had to contest his seat in two successive Parliaments at a most enormous expense and trouble."

(Answer. Government will not interfere with the patronage of a Bishop.)

From Col. C. to Mr. Gregory

"Dear Sir,—I had the honour of your last letter, and cannot but observe that I am the only member for a County in Ireland that would have been refused such a request as my last. I have always understood that every one of those small situations that become vacant in the County was and is given to the member who supports Government even without applying for them. I did apply the moment it became vacant and I have been refused. I have experienced similar refusals before.

"I wrote to Mr. Peel some time back relative to a conversation that took place between you and me on the subject of Clerk of the Crown for this County, having in consequence of that conversation promised it to Mr. John Hurley should it become vacant. He has now brought me the resignation of the present clerk, which I enclose, and I hope there will be no difficulty in naming this gentleman to the situation. He is in every respect fully qualified to fill it."

From Mr. Gregory to Col. C.

"Dear Sir,—In answer to your Letter expressing your surprise that you should have been refused the nomination to a small revenue place in the Co. of Kerry, as you considered when such situations became vacant they were always granted to the Member for the county in which they are situated who supported the Government, I am directed by the Lord Lieutenant to refer you to your letter of the 3rd of February last, to Mr. Peel, in which you declared the conditions on which you had given your support to the Government, and as his Excellency has no prospect of being able to gratify your Expectations he concluded it was not your Intention to continue your support."

Mr. Gregory to Mr. Peel

March 30, 1816.
"Nothing will drive the Irish members to Parliament unless convenient to themselves, and yet if they declare themselves for the Government, they think they are entitled to every branch of Patronage as much as though they gave a useful support."

Mr. Peel thus notes some of the letters he returns to Mr. Gregory.

(Application for increase of pension from a Comm. of Appeals.) "A modest request! Use my name as you please in discountenance of it. R. P."

(On one from Baron Smith.) "Dear G., I would rather give Judge Smith 5 Gaugers' places than receive one letter from him."

(On Mr. Hans Hamilton's letter recommending Johnston, an honest man, to fill the office of Coast Officer of ruck.) "Pray reward him then—rari nantes in gurgite vasto. R. P."

In reply to Mr. Gregory's question whether the clerkship he had asked for Mr. Sargent should be kept until some work was done, Mr. Peel answered, "Yes, but it will be kept ad Gra. Calend."

May 13.—On the Stamps letter saying that James Norton was unfit for a stamper, and in reply to Mr. Gergory's comment that he must be a wretched devil if unfit for that situation, he observes that he is, and directs that Pole's man may be appointed.

But the last letter I will give is a kindly one of his, on a case where he thought help ought to be given: —

[No date.]

"I really think Mrs. Farina well entitled to some provision from the Irish Government.

"Poor Farina was a most indefatigable, zealous, and faithful Servant. I am not afraid of any pension granted to his wife being drawn into Precedent, if granted on account of his services.

"Few, I fear, in his situation will equally deserve such a posthumous reward . . . and if they do deserve it equally, I hope they will receive it."

LORD TALBOT IN ENGLAND

These comments of Lord Talbot on the changes that led from the old order to the new, and the glimpses given of his own home life, are full of interest and of charm. His life had a fair sunset after the clouds and sorrows we have seen it darkened by. But he is full of anxieties for his motherless children, especially when they grow up and he takes them out in London. He sits down sometimes while they are amusing themselves, and writes his cares and fears to his old friend. But his boys seem to do well as he sends one after another out into the world. As for his adored Cecil, Marchioness of Lothian, though he loses her it is with a smile as well as with a tear. "Depend upon it," he writes from her Scottish home, "this marriage does unco well."

There is a packet of letters from her also to Mr. Gregory, whom she claims as "a second father," showing much sweetness and nobility of character.

In 1831 she writes to tell of a sad disappointment she had met with. She had been on her way to England, meaning to stay with Lord Talbot while Lord Lothian attended the Coronation. "Well, we were actually at Mounteviot on our journey to Ingestre when I got a letter from Papa, saying he was induced for sundry reasons to go up to town for the Coronation. There was no time for communication, so, after having long meditated upon the pros and cons, I settled that I should be more sure of being in nobody's way by remaining in Scotland. I thought that Papa once in London would probably stay to vote on this odious bill, and that there would be some bother of the how and where I was to join my husband. The long and the short of the story is, that I am left here by myself entirely for the *two next months*, for I fear that there is no chance of the bill's being out of the House, so as to admit of Lothian's return, before then. You may suppose what a bitter disappointment it was to me to miss my looked for visit at Ingestre, and how painful to have to decide on so disagreeable a measure for myself. I feel quite in a strange land here, for I have only been here a week with Lothian, and literally don't know my way about the place (Newbattle), added to which there is not a creature I know about, every face in doors and out is new, and I have no maid into the bargain. I continue, however, to amuse myself very well; indeed it would be a shame if with young legs and eyes and plenty of books I could not." But a week later she writes again, "I really do not deserve to be pitied for having been alone, for I have found plenty to occupy my time fully. I think it has been of service to me among the people about, who rather dreaded that I should be a fine English lady, and that I should induce Lothian to live away from here. This they are now persuaded is not the case, and they are all quite fond of me already. They are flattered at my having voluntarily remained amongst them instead of going to England. It has also given me leisure to become personally acquainted with my poor neighbours, which I was most anxious to do. I am sure you will be happy to hear that I expect Lothian back here to-morrow. This is a most unexpected pleasure to me, for he had intended to go to Norfolk to his Aunt Lady Suffield between the Coronation and the "Bill;" but finding that a fortnight at least will elapse before he is wanted, he, like a good dear man that he is, has taken his place in the Steam Packet in order to rejoin me. He says he shall carry me off to England with him. That we shall see about when the time comes. . . . I enclose a letter I received yesterday from A—— which explains his History better than I can. I think Lady G. W. has acted a *base* part by him, and the whole affair has ended as I always predicted it would. Those confidences which women are so fond of receiving about young gentlemen's love affairs, are in fact nothing less than a second-hand flirtation they carry on for themselves, and I think seldom or never end well for the confidante. I think one should endeavour as much as possible to steer clear of all such affairs."

In January 1832 she shows the same good feeling and devotion to duty:—

"The Cholera is at this moment raging around us, we have it *close* to the House on all sides. A poor man was taken ill of it and died in the course of a few hours not 100 yards from our door the other day. I am afraid too that it is only beginning, and that we shall have it in all its horrors ere long. Of course we don't see a soul, nobody would come near us, even were we to allow them so to do, surrounded as we are by Pestilence it would not be right to do so. We might go away, but we do not think it right to run away when the chief part of the community are exposed to it without any possibility of escape. Lothian wanted to pack me off, but to this I would not submit. Had I gone I should be much more likely to catch it, for I should be in a perpetual fidget and fright, knowing him here in the midst of it all. Now I am not the least bit frightened."

After some years, in the Duke of Northumberland's viceroyalty, Lord Talbot came back on a short visit to Ireland, but begged that it might be quite a private one. He writes, "No, my dear Gregory, my visit is purely to you, and has no ulterior object. What shall I do on my landing? Shall I go to the Hotel or drive straight to the Park chez vous?"

Tradition says that he was so anxious to avoid notice that he came without a servant, hailed a car, put his valise on it, and drove to the Phoenix Park.

"I don't think much of your horse," he said to the driver on the way.

"Faith, he never did a ha'porth o' good since the day *your Excellency* left," was the reply. So after that he gave up the attempt at incognito, and even dined more than once at the Castle. Mr. Gregory notes his arrival on October 23, and the friends invited to meet him at dinner during his stay, the Leinsters, the Primate, the Leveson-Gowers, Sir Philip Crampton, Saurin of course on the first evening, and Joy the Attorney-General.

But as he grows older, the rush and tumble of the times distress him. God knows what will become of the country now Catholic Emancipation is being granted! And the Reform Bill coming on too, "what times we live in!" He is not to be persuaded to turn his coat, and writes with a pained and affectionate sadness about Peel's defection.

Mr. Gregory visits him more than once, and meets other friends there. "Peel and his Brother William came," he writes at Ingestre in 1827, on September 19. And next day "Two Peels Killed forty Brace of Partridges." He may have taken it as a compliment to his nationality that the battue had been kept for the opening day in Ireland, the 20th. They go over to Drayton also to see the new house "which when finished will be excellent."

The good Earl's pleasures are simple. "My children, my library, my garden." He laments a storm in which "the poplar, you remember it—near the garden wall," has been struck by lightning. He imports the aboriginal Kerry cows from Ireland, and is "looking forward to the arrival of my roses from France." These pleasures suit him better than those of "Babylon," as he calls London. "Yet one must go there or be counted among the dead."

One can fancy when he and Mr. Gregory meet at Ingestre how

cordial is the welcome, how courteous the attentions to "Lady Anne and your daughter." How the old heads wag over the walnuts and the wine as they look at the political world wholly given to wickedness and the Radicals flourishing like a green bay tree.

Well, the world is seventy years older since then. The Catholics have not sold England to the Pope. The House of Lords still stands. Nonconformists are decently buried and the ghosts of good Churchmen have not come out of their graves. The sun has not yet set upon the Empire.

The wine is older now, but the walnut trees bear fresh fruit. The elders of another generation sit and hear each other moan, and shake their heads over the Local Government and Welsh Disestablishment that will bring the world to an end.

E pur si muove. And we still live and plant roses. And the fall of the poplar at Ingestre and of the pocket boroughs moves no one any more to regrets or to fears.

I have chosen those of his letters which contain matter of general interest to give here. They do not require any comment.

"Boodle's: March 30, 1824.

". . . I am in search of a House for 6 or 8 weeks to complete my residence in Babylon . . .

"Our friends in Grosvenor Square are particularly well, indeed Lord Whitworth is better than I have seen him for many years. He is lively, upright, riding out in all weathers, and looking younger than ever. It does me good to look upon his cheerful countenance. His appetite is just what it ought to be, and under very fair control. I dined in company with him at Lord Camden's yesterday to meet the Duke of York.

"Our politics here are more placid than common, and the State of the Country free from discontent and prosperous. Not that I quite like this philanthropical System of universal toleration, and levelling all the old fences which have so long protected us, and brought us safe through so many storms. I have heard it said that some of the oppositionists say, Ministers are more *opposition* than any of their party, and carry reform and liberality and freedom further than they either expected or desired. This is one of the mollifying effects of the C—ites' introduction into office. I never can consider this person but as a slippery friend. Whether I am right or wrong will be seen I think at no very great distance of time. The premier is quite modernized, meaning, I am told, and supported by the Bishops, to vote for the bill Lord Lansdowne is to introduce respecting the marriage of

Dissenters. The Chancellor and a few of us old-fashioned politicians will go against the principle.

"The King is said to be well, and is to have a Levee before the Birthday. . . ."

Ingestre: August 28, 1824.

". . . I have been very busy in superintending my agricultural concerns, and thanks to a most bountiful Providence, and a little more personal activity, I should not again have to explain to you why my Rickyard is not full. This year I have not room for my hay, I have one superb rick of 80 yards long. . . .

"I have not heard of Lord Whitworth very lately. I did not think him quite well when I last saw him, but I trust the sea air which he went to Sandgate to enjoy has re-established him. He was sadly feeble.

"Peel has been very kind to me, having given me a situation for Ginder's son which has comforted him in his affliction, poor fellow (he has recently lost his wife), and has gratified him very much. The manner in which Peel made me the offer was so peculiarly kind that it reminded me of old and happy Times when he, you and I considered how places were to be disposed of.

"The Duchess of K. seems to have behaved herself with great prudence, and if the small number of her husband's friends that remain did not remind her of the rapid change that takes place in human affairs in too melancholy a manner, she must have been gratified by the cordiality with which she was received. . . ."

May 15, 1825.

"It is with a bleeding heart that I communicate to you (although you have probably heard it before), the departure from this world to a better of our dear friend Lord Whitworth. 'He was taken ill on Wednesday and expired on Friday evening. He had suffered much, but expired without a struggle. He was conscious up to the last, and was not aware of his situation.' Thus writes Plymouth from Knole.

"I will not attempt the description of my feelings on this painful occasion. They are such as will be common to you and all his friends. A greater private loss cannot be imagined. Honest, upright and sincere, he was a pattern to his equals, benevolent, humane and affectionate; his loss will be felt by all classes.

"In him I lose a second Father, a friend in whose honest judgment I always could depend, and a minister in whose indulgence my failings always found a lenient judge.

"May we, my dear good Gregory, be allowed to meet him and others who have preceded us, in regions of happiness, never again to be separated. May God bless you and yours, and believe me always your truly attached and affectionate

"TALBOT."

Jan. 28, 1826.

". . . The rumour of a change or changes in your executive daily gains ground. I fear this country is in a very precarious state. The extent of distress in the manufacturing districts in Cheshire, Lancashire, and parts of Yorkshire, is, I fear and believe, very great. In Staffordshire we are as yet flourishing, but God knows where the evil of over-speculation and trading upon others' capital may reach.

"I had hoped never to be called upon to go out with our local force again, and to repose under my Laurels, faded as they have been. Yet I assure you I am by no means tranquil on the subject. I wish to my heart that Peel would organise and head an administration on old English principles (I mean this expression to be taken in its best acceptation) in our trade and politics, which really alarm the jog-trot friends of the Country, among whom ranks himself

"Yours ever affectly.,
"TALBOT."

71 Liverpool Street: May 31, 1826.

"My dear Gregory,—It has pleased the Almighty once again to visit your poor friend with a most heavy affliction, in having called to Himself my dear *Son Ingestre,* of whose melancholy death I have this morning received intelligence by express from Vienna.

"It appears my poor Boy was in the habit of taking early rides in the Prater (the Park) near Vienna, and that in conformity to this practice he went out on Tuesday the 23rd about 10 o'c.— that his Horse was seen to turn restive and to break away with him towards the Town, when he rushed into a muddy pool, where throwing his Rider, my poor son fell into the water and was suffocated in the mud.

Assistance was procured, but, alas! too late; and thus am I once more thrown into the deepest affliction. Of Ingestre's amiability and virtues there is but one opinion, and this carries consolation with it, yet it aggravates my misery at the loss of him.

The Almighty gave him to me, it has pleased Him to call him unto Himself. Blessed be the Lord. . . .

"I am sure you will feel for yours

"Always most affectionately
"TALBOT."

Mr. Gregory to Lord Talbot

Dublin: June 18, 1827.

"My dear Lord,—Next to seeing you in the situation I most wish will be the gratification of seeing you in my house, and to which I look forward as no distant event. Whoever may be the successor of Lord Wellesley, he could not have the slightest objection to your visiting this Country. As nothing to my knowledge has yet been settled respecting the appointment of Lord Anglesea, I suppose he declines accepting it; so many Protestant noblemen have refused the Viceroyalty of this Country that I fear the King will find it difficult to nominate one according to the declaration he made to the Bishops; the objections made by others would not hold with Lord Anglesea, they refused as I understand because they would not act with Mr. Canning. Lord A. has acted with him, and could not therefore refuse on that ground. To you I never scruple to open my mind, and therefore say that if Mr. Lamb is not to remain Chief Secretary, I sincerely hope Mr. Frankland Lewis will not be appointed his successor. I know your intimacy with him, but you are not aware of the strong line he has taken in Popish Politics in this Country, which in my mind makes him totally unfit for such a situation; he is far from a moderate Politician, and would be under the influence of Persons the most prejudiced against our Church Establishment.

"What a retreat old Norbury has made! Tho' loaded with so many honors some of his friends are of opinion that he will feel unhappy when out of office. Whatever may be thought of the terms by which he has been induced to resign, no one can doubt but that his removal at this very advanced age from the judgment seat is a public benefit.

"Just as I had finished the last sentence the English mail arrived, and brought an account of the defeat of the Corn Bill. I am aware that the measure was one in the success of which the Ministers were much interested, but being ignorant of the present state of Parties I am incompetent to form an opinion of the

effect such defeat may produce in Ministerial influence. It must
be very mortifying to Mr. Canning.

"W. GREGORY.

"P.S. We had yesterday our last Beefsteak meeting for the
season;[1] it was excellent. Your health is never forgotten there,
and I am happy to say that at each time it is given the applause
with which it is received does not diminish."

Lord Talbot to Mr. Gregory

Ingestre: July 4, 1827.
"My Dear Gregory,—I did not obtain a sight of Lord
Wellesley's most handsome letter to you until this day. All I
can say is that it is strictly what is due to you, and complete
triumph as to the correctness of your Principles.

"I dare not look forward, my dear Friend, to a political future.
What is to happen a wiser and greater Power alone can foresee.
With a Catholic Home Secretary, a d[itt]o. Irish Secretary, with
Mr. Spring-Rice for an Under Secretary, with a L. L. who always
had been a Catholic, who remains till Xtmas, and is to be succeeded by one who, though he has voted against Emancipation,
is not a decided Protestant, I lament and grieve from very soul
for poor dear Ireland.

"The political changes are to me quite appalling. I feel as if
some sad Calamity had fallen me, having for so many years supported, and with all my heart, the Government, I cannot conceive
how and why I find myself opposed to it. You will not, indeed
you will not expect it, find me among the very virulent hot-headed
opponents of Ministers. But I cannot stomach Whiggism, and
Whiggism of the Geneva school too.

"You will, I think, have Lewis—but do not misunderstand me
—tho' I like him as a man I dislike his political views and
principles totô coelo, and since I have known what he has been
doing in Ireland, he is just the last man I should (were I L. L.)
wish to have as my Secretary.

". . . You will be glad to know we are all, thank God, quite
well. My little fellows are at home. Gerald comes on the 28th. If
Ingestre can be of any use as a resting place to dear little William,

---

[1] The Beefsteak Club began as a musical, but afterwards became a Tory
place of meeting. It was here that, when Lord Wellesley's removal was
announced, "The Exports of Ireland" was given as a toast to his great
indignation.

you of course will make use of it. Adieu, with kind regards to Lady Anne, your Daughter and Saurin."

Cardiff: August 10, 1827.

"I last night heard, to my great surprize and concern, of Mr. Canning's Death. The only remark I shall permit myself is, that the ways of Providence are awful and mysterious. Who would have thought that the Successor of a Minister afflicted by a mortal disease should be called to his last account before his Patron and predecessor! That everything ultimately tends to good I have long been intimately convinced. May this awful Event prove a benefit to the Country.

We Protestants have another Squeak for our Establishment and principles.

Remote from my friends, being on a survey of my Welsh Wilds, I have no chance of hearing what is going on in the political World. My confidence is in Peel, whether or not his party be strong enough to carry him through the Struggle I have no means of judging. Sure I am that the Whigs are not popular. I pity the King, he must be in a state of great annoyance and distress. . . ."

Jan. 21, 1828.

". . . How shall I frame a letter to you in these eventful Times,[1] and not tell you a thousand Lies? If I venture to commit anything to paper it shall be without *pretending to communicate more* than I hear in the streets, for to no other source of information have I any access or pretension. You are aware that every person that tells news either gives it the coloring that best suits his party feeling, or else retails the Gossip he has collected from party followers or persons as ignorant as himself.

"I am afraid that all matters relative to the Chiefs of departments are settled, and that the minor dependencies are now in cogitation. You will have been told that the List in the Chronicle is mainly true, and I believe it is so. Some discussion, report says, has been held whether Mr. Herries shall be in the Cabinet. Lord Anglesey is better; he was riding yesterday, and intends to assume the reins of his Government in a month or six weeks, if his health permits. Should he not be well enough I have heard Lord Melville is likely to be appointed. Dr. Luton said that as far as Lord Anglesey's Health was concerned, he wished he was on his road now. Some medical men then seem to think he will never be well

---

[1] Alluding to the fall of the Coalition Ministry under Lord Goderich and formation of a Government under the Duke of Wellington.

enough to go. As yet Lord A. has had no communication from Duke of W. This, it must be allowed, is natural, until the Government be formed and the Basis of its policy fixed. Lewis, I think, remains, and there are not wanting those who think that the principles of free trade, &c., which the old Tories objected to so much last year, will now have more free course than before, as Huskisson, Grant and Lewis will be uncontrolled by Herries, whose Mastership of the Mint will not give him that Authority which the Chancellorship of the Exchequer had conferred.

"The Duke of Newcastle, report says, is furious, and will not support Government.

"Lord Wharncliffe is also violent, deprecating the Desertion of Huskisson from the Canningites, but he will support (p.s. this I hear since is false).

"Lord Eldon, *I have been assured,* has not had any Communication from his old Colleagues, or been consulted in any way.

"Much as I respect the leaders, I confess this omission appears ominous to *our* Cause. I dare not make any Comments upon the public feeling before the whole is settled, yet I think I discern great rancour.

"The Whigs are dissatisfied with Huskisson, and some with Lord Lansdowne. The Canningites with Huskisson. The old Tories with the admission of the Leaven of Liberalism in the persons of H. and Co. In short I do not think any party are quite in good humour.

"However these feelings may be justified or reconciled, it is but fair to say that situated as public men now are, it is extremely difficult to form any Administration without *concession.* For myself I feel glad we have such a man of peace and strong commanding Sense as the Duke of Wellington is, at the Head of Affairs, altho' there are some points in the Arrangement I should *have liked* to have seen different, as I am sure some of our friends in power would, if possible, have managed. . . . Lord Liverpool is something better, he has been informed of Canning's Death, and was much affected."

Ingestre: Sunday, January 28, 1828.

"Many thanks, my dear Gregory, for your kind and satisfactory Letter, which has soothed my ultra-Tory feelings. I do trust to the principles of the Premier and Peel, but I do wish they had been able to form an administration on really pure Protestant principles, tho' I admit that great difficulties may and probably have arisen to prevent so desirable an Union.

"I had nearly forgotten the object of this letter, which was to tell you that Arthur has been ordained and did duty to-day here! He really acquitted himself vastly well. May he prove himself of the Vocation!"

Boodle's: April 17, 1828.

"I arrived on Saturday, and have just begun my Town Life.

". . . I was accidentally told a curious thing today from which some little explanation [is furnished] to your Letter requesting to have the one you had written to me, and which you suspected to have been opened, to be returned, to satisfy you on the point.

"It appears that there is a solicitor by the name of Talbot, who being accidentally from home left a Clerk in charge to open his letters. Among these it would seem was one from you to me; this was, the young man says, inadvertently opened in the first instance, but then *read as he confesses*. Conceiving that some wishes expressed by you to see me in my old post as L. L. again, imported a conspiracy between you and me to rid Ireland of Lord Wellesley, he deemed it right to send this treasonable Document to Mr. Canning! Mr. C. answers him very coolly, telling him he had been guilty of an unpardonable breach of propriety, and that to save all further discussion and difficulty he had burned the Letter in question.

"*Lewis* I believe has seen Canning's answer, tho' I have not this from him, nor does he know that I am in possession of these facts.

"Can all this be true; can it be an answer to my having once inveighed against Letters having been opened; was the Letter the one I have (which I returned to you)? In fact it is a surprising Mystery, and I cannot quite fathom the thing either itself or its being now communicated to me.

"I contented myself with the observation that it was passing odd you should have mentioned a wish about my return in that Letter alone.

"Can this be preparatory to any attack? What can it mean?

"I had better tell you that my friend Peploe told me the story under some reservation. To you I have none, in this case I ought to have none. He is incapable of any underhand conduct to anyone, Especially towards myself or you, whom he, I know, likes as a man; as Tories and Protestants he pities our blindness and Bigotry."

London: June 13, 1828.

"As Enniskillen wrote to you after our Catholic Debate, and

I believe he entertains the same opinion that I do, that the Question is 'virtually carried,' I did not write to you, especially as I had it in contemplation to go to Iver, and I thought you would like to hear how your Grandson does. I went yesterday, and I can report William is in great health and good looks. He told me he was quite well, which Mr. Ward corroborated.

"With regard to these catholicks, I can have no doubt that some overtures will be made, and I should not wonder if some measure was brought forward. But you, I think, will agree that until these Gentlemen can be induced to act a little more like good and quiet subjects, there is but little chance of anything like arrangement to be expected."

Ingestre: July 11, 1828.

"Well, my dear Gregory, things are now assuming a dreadful aspect, and a Crisis which I own I did not expect quite so soon is now at hand, and a dreadful one it will be. Separation O'Connell now avows. It would be heartless that we should triumph in the correctness of our Estimation of the real views of the Emancipators. Their real object is now unmasked by their Idol. "Separation" from this Country alone will satisfy these agitators. Good God, what will happen? It has been remarked in this neighbourhood that fewer (indeed scarcely any) of the Irish laborers have come over this Harvest. This cannot be accidental, this is part of the system of the Priestcraft. What security can this Country now pretend to if the Catholic Claims be admitted? None, but there will be a collision between the 2 Religions.

"I begin to think that Catholic Emancipation is positively dreaded by the R. C. Clergy, and that they never will consent to any Terms by which their influence would be lessened, if indeed any such could now be advised.

"Poor dear Ireland! I feel for you!

"How the noble Marquess feels I do not presume to suppose, but if this be not *dragooning* I cannot interpret the word, and if it be, we have his assurance in the H. of Lords that he will not submit to it.

"I do indeed think he is the last man in the Country that will brook such outrageous conduct.

"We have a firm administration too, I think, at head-quarters, and of such a one shall we stand in need.

"I enclose a few lines of congratulation to our friend Saurin on his son's Marriage. The Lady is a neighbour of mine, *entre nous* report says she is rather a swaddler. . . .

"How you will like your new *Chef*[1] I cannot surmize. He is a very gentlemanly and clever young man, but I fear his melancholy cast of countenance will scarcely suit your vivacious Countrymen. Henry Greville, his brother-in-law, is a great friend of Jack's; he is rather a dandy, but I think not an unpleasant man; he is quite up to the "Snuff" of the world. I do not think that either of them are strictly men of Business, but both of them are too keen not to know they must become such if they mean to retain their Situation with credit. . . ."

July 13, 1828.

"I told you in my last I should write soon again to you. This I did in the expectation that Ingestre might succeed in obtaining the Consent of Lady Sarah Beresford to become his wife.

"This is now effected, and I lose not a moment in communicating the happy event to you."

Foxley: August 17, 1828.

"It has not been without a struggle, I assure you, that I have given up my intention of visiting you this year. . . .

"I felt, however, some doubt on the propriety of my arrival in a Country where my political principles are so well known, at a moment of excitation like the present. . . .

"I am afraid of asking you whether you can give us a little of your company.

"With a young L.L. and a still younger Secretary your experience will, I fear, be too much wanted for me to expect to see you at Ingestre.

"Henry Greville was with me some time before he went over. I hope you like him. He is good-natured, with some cleverness—but very unused to such serious Business as he has engaged in."

London: 12 o'clock Feb. 5, 1829.

"When I left home on Tuesday I little expected to be greeted on arrival in London with the Intelligence that the Catholic Question was to be carried, that Peel had offered to resign his seat in the University, and that the King had assented to the Measure. Until this moment I was not aware that I was so sensitive a being—but I confess I am quite overset with this, to me at least, unexpected Change in H.M.'s Councils. What I may do, that is, how I shall vote, I am at present quite ignorant—to exhibit a useless opposition to a measure which both sides

[1] Lord F. Leveson-Gower.

of the House will unite in defending would be as the expression
'useless' imports, *nonsense*, but if the Veteran protestants who
can speak array themselves in opposition to it, I probably shall
be found among them.

"This is the blessed fruit of Charles Grant's appointment, and
thus are Cities often carried by Sap whose fortifications resist the
bolder attacks by Storm. . . .

"Pray let me have one line from you to *this place*, where I
have not much inclination to dwell, on this important and unfortunate subject.

"A casual visitor has just told me our Premier's politics on the
Cat. Question are quite changed."

London: Feb. 6, 1829.

"You doubtless will hear that all our apprehensions have been
verified, and the great Question of Cath. Eman. is carried. I
could not, I would not believe it.

"But, alas, the strong Tone assumed by the Duke, and Peel's
speech of last night, leave no doubt of the Fact.

"I was sorry to observe the Tone in the House of Lords. It
should seem we had all been of the opinion now manifested by
Ministers since the world began.

"Yet it may be a politic prudent measure. Then why not state
the facts that make it so.

"Why throw over your former friends and co-operating fellow
labourers in opposing the Cath. pretention, by giving them no
notice of change in your policy.

"Lord Winchelsea told them it was disingenuous, it was base.
Lord Eldon made a good speech—but was rather 'wordy.' Lord
Anglesey spoke with great dignity and ease, and wisely availed
himself of this momentous change not to trouble the house with
a detail of his personal wrongs, the right to detail which he,
however, begged to be understood he would not abandon.

"I really am sick at heart. That the measure cannot be success-
fully opposed I am satisfied. Shall we content ourselves with
watching the progress of the measure, or let those protestant
ministers defend the Church by themselves. That the opinion
here is against the measure I think no one can doubt. How far
it will be expressed, Time will show.

"For me, I am rather inclined to require no Securities, as if
given they will form new reasons for disquiet, and ultimately be
cancelled. The word *toleration* should now be obliterated. We
have all a right to everything, and are fast verging to the doctrine
of Tom Paine of the rights of man.

"But eno' of this d——m subject. I saw Lord Manners, who appears quite well."

Ingestre: Feb. 28, 1829.

". . . I feel acutely the blow that is about to be inflicted on the Country.

"As at *present* informed, my vote will be as it ever has been; but if in a conscientious examination into the Arguments to be adduced and facts which we *Hear* are to be brought forward, I see reason to alter that opinion, I shall do so. If you ask me what I think, I think you will find me the uncompromising defender of those principles in which I have been brought up and have ever professed. I am not one who will give up deep and firmly rooted principles because a Duke of Wellington may be driven from his post . . . fiat justitia ruat Coelum. I can safely say I have never felt a political Question so deeply—it has positively made me ill—deprived me of all comfort and peace of mind.

"Depressed in spirits, deprived of hope, I wandered about London like one possessed with an Evil Spirit. Yet the Question will be carried at all risks and at all events. I shall be at my post tho' I cannot summon up resolution to speak (tho' I will not say to what I may be goaded). I intend to watch every clause, every word of the intended Acts of Parliament. I cannot but think Peel conscientious—he has lost everything to gain nothing. I have not seen him, but I hear he says he is *conscientious* in adopting ·he Line which he has painfully taken.

"Hoping your Daughter is restored to you in health, with Cecil's Love to you all, believe me, unalterably yours."

London: March 25, 1829.

". . . I have not seen Peel, nor do I know that I quite wish to seen him—for although I give him every credit for *honest conviction* on his part of the *expediency* (that is our new and fashionable phrase), if not absolute necessity for a change, I cannot forget he is no longer the bold assertor of those principles in which I have been brought up, and which notwithstanding all his oratory I still conceive to be necessary to the well-being of the Country. But I will call when he is more at leisure to see individuals who have no demands upon his time.

"I saw W. Peel yesterday, and I told him I was not yet arrived at that pitch of political proficiency when I could reconcile it to myself to sacrifice *principle to expediency*, neither would I do so. If you recollect the W. Peel at Grenden you would scarcely recognise him in London. I mean the expression, not the person of the man.

"I am told we shall be beaten by a majority of fifty-eight in H. of Lords. I fear the *Reaction,* for certainly the feelings of the public are against the measure. W. Peel having stated some difficulties which in his opinion justified the bill, said to me, 'What would you do?' I replied, 'Upon my word I do not know, but allow me to ask you, what do you expect to do now?' I got as little satisfaction from him. I hear six Irish Bishops are come or coming over to see the King on this business. This is all very well—but they might as well have staid at home. The present Premier will not consent to retrograde, and the doors of the Constitution are to be set wide open to all persons wishing to enter them. Some people doubt of Lord Manners. Surely he cannot after his Uniform opposition to R. C. Emancipation turn round and vote for it. But you will say, 'Look at Peel!' I can only shake my head and say, very true!

"Yet I think 'Tom' staunch. I have heard the magnificence of your present L.L.[1] is unbounded, quite princely. Yet a more unassuming person cannot exist. I hope you will like them both! They are amiable in private life. . . ."

London: April 1, 1829.

"The bill for R. C. Emancipation was yesterday brought to the Lords, by Peel in person. Little did I ever expect to have seen our friend at the bar of our House upon such an occasion. Had I been told of such a circumstance two years, nay one year ago, I should have scouted it as impossible.

"As I have a perfect conviction of Peel's honesty, morality and religious principles, I cannot entertain a doubt of his *motives,* but perhaps I should say *fears* which have induced him to sacrifice his Character for consistency and firmness. But having so far given him credit, I hope I shall not be reproached with a wish to derogate from his character if I say that in future I *cannot confide* in his stability. *Expediency* is a sorry word. I say give me *principle* as my watchword.

"No one in future can be fairly reproached with abandoning principles, friends or party—all, all, must yield to expediency! Be it so; when we know whereof politicians are made we can measure the proportion of faith to be reposed in them by that Scale. I am glad you approve of my line of conduct. I wish so to vote that I can say to myself, 'You have acted conscientiously and done your Duty.' . . .

"I hardly know what to think of Lord Manners. He is

---

[1] Duke of Northumberland.

decidedly against the Bill, but they say he has many crotchets on the subject.

"The minority (the other side will far outnumber them) will be very respectable, highly respectable, for independence, character and weight in the Country and public Estimation, but this is of no practical use.

"Whenever you come to London you know where to find a Bed. Cecil sends her love to you all—she is well."

Lower Grosvenor Place: April 24, 1829.

"It is with very sincere pleasure that I have received yours of the 21st, inasmuch as I applaud and concur most truly in all the advice your Friends have given you to remain in office, until at least you know what the Government is.

"For the sake of Ireland I rejoice, for yourself I hope you have not acted wrong.

"Among the many contradictory reports I sent you, the news I collected yesterday proves correct, and it will enable you to form some judgment as to what is likely to be done in Ireland. This much is proved, that the future administration of that Country forms an important feature in the consideration of Government. I believe Lewis will be your Chief Secretary. W. Horton and Lord Binning have both been talked of for this Office, but from all I hear and see, Lewis will, I think, most likely be the man. He is a decided Catholic Emancipator, but disposed not to lend himself to any party.

"You will have heard with some surprize, I doubt not, of Mr. Plunkett's having declined the Rolls, but this is accounted for by the dissatisfaction expressed by the English Bar at the appointment. I see farther. It may be he does not like to face public disinclination, but, alas! I fear he has views incompatible with the Elevation of one for whom I have the liveliest affection, Esteem and Regard. This may not be the case, but we live in such times of Juggle and Trick that GOD knows how far anyone may look, or what we plain dealers may dare to encourage a hope of. . . .

"Public opinion, as far as I can learn, is not in favor of the long continuance of this (by some called) strange coalition. This grand sentiment (pub. opin.) is decidedly in favor of our friend. I saw him a few days since, a more manly, conscientious, distinct Line no man could have pursued. He acted and fell like a man— like a Protestant.

"Such conduct must meet with Reward, the mens conscia recti never needed consolation. The train for all this has been long and

deeply laid. May it all turn to the advantage of the Country. . . .
Peel is very well. Lord Eldon, they say, is equally so."

London: June 4, 1829.

"O'Connell's impudence is just what I expected it would be.
Among the many results of the late Act of Parliament, this I for
one anticipated, that the radicals in Ireland would only be
exasperated, in short, what can satisfy disaffection? Nothing but
the overthrow of Existing Establishments.

"I fear we are not very comfortable in our home politics.
Disunion is said to exist in the Cabinet, a want of confidence I
am sure prevails among the more moderate partizans of the
Government. The Evils of over production and a superabundant
population become daily more apparent. How will it all end, Dieu
sait. Many changes must take place before all is settled, but
among them do not suppose any will take place in the affection
of yours truly."

London: June 18, 1829.

"I hasten to assure you that both Cecil and myself are in good
health. *She* was at the Ball at St. James's. *I was not*, because the
invitation did not reach this house till Tuesday evening, and I
being at Ingestre for my sheep show (which I have established)
did not hear of the command till it was nearly impossible to obey
it, which suited my Book indeed, as I had several friends to meet
me at home. We sat down 32 to dinner the Friday, the day after
the Ball, so that had I attended I must have disappointed many
people. And as I can conscientiously say, nothing but travelling
all night, after having been running about Leicestershire in the
morning, could have brought me to Town in time for the Ball,
I felt justified in saying I did not receive the Command in time
to obey it.

"As it was I left my Company early to be in time for a great
dinner at Peel's on Saturday—for whom, notwithstanding all that
has passed, I cannot help entertaining a sincere regard and
perhaps affection.

"That circumstances compelled him to do what he did, I must,
unless I accuse him of everything odious, believe, but I cannot
help feeling that *I* in common with everyone of the same opinion,
have been *gulled* and *misled*. I fear too for nothing, for unless I
am deceived, and I pray sincerely I may be, the same opposition
to Government will be experienced, tho' under other names and
far more favourable circumstances to the oppositionists, than the
Emancipation of the R. C's called forth. I hope I may be wrong.

Alas, I fear I am but too right. Certain it is, Government has *few real* friends, such as it possessed before this stroke of policy. I conclude some changes in the Admiinstration must be made before Parliament meets again. We are to be dismissed next week. . . .

"We are suffering much from drought. I fear the country is in a very deplorable state. I own I *croak*. The Town is emptied for Ascot, where much sport is expected. I hope H.M. may win *his Cup*, he sets so much value upon the doing so."

London: June 24, 1829.

". . . As for your Catholic Gratitude, I confess I should have been disappointed had it turned out different from what it has. We always said that C. Emancipation was only a pretence, a stepping stone—for ulterior objects—and what your present L. L. thinks of himself now he sees things in their *true* colours, I cannot very well imagine, as at heart he is a *true protestant*. If no serious mischief ensue I should be glad to find that some of the wise politicians should be made to feel that *ratting* is not always *wise, safe,* or *dignified*. But as you say *the deed is done* . . . I will not disturb it or rake up any ashes."

Ingestre: July 5, 1830.

". . . So Parliament has begun its sittings. The weather is so severe that I have not been tempted to go up to it, especially as my last year's zeal in going was *so well* rewarded. I cannot say that I am in opposition, but I feel all my old ties relaxed, and I cannot feel I am as I used to be, disposed to act without suspicion of reserve with my friends. Yet I confess there is no one I should wish to see at the helm rather than the present Premier and Peel. The effect which we predicated, that the Priests would not be less unmanageable than before by the repeal of the R. C. disabilities, has been proved by their conduct in Limerick, and therefore I hope that the Duke will not forget his promise of taking effectual measures to restrain disaffection, if after the boon thus granted such steps should become necessary. Yet I cannot but fear the gallant Commander finds it less easy to control a whole Nation than a large Army. He seems bothered, if I may judge from the king's speech, which I have just read; Government scarcely knows how to act or what to recommend. Distress is at its acme in many districts. Here, thank GOD, we are comparatively well off—though I have just seen forty-five men emptying one of my ponds, whom the various Overseers of the works at Ingestre have no work for. I like Ginders for his extreme kindness of heart. He never will discharge a poor man. In my heart I bless him.

"My rents are tolerably well paid, so far so good. I hear your noble L.L. remains. Old Charles Greville has been here (I mean in Staffordshire) saying that nothing ever equalled His Grace's magnificence, and that *Justice* was *for the first time* impartially administered in Ireland; to which observation Arthur replied, 'That is not true,' and said no more, nor was anything of the kind attempted afterwards. The Duke has given Lord F. Gower a magnificent Snuff Box with Brilliants for New Year's Day, telling him he was the most efficient Secretary, &c. . . . Do we live, my dear Gregory, among sensible people, or were there in our days dolts, fools. Else all is now Humbug. I really Know not what to think. I often ask myself, am I alive, can such nonsense really be?

"You will be glad to hear we are all quite well. I am as happy as a King, with my daughters only in the house. We meet at 9 every morning. I read after breakfast for two hours, walk for three. I am improved in walking. Then we write letters and dine —play music, read German, play at double patience and go to Bed. I am also improved in my Magisterial knowledge, in which Capacity I really think I begin to be of use. Cecil asks in the imperative mood, Have you given my Love to Gregory? Therefore *I beg to do so*. She is really vastly well. . . . What a yarn! This will, I hope, find you warmer than I am, tho' I am close to the fire whilst writing this. . . ."

London: July 15, 1830.

". . . The new Monarch begins well; if he should confine himself or restrict himself, I mean from over-doing his Duty, he will become a most popular Sovereign. His heart is in the right place.

". . . I believe I ought to have attended the Royal Funeral. But here I am in London, when the others are at Windsor. . . ."

Ingestre: Sunday, July 25.

". . . The weather appears to be taking up. I have had 80 acres of Hay spoilt. The Judges dine with me next Sunday. Jack goes this Circuit, he is retained by Lord Salisbury at Hertford with a 100 Gn. fee, and in other things he is beginning well.

"The Wharncliffes and Dartmouth come Friday. Lady Anne will be delighted to hear Lord D. has entrusted me with my dear little Grandson "Lewisham." He is indeed a lovely child, full of goodness and kind-heartedness. We are all delighted with him.

'Tis funny to hear him call Gerald and Pat 'My Uncle Ge, and my Uncle Pat, and Uncle Gustavus'— 'tis very odd. . . ."

London: November 9, 1830.

"Many thanks, my dear Gregory, for your letter. I fear we, the Country, and the Government, are fearfully situated. Whatever may be our fate, however the Country may rally, I doubt and fear the Govt. must succumb. The indiscreet, or by whatever name the determined declaration of the Duke *not to entertain the question of reform at all, or under any circumstances,* may be designated, has placed his political existence on the chance of a Die, and therefore it is, I fear, the H. of Commons, by their vote on Brougham's motion, will virtually turn the Administration out.

"The Events of yesterday, the advice Government gave the king *not* to go to the City, will give a helping hand to their fall.

"For one, I conscientiously think Government *did right,* but then I do not *want place, nor do I want to see them out of place,* which I grieve to say many who are not hostile to them individually do.

"This change will, I fear, be followed by your going out too, unless, now you are no longer a detested Orange Man, they may wish to secure the benefit of your services and advice. Then follows, Will you do so? I cannot think you *will not,* altho' Stanley is a clever man, yet you will not like a Whig Government.

"The Country and this Town is in a very delicate State. There can be no doubt of the existence of French Influence and money among us, a decided revolutionary spirit is abroad—can, will, the Whigs check it? I fear not. *The spirit here is bad.* I go to Court to-morrow, and Cecil and I go to the Queen's party on Thursday. It is impossible to give you any adequate idea of the royal pair's popularity, a great circumstance at this anxious moment. Lord Londonderry joined Govt. yesterday! And Devonshire had better have remained in opposition."

Dunchurch: November 25, 1830.

"I arrived in Town yesterday three weeks, for the express purpose of supporting Government.

"In the short period of twenty-one days that Government is not only turned out, but another formed and in full activity, having filled up a greater number of situations in a Week than was ever known before to be the case.

"Although I am in no way individually concerned in the change, I cannot help feeling like a Dog with his Tail between his Legs. I heard it so confidently reported that you have received your congé, that I fear it must be true. If you regret your leaving office, so I do for you, but if you do not, and under existing circumstances I doubt much if you would have remained, I will congratulate you upon the termination of the severe labours, which have been very fatiguing to you of late years.

"Cecil desires me to say she hopes you *are out,* as you will have more leisure to take care of your health, and more time to bestow upon your friends. Everything kind to Lady Anne from us both. I am afraid that poor Saurin will have another bitter pill to swallow in having to plead before Lord Plunket. The luck of some men is astonishing. I still hope all will come right at last. The burnings continue. I fear that if Peel failed in finding the Rascals out that Melbourne will hardly succeed."

Ingestre: January 4, 1831.

"Letters on which I think I may depend assure me the Government is far from united—indeed, it is said many of the Cabinet are not upon speaking terms.

"I expect Peel will come here this month. I shall be glad to see him, though his erroneous View of the Catholic Relief Bill has more or less been the cause of these evils. It has been the irritamentum malorum.

"So poor Saurin has retired. I have had a very affectionate and kind Letter from him. I trust he will have plenty of chamber business.

"It is sad that so eminent, just, and good a man should at so advanced a period of his life have no retreat, but be left to struggle with younger men in the daily routine of dry, dull and fatiguing Business. . . . I have been very busy in my County, and have, I believe, the happiness to think that I have a quiet dominion.

"But I have had some running about to maintain peace. Lord Melbourne has handsomely acknowledged my zeal."

January 11, 1831.

"I have to thank you for the newspaper in which the Address to you from the Lord Mayor and Corporation of Dublin, and your reply to it, are inserted. A very satisfactory, and at the same time just, compliment to you, such as was every way your due, and which will be lasting testimony of the sense which your fellow Citizens entertain of your conduct and Services, who, from long experience and local means of judging, were the best Judges possible in the case.

"At a dinner where I casually assisted the conversation turned upon your dismissal from office. Some one of the friends of the existing Government said: 'Oh, it is well known that Gregory interfered against Lord Anglesea when he came to England (to see you I believe),' said the person, addressing himself to me. I replied that Gregory never mixed himself up, or rather suffered his Office to be mixed up, in party politics, this I boldly deny. And then with less discretion I added, 'Perhaps a more genuine reason for his dismissal may be found in the fact that Lady Anne *would never call* upon Lady A.' My friend said: 'Very likely, it is abominable how feelings of private society are suffered to influence political affairs.' To this I assented. I hope I did not step beyond the Truth, then I heed not. I am become a rank radical I believe, that is, whenever I see an abuse I denounce it boldly. I am engaged in *reforming* all the abuses of our *county* Establishments, and have been calling a Gentleman to account (not hostilely) for hinting *I am one of the oppressors of the people,* whose firm friend I tell him I have always been. Indeed, I flatter myself I have been of some use in keeping people quiet, as in my own neighbourhood, thank God, the poor man does consider me his friend.

"Well, proclamation succeeds proclamation, and if the Courier tell true, the recreant caitiff O'Connell begins to show his white feather. I shall be glad to hear that you can occupy yourself without red Boxes. The change, however, is great.

"Have you yet dined at the Castle, for I suppose you will be asked, and be expected again to show your good humour and your magnanimity by going, as if nothing had happened. Is Wilkie still your Servant? Have you a garden for Lady Anne at your new abode? Adieu, my dear friend, believe me always yours most faithfully and affectionately."

Ingestre: Feb. 1, 1832.

"I am getting anxious to know how you are—and most happy shall I be to find that you have shaken off your Attack. These are not times for us to *indulge in* sickness—our very best energies both of an active and passive description may at any moment be called for.

"Not that I am so disheartened about things as many of my friends are, for I think that many persons who were bit as it were with the madness of Reform have seen their Error (thanks, I believe, to the horrors at Bristol and Nottingham), and would rather take the part of the old Institutions than join for their destruction.

"In short, I see the conflict must come, but I hope to go into it with better spirits and companions than had the Crisis come last year would (I imagine) have been the case.

"Lord Harrowby had many conversations with me when in the Country about the expediency of endeavouring to mitigate the evil which we could not avert, and I agreed to the proposition to consent to the suppression of the nomination Borough, which however true the position may be 'that they have worked well,' must be admitted theoretically speaking to be a blot in the constitutional representation, and being *hit* they could never again be of the Use they have heretofore been.

"Well, I agreed to their going, to the giving members to the unrepresented large Towns, and also to the extension of the elective Franchise in Counties. I required on my part that the qualifications of the Electors should be altered and raised, and that the Schedules R, C, and D should be improved.

"All these negotiations ended in smoke, and I said that I again conceived myself a *free man,* as at liberty to take my own Line. This was fully admitted. Last week I received a very remarkably clever Letter from Lord Harrowby, telling me how matters stand, and deprecating the *swamping* the House of Lords by the making so many peers—and stating his opinion rather to be that it would be better to avoid opposing the 2nd reading of the Bill, and thus prevent ministers feeling it necessary to create Peers to carry the measure. No letter can be better adapted for its purpose—it is remarkably clever, well defined, shrewd and argumentative. I have answered it at some length, the pith of my letter is that as Ministers would not come to terms upon the basis of mutual concession, that I could not pledge myself to the *not* voting against the second reading; that as the ministers have shown themselves pertinacious in driving the Bill through both Houses of Parliament, I thought that our only resource left was to be equally firm in opposing it.

"I cannot, indeed I cannot, give up resistance to a measure of this obnoxious tendency which Ministers carry forward with a total disregard of everything and body not of their own persuasion.

"I hope, my dear Gregory, I shall receive your Sanction to this Line which I have chalked out for myself. I am friendly to mutual concessions if thereby we can mitigate the horrible Evil which is now hanging over us.

"Some day or another you shall see the correspondence. I wish I had more talent to fight it, but I am so *innately satisfied* that my view of the question is in concurrence to my feelings and principles that I cannot alter my opinion even if the world was against me."

Feb. 10, 1832.

". . . Your letter is also very satisfactory to me, it gives me confidence in the opinion which I entertain, and which I ventured to give Lord Harrowby in reply to his beautifully written, and I may say almost unanswerable Letter. Yet superior as he is to me in endowments, in political knowledge and expediency, I learnt sufficiently when in Ireland, that the straightforward Course is the only System which never fails a Man, and as I can honestly and conscientiously say that I have in my Letter spoken the genuine Sentiments of my mind, eye and heart, I am satisfied that I shall never regret the having done so. I may be wrong, but if I am, it is the fault of my head and not my heart. I have been told that "Evil is never to be done that Good may come," why may I not apply this maxim to my political conduct? Honesty and Uprightness are infinitely more valuable in politics than cleverness to manage matters, and sophistry in argument and conduct, however specious and seductive.

"Upon the intention of being honest I must rely, and hope that we shall at length see through all our difficulties.

"I am sure the spirit of this Country is improved, the senseless cry of reform is seldom or never heard in the way it was. I do not deny that the Country expects reform, but not to the extent of our ministerial reformers. Lord Grey has at length avowed himself a protector of the Irish Church; pity it is this declaration has been so long delayed, but better late than never. Lord Plunket, too, is (he says so at least) a supporter of the establishment. Report says Lord Anglesey is to return. He has certainly added neither to his own fame or the welfare of Ireland, either by his Counsels, Acts, or by the choice of his advisers.

". . . I am sorry to say I hear my dear old Aunt Lady Salisbury (now 82) is reputed to be unwell and much changed. Having always considered her as a second mother and been treated by her as a Son I shall not leave Town if I can be of any comfort to her."

Mt. Teviot: Sunday, Oct. 7, 1832.

"Thus ends my Scotch Tour! To-morrow I leave Scotland for old England with this subject of regret, that I leave my beloved Cecil uncertain when I shall see her again. This is one of the miseries of life—to be parted from those we love the most truly. Yet let me not repine—it would be unjust, ungracious and selfish were I to do so—as I have the great satisfaction of knowing that she is supremely happy, loving and being beloved by one of the most amiable excellent men that ever lived. In fact they are, I honestly believe, as happy as possible, so that if I could command the power of seing her with more facility than is the case, the thing would be too perfect. Nothing can have succeeded better than our progress thro' the Country. . . .

"Among the places we visited, Gordon Castle, Scone Palace, Dalmeny Park, Avistone rank among the best. As all these places, with the exception of Dalmeny, Lord Rosebery's (one of the loveliest things I ever saw) belong to Conservatives, I am afraid my friend and companion Peploe, who is an old and staunch Whig, has had his dose of conservatism.

". . . Has Lord Anglesey really had an attack of the Tic douleureux, or did he wish to shirk the attendance at this high protestant Lord Mayor's feast, where it seems the old Toasts were given and enthusiastically drunk. . . . Do Stanley and the L.L. hit it better than they did? I am told Stanley dislikes his station, and is disliked, and that the family of the other wish him home again."

Ingestre: Nov. 16, 1832.

". . . We hear rumours of changes in your administration, but till I see them effected I shall not give credit to them. It is said the Ld. L. is recalled (Uxbridge denies it), and that Richmond succeeds him, with St. John C. Hobhouse for his Secretary. Unquestionably St. J. C. H. is one of the cleverest men they have, and will, I daresay, make a good Secretary for Ireland—but I do not think Lord A. will come away yet. As for our war with Holland, it is little better than a civil war—to cut up our old allies to strengthen Belgium or *rather France,* appears to me as absurd as it is unjust. Surely no victory in diplomacy was ever so complete as Talleyrand's over our imbecile Governors. I look upon Sir Thos. Denman's appointment as alike wicked, unfortunate and dangerous. The Whips, I have learned, regret the necessity of the appointment. You and I used to ask *who* is the fittest man to become Judge—not whose politics accorded with ours? *Mais on a changé tout cela*—and I fear that our judicial appointments will for the future be political, than which system no greater Curse for the Country could be invented.

"We have had the Duchess of Kent and her little Princess in this County. Lord Lichfield received them at Shugborough with princely magnificence. I never saw anything better arranged or more high bred Attention paid by any Host or Hostess than Ld.

and Lady L. paid to everybody. No hurry or fuss, but every wish was forestalled and every want supplied with magnificence. They had a Review of the Yeomanry Cavalry which went off well.

"Nothing could exceed the affability and condescension of the Royalties. The effect the visit has produced in the County I think has been good.

"I am to meet Peel, I believe, at Dartmouth's next week, and am going to Drayton as soon as I can. But I fear I shall not get our friend to open himself. He is one of those who think that the least said is the soonest mended. I am informed, however, that he is in better spirits, and says *there will be no revolution*. But surely there has been one, and one is going on now."

Ingestre: April 23, 1832.

". . . I left London on Sunday night so as to get home on Monday. I am now surrounded with schoolboys, among whom is Gerald more improved and strengthened than I confess I ever expected to see him. He tells me that your William is a clever and a popular Boy. I hope he is with you, and that you have among your several *Gregorian* difficulties this happy rallying point in which, Phoenix like, you see yourself renewed again. . . .

"In the last parliamentary struggle I have voted strictly in conformity to my conscience, so much so that I feel I smile at what occurs. I have deeply thought as to what line it was my honest duty to adopt. I have made my Election, the consequences are in better and wiser hands than mine. I can only say, come what may, God's Will be done.

"Of Ireland I can say nothing excepting, that if it has been misgoverned for centuries, the present mode of governing has by no means destroyed the charter of Misrule! . . .

"Lord Anglesea says he is quite well. I hear his Complaint has ceased. The *political tic* will be *douleureux* eno', I fancy, let what will happen. . . ."[1]

"Potatoes only fetch from 6*d*. to 10*d*. per bushel! and this at seed time too!"

Ingestre: Xmas Eve, 1832.

"Many and very happy returns of the present season to you and yours, my dear Gregory, though I dare not anticipate that we

---

[1] "It is an extraordinary thing, and the most wonderful effect I ever heard of the power of moral causes over the human body, that Lord Anglesey, who has been scarcely out of pain at all for years, has been quite free from his complaint (tic doulourteux) since he has been in Ireland. The excitement of these events, and the influence of that excitement on his nervous system, have produced this effect."—*Greville Memoirs*, Jan. 21, 1831.

any of us shall experience any quiet or happy times for the future.

"The Elections have gone so against us that I give up all idea of successful resistance to our reckless Ministry.

"In this County the conservative Interest has been beaten out of sight. The radical is the Strongest Interest of the day, therefore we must yield to the superior luck of our adversaries, or perhaps to their superior good play. Ingestre carried Hertford gallantly, and Grimston succeeded in his wishes to represent the County— much to Alstone's disappointment, who is a warm radical. What is to happen God alone knows! I think people are very low about things in general. . . .

"There is a report that Stanley is not upon good terms with his Colleagues, as he will not, it is said (I answer for nobody) consent to the spoliation of the Irish Church."

Ingestre: February 10, 1833.

". . . You talked of coming over in the spring? When do you consider that this movement is likely to take place? God knows! you will say; for who can venture to say to-day what will happen to-morrow in your ill-fated Country! Poor dear Ireland, I feel for you as an affectionate and grateful friend.

"What say you to the proceedings of the new and reformed parliament. Surely Lord Althorpe and Lord John Russell must have qualms of conscience, must regret the old system of things when they witness the fanatical disposition of the delegates to parliament? Four days' debate upon a King's speech! ! ! Was such a thing ever heard of! ! O'Connell seems to have thrown off the Mask, and appears in his native Colors, so that, if I mistake not, the Rebel will be confessed at no distant period.

"Were not the subject of too grave and serious a nature, I could laugh at the difficult position into which these Whigs have brought themselves, but alas it is not only themselves they have thus brought into difficulty, trouble and danger, but the whole Nation. Peel seems to have taken a bold, manly, generous line. I hope he will gain some credit, for he has been abundantly reviled by the Ministry and radicals. We must regret the false step, irretrievably false step, of granting Emancipation to the Catholics! I believe the Duke now sees that he made a fatal Mistake. Nothing but force can produce quiet, but what force can subdue a Nation, for now I take it the protestants are from previous neglect and ill-treatment disinclined to the Govt of Lord A., *who they say returns as L.L.* I don't know who would make a better, but his Lordship has not succeeded in rendering the

Country quiet! When one remembers his advice, 'Agitate, Agitate, Agitate,' one is tempted to exclaim, 'How the devil should he?'

"You remember my offering you a place of refuge here, do not imagine the offer was a string of unmeaning words. I honestly meant it, and beg in all sincerity to repeat it now once more. God forbid its being necessary!"

Ingestre: June 20, 1833.

". . . As for politics, let us not mention them! I am tired of the subject. I have taken my seat, but not till the Friday (the last day I could) before I left London.

"I suppose I shall go up when the Irish Church reform Bill comes before the House. I dined with Peel last Saturday. I never saw a more splendid and sumptuous repast in my life. Beautiful and excellent in all its parts. He was in fair spirits. The Duke of W. was one of the Company.

"When in Town I heard that Lord Melbourne would succeed your present Lord Lieutenant. I know not with what Truth!"

Ingestre: June 20, 1833.

". . . We had a most violent Thunderstorm here last week. The Lightning struck a tall poplar tree which you may remember in the grass field near the farm, and altho' it did not affect my Gardener in fact, it drove him and one of his Men against the Wall in the Garden about 3 or two yards from the tree I have named."

Drayton Manor: October 2, 1833.

"I came here this morning for one night. A confounded Justice meeting requires my presence at Penteridge to-morrow. There is hardly anybody in the county, and fewer Justices than are required for the necessary duties of the Magistracy. My friend Monckton and myself work at two places. Yet we are Tories, a proscribed and useless Race.

"The works at this place are getting on rapidly, and upon my word a very handsome house with every conveniency and even magnificence will be constructed. The place you know is not naturally fine or picturesque, but somehow or another it has been so twisted about that it is by no means ugly or dull, as formerly. I like to think that I am perhaps sitting in the room which you perhaps occupied, my good friend, when you were here."

London: May 16, 1834 (?).

"There has been a long interval in our correspondence. I have been in Scotland, and am returned again in good health, having left my beloved child better than I for some time had seen her. The children are all the fondest Grandpapa (that hits you, you old rogue) can wish.

"The Country seems progressing to evil as fast as it can. Rents must fall if things do not mend, and I must go too if such be the Event, so come while you can. My Tenants and I are on the best of terms, and they have not complained, but I know they suffer, and suffering has its term.

"The Government bolstered up by the Tories seems stable—more so indeed than it has been—of themselves they can do nothing, but as our policy is not to turn them out I think we shall be blessed with Whig Rule some time longer unless their internal divisions blow them up, which I should not wonder at. We have a report of their having offered terms to O'Connell. Surely they cannot be so weak, so short-sighted. It is said he has refused their advances. A great man is said to be queerish!"

November 28, 1834.

"Only think, my dear Gregory, that not a line has passed between us since the overthrow of the Whigs. *If* you should like it I hope to see you employed again. If not *I shall like it better*, as it will give me a better chance of seeing you. Will they give Saurin anything? I hope most devoutly that this most excellent Man may receive some mark of Respect, some Tribute of regard for his exemplary conduct when in office.

Lord Rosslyn, it is said, will be your L.L., and I hope Sir Henry Harding your Chief Secretary. No man is fitter than Sir Henry is for that now most arduous situation, and no one can be a better man to succeed than Littleton.

"The King seems to have acted like a wise firm Man. I hear that things *look better daily for us*, and that Lord Brougham has written a Letter to Lord Lyndhurst offering to become one of the Chief Justices at a reduced salary! This I do not, cannot believe. Yet my letters speak of the transaction most confidently."

Ingestre: January 3, 1835.

"I am glad to find that your merits are *thus* acknowledged.

"You will so much better know how to deal with the subject, or object of this letter than I can at such a distance from you, that I think I had better send it to you without any further remark.

"As the days of franking are gone by, I send this without an envelope to save your *Tin*."

[Enclosure]   London: January 2, 1835.

"My dear T,—I write at the express request of Haddington, who implores you to excuse him for thus writing by deputy, but he is wild with business. He is to start to-morrow morning by himself to Dublin.

"He bids me tell you that at the suggestion of Sir R. Peel he earnestly begs you to have the kindness to write to your friend Gregory in Dublin, to request him to put himself in relation with him (Haddington) upon his arrival, and to give him the benefit of his private assistance and counsel in all such personal matters as a new Lord Lieutenant must require to be instructed in *en debutant*.

"Now pray do this, and you will be his and my magnus Apollo.

"Yours most affectionately,
"C. BAGOT."

                                    Ingestre: January 17, 1835.

"How very good-natured of you to go to Dublin. To tell you the truth, not knowing of any communication having passed with you which tended to make you feel that you had not been forgotten, I hardly knew in what terms to write to you, to convey Lord H.'s wishes to have the benefit of your advice.

"That you are gratified I am glad, the more so as I think Peel has shown very distinctly that he really esteems you by conferring the P.C. upon you. You may justly be proud of the distinction, which is alike honourable to both parties.

"Joseph Hume will, I fear, be returned for Middlesex, and I also apprehend that O'Connell will succeed at Dublin. His power has been shaken. If Sir H. Hardinge sticks to him, he will be the Agitator."

                                    Ingestre: March, 1835.

". . . I think that Shaw grilled Dan well. It is, I believe, now admitted that we must talk and speak out as well as our adversaries.

"Peel, I think, rises! He is sure, John T. says, of a majority to-night, but a victory will be almost as bad as a defeat.

"What times we live in!"

                                    Ingestre: March 4, 1835.

". . . Peel appears to be quite equal to the arduous task which he has in hand. I hope, indeed I expect, that Lord Stanley will join him. My Idea is that the Duke will go to the Horse Guards, that Aberdeen will succeed him at the F.O., and Lord Stanley, Aberdeen. This may be visionary, but I suspect it will sooner or later be the case. If I could see Peel and Stanley cordially acting together I should then consider the thing safe.

"I wonder how Lady Haddington will be liked. She is a highly principled virtuous woman, but I fear that neither her appearance or her manners will suit your vivacious people. When known she will be liked and esteemed."

Ingestre: April 10, 1835.

"I cannot find words to express the state of despondency in which the resignation of Peel has cast me.[1] The Game is up as far as mortals are concerned.

"But thank GOD I have a firm reliance in the Almighty's Mercy, and if we are to suffer here, it will, I doubt not, turn all to our ultimate happiness, if we conduct ourselves in heavy hour of Trial and Adversity with propriety and resignation.

"So courage, mon Ami.

"We have addressed our Sovereign and Peel on the occasion.

"We have also formed a Conservative Association, from which I hope we shall derive some strength, and not suffer ourselves to be *be-Whigged,* as this formerly loyal County is now.

"I conclude Haddington has resigned."

Ingestre: May 7, 1835.

". . . By a letter from Haddington, to whom I wrote to congratulate him on not serving under these O'Connell be-ridden Whigs, and on his having gained the good opinion of all that was good and honourable in Ireland, I find he is, like me, warmly attached to your Country. By the by he thanks me for having obtained for him your acquaintance, and, he adds, 'I hope his friendship.'

"What work these O'Connells are making! I am not without hope that it will all work to a good end, although much dirt must be thrown aside before we are safely through our dangers!

"Alvanly has behaved *well.* Mr. O'Connell had a shot more than he ought to have had at him."

---

[1] On the defeat of his Government on the Tithe Bill.

From Lord Haddington to Mr. Gregory

London: May 30, 1835.

"My dear Sir,—Your very kind answer to the very hurried lines I wrote to you on the morning of my departure reached me soon after my arrival here. I wrote in haste, and in a state of mind not very likely to produce an adequate impression of the feelings I wished to convey to you. You will, however, believe that I entertained them very sincerely, that I truly value your friendship and good opinion, and am duly sensible of the advantage I derived from the kindness and frankness with which on several occasions you answered my call on you for your opinion and advice.

"I will not dwell on the feelings with which we left Ireland, and continue to think of the day of our departure. You understand them, I am quite sure, and will believe me when I say that Ireland is never out of our anxious and painful thoughts, tho' there is much to dwell upon that is deeply gratifying to us. The kindness we met with during our stay and on our coming away was too remarkable ever to be forgotten, or to be remembered during life without gratitude and delight. But these very feelings aggravate the painful necessity with which we think of the present position and future prospects of a country doomed, it would seem, never to be at peace, and yet requiring but Peace to make it one of the happiest and most flourishing regions in the world.

"I will leave that subject, however, as I think it will be more agreeable to you to hear about the state of things in this part of the world than to read reflections and lamentations about your own Country, from one whose knowledge is so imperfect as compared with your own as to her real state.

"If speculations on politics have ever been doubtful, true it is that under the reform régime they are more uncertain than ever. My speculation, however, is, that the present Government will outlive the Session. In the first place I think they are determined to do so, and that is no small help to a party not overburdened with high feelings of honour, nor embarrassed by much political principle of a very squeamish character. In the second place it is obviously not in Peel's intention to press them with a view of turning them out. He will deal with their measures, but they are determined to afford him very few measures to deal withal. They have unblushingly thrown everything overboard, and the radicals and dissenters are too wise in their generation not to play into their hands and wait their time, by which they diminish the chance of a Tory resurrection, and increase that of ultimate radical preponderance and domination.

"They will not quarrel among themselves, because pressure from their Radical allies is the only thing likely to create dissension, and to that, during the Session at least, they will not be exposed. They will keep the O'Connell influence as much as possible in the background, and the Daniel himself will in that respect play into their hands. Satisfied with its real and vital existence, he will be content not to display it in the meantime, reserving himself for the moment when its manifestation will not endanger the Government and help the Conservative cause.

"They will produce nothing of importance but the corporation question for England and Wales, and the Irish Tythe Bill. The first they will carry. The second is their difficulty, and offers the only chance of their overthrow. I think they will overcome the difficulty. If Peel (which is very likely to happen) defeats their appropriation clause they will submit and take the Bill without it. If he does not succeed in this, and if they succeed in sending it to the Lords in the shape of a money Bill, the Lords will throw it out altogether. If it comes to the Lords in such a shape that they can alter it, they will return it to the Commons without the obnoxious clause. In either case they will acquiesce, in the one, throwing the loss of the Bill on the Lords, in the other abusing them for its mutilation, by which they will have deprived it of its most valuable principle. If they outlive the Session—what are their future prospects—and what are ours?

"Into this speculation I cannot enter—it depends too much on the chapter of accidents. But outliving the Session they outlive the present danger—which in these times is all that a Government can be expected to perform.

"In the mean time Conservative feeling is daily increasing in England. Were England only the question I am not sure that I should not wish these Gentlemen to keep their places till next Session. What overpowers every other consideration in my mind is Ireland. What may they not have done in that devoted land by next Spring? I hate to think of it, and will say no more about it.

"Peel does not wish to be exposed to the chance of being again compell'd to attempt to govern with a minority. In this no one can blame him, but I see little prospect in the course of the next six weeks or two months of anything arising to present him with a majority of the present House of Commons on which he can rely.

"In short, my dear Sir, we are under the régime of that blessed Act which has made over the fortunes and the interests of this great nation to that class that is at once the most dangerous in its principles and the most infatuated in the plenitude of its ignorance and presumption.

"I hope we shall get away to Scotland next Wednesday. We certainly shall if Londonderry will but present the famous Down petition on Tuesday. I have already deferred my departure on that account.

"I shall be happy to hear from you if you have anything to tell me, and shall be obliged to you to enlighten me on the practical working of the existing state of things in Ireland. I am sorry to see in your letter that Miss Gregory has been called to the country by a serious accident that has befallen Lady Castlemaine. I hope her recovery is as favourable as that of Mr. Saurin, to whom I beg you will present my best and kindest regards.

"Lady H. sends you her best regards and good wishes, and I am ever my dear Sir, Most sincerely yours,

"HADDINGTON."

Lord Talbot to Mr. Gregory

London: 16 June 1835.

". . . Yes, I was desponding at what I deemed the rapid advance of revolution! As it came a little nearer home than usual you will excuse it. In the potteries the custom is to engage workmen at stated fixed prices for a given term, say 6, 9, or 12 months. It so happened that a Mr. Hawley agreed with these men for what appeared equitable—in three Months they were under *the order of the Trades Unions* (which prevail there) turned out for advance of Wages. Hawley had 18 of them before the Magistrates, who committed the whole of the 18 to prison courageously and legally for 3 months.

"I had taken the precaution to have a troop of Cavalry at Stowe ready to protect the Magistrates—this was *known* tho' the Troops did not make their appearance. *No row ensued*!

"Well, a petition signed by 7,000 people (all Unionists I hear) was sent up to Lord John Russell. He wrote me word that the Military have been frequently called in to our County—talked of the Petition and of establishing a stipendiary Magistracy.

"I replied that the Military had never to my knowledge been called in without justifiable reasons—and that the Magistracy had never been complained of to me. *The weakness* of our chief—this listening to or proclaiming to me that he meant favourably to consider the petition, which is in truth only levelled at those

Men who had the Courage to resist the Unions and to do their duty, I confess alarmed me. Supported as I ever have been, and by no one more effectually and generously than by 'Melbourne,' I dare put myself in the Breach, but if I am to be left in the Lurch by those whose Duty it is to stand by the Civil Power, I confess I tremble for the result. I have left my name with Lord John since my arrival, but have not been sent for yet. Peel is in high force and spirits. He laughs, and *so will I*, at the imbecility (he did not *say so,* it is merely an inference which from his cheerfulness I have drawn myself) of this untalented un——Ministry.

"By the way, Peel told me how completely your dear Boy[1] distinguished himself at Harrow the other day. Peel says he surprised *him*. Thus do you reap a highly gratifying regard for your sacrifices in his favour. May William's future career gild your remaining Years, my dear friend, with comfort, and the high gratification of beholding his success.

"Lord Haddington is gone to Scotland. Your L.L. is an agreeable Man, and his Lady a most amiable, excellent person. She was bred a Tory. The prevailing opinion here is that these people will stay in. Why? Because they will do nothing. I am glad to hear from a Bishop that the Church Commission was likely to go on well notwithstanding the influx of new Members. . . ."

Ingestre: Sept. 13, 1835.
"I think People were getting less angry about Peel. When I wrote the universal cry was even among our enemies, Peel has thrown the Lords over. In the city as I believe I told you, the universal belief was (this is too strong, I will not say *universal belief,* but the *report* was current on change) that he had deserted his party. All this was gall to me, who knew the impossibility of the fact, but who also know how little confidential he was in his intercourse with his friends. I know, too, that he had left London without communicating to the Duke his opinion as to what the Lords should do with the Municipal Reform Bill—and angry I was told that evidence was to be called before the House. All this quite chafed me. I was miserable at hearing Men I knew abusing Sir Robert. What could anyone say who had voted as we did upon the question. I hope, however, his speech at Tamworth has done him good with our friends, and that mutual confidence, if it ever was shaken among the Leaders, will be restored among us."

[1] Mr. Gregory's grandson, afterwards the Right Hon. Sir William Gregory.

The last letter I will give from Mr. Gregory's letter-box is from the Harrow grandson of whom he was so proud.

Harrow: July 20, 1835.

"My dear Grandfather,—I am going to inflict on you a shocking task, namely to get a number of copies of the *Harrow Magazine*!!! sold in Ireland. This great and interesting work was planned this quarter, and I am happy to say that you, I am sure, will like our first number. A great number of clever articles have been written, and we are all confident that it will be of the greatest advantage to the school, without in the least interrupting the studies, which latter effect has been produced by the publication being issued only three times a year. I have had the great honour done me of being unanimously elected president, and I am of course most deeply interested as to its ultimate success. . . .

"Do make *all* and *every* friend of yours buy it, as nobody in Dublin will refuse you except Dan O'Connell, and you know all but him and Ruthven, and the price is *only* half a crown. It will be published about the middle of the Holydays by Murray we expect, we have not yet, however, determined by whom. . . .

"Your affect. Grandson

"W. H. GREGORY.

"P.S. We are sadly deficient in English poetry, every fellow is so modest that he does not like to write any, and they have insisted on my composing an ode on the death of Zumalacarrequé. What am I to do, my principles are entirely against him. I proposed to begin thus:

O! Zumalacarreguy
Thou wert the Christino's plaguey!

but they were very angry at such profanation."

So the generations come and go, and the whirligig of time brings in his revenges. A son of Lord Talbot became a Canon of the Church of Rome. The "dear boy at Harrow" broke from the Tory traditions of his grandfather, made friends with Dan O'Connell, and helped to disestablish the Church of Ireland. To-day, it is Mr. Gregory's great-grandson who is a Harrow boy, whose mother hopes he may put into the work he has to do as much good will as she has brought to this self-imposed task of hers.

APPENDIX

To *The Times*, 12 August, 1907.

Sir,—The enclosed letter from Major Poppleton, 53rd Regiment, who had charge of Napoleon's person at St. Helena from his first being sent there till 1817, may interest some of your readers. It was written to the Right Hon. William Gregory, at that time Under-Secretary for Ireland. These two letters were not among the contents of "Mr. Gregory's Letter Box," which I edited some years ago, or I should have used them then. I found them the other day in a pocket-book apart.

We still possess the lock of Napoleon's hair, and also a Cross of the Legion of Honour given by Napoleon to Major Poppleton.

Yours faithfully,

AUGUSTA GREGORY.

Coole-park, Gort, county Galway, Aug. 4

St. Helena, 9th April, 1817.

My dear Sir,—I return you many thanks for the trouble you have had with my correspondence—any letter addressed to you I feel confident of its safety and am greatly obliged by the liberty. When Buonaparte first arrived at Longwood, he rose early, mounted his horse, returned to breakfast about 9, afterwards confined himself to his room, but constantly complaining of the humidity of his residence—he said he was either in the clouds, fog, and rain or under a burning sun. In the evening he saw most people who wished to be introduced. The carriage was always ready for him at that time, and he frequently asked some visitor or other who happened to be there to take an airing with him, always extremely condescending and affable. I never saw him in a rage but once, and that was in consequence of a communication made to him by the Governor and in the presence of the Admiral (by order of the Minister, I presume)—they both left him in consequence of what he said and what I cannot repeat; from that day to this the Governor has never seen him—this occurred many months since.

His *rencontre* with me is not without foundation, but mis-

215

represented. I neither spoke to him or he to me. I sent a very polite message to him in plain terms that when I rode with him I expected to be treated as a British officer and a gentleman, not as his servant, the light in which his suite seemed to think me. This I have since found out was wilfully misstated to him—nothing further took place, and we have not rode together since. After Admiral Sir G. Cockburn left us fresh restrictions were placed upon him; from this period he never quitted Longwood—for many weeks he never quitted his room—within a very short period only he has quitted the house for a walk in the garden. He bears his confinement most heroically—amuses himself in writing his own history, assisted by his officers, and reading, and is always happy to get hold of any book that abuses him, even in the most gross language. Many people call him sulky—what he was formerly I know not, but since I have known him he does not deserve such an appellation—very few would have borne so sudden a change of fortune with the stoicism he has. His officers were always full of complaints and never pleased—from him no complaints ever came, except regarding the restrictions which deprived him of the exercise he was accustomed to and injured his health.

He is lustier than he was and much paler, but altogether not in bad health. He was very unwell at one time in consequence of his confining himself to his house and room, but never could be persuaded to take medicine. He would diet himself and go without food for many hours, but nothing more.

He certainly has a most dreadful antipathy to the Governor. He wished everything to remain in the same state as when Sir G. Cockburn was here; this would not be granted, and in consequence he refuses to see any one passed to Longwood by the Governor, says he will not be stared at or shown as an elephant, as he himself terms it. Be assured all reports of his escape from St. Helena must ever be false. In the first place I must prove false to my trust, as I myself and the surgeon who attends him are the only two persons who absolutely know he is there, as he is not seen by others for frequently long periods. I report his presence morning and evening. I am very little better than a prisoner myself. He cannot quit Longwood without my knowing it. In the next place he has now lost all activity of body, takes his bath very frequently—has confined himself to his house and room for so long a time that he could not walk a mile—complains always of the damp and of the least wind—and his descending any of the precipices surrounding this island to escape by a boat is morally impossible. His habit of body alone would render such an attempt abortive. No vessel can be within 60 miles (afternoon) of the island without being seen in fine weather, and no vessel in thick weather would approach the island with the idea of taking him away. We must be regularly besieged and taken, that only will release Buonaparte. Mine is a situation of great responsibility, but I do not expect to retain it—I have no interest, and I daresay Ministers have plenty of friends of their own. I have memorialed for promotion, but do not expect to succeed. Admiral and Lady Malcomb and Buonaparte are on the best of terms. He receives their visits when they choose to call upon him, and indeed any of his old acquaintances. But the Governor and his Staff are out of his book. Lady Malcomb played at chess with him the other day. He does not play well according to my knowledge of the game. All those who do see him are greatly surprised, expecting to see a morose and unpleasant man from hearsay, but they find him just the contrary. Las Casas when here has often given me most extraordinary accounts of the Tallents of Buonaparte. I listened to his description as I would to a noted and determined flatterer. I gave Nap. credit for a great deal certainly, or he never could have been what he was, but the more I see of him the more I am inclined to credit what I thought the courtierlike description of Las Casas or a Frenchman. You cannot deceive him, he penetrates the every motive and action of another. His surgeon, Dr. O'M., often repeats his conversation. His language is forcible and his meaning conveyed in fewer words than I ever heard or read of. I know his opinions and reasons for a few of the most extraordinary events of his life in which he is held up as a monster of barbarity—if he is to be believed he refutes some and gives reasons for others. My letter is written in a hurry and I fear very carelessly, but you must excuse me, I cannot boast of the Tallents of Buonaparte; but I certainly write a more intelligible hand than he does, that I'll give myself credit for. The newspaper accounts are not to be believed, the people in the town know little or nothing of him, and their descriptions to the passengers in ships are ridiculous. Occupied as your time is, I am sure the reading of this will give you but little pleasure—should it, I shall be repaid. I have now only to beg of you to confine the contents of this to yourself, however uninteresting. I believe it is wished at home that little should be said of this one great personage—remember my request. With best compliments to Lady Anne, your son, and a Miss O'Hara that was, believe most truly yours,

J.P.

26 June, St. Helena.

My dear Sir,—The enclosed is rather a weighty concern and requires a weighty apology.

Napoleon continues as when I last wrote to you. His answer to Lord Bathurst I presume will reach England at the same time this does.

My situation at present is no sinecure. Lord Amherst not yet arrived, but may before this letter leaves the island. Admiral Plumpir not arrived at the above date, but expected hourly.

Napoleon is perfectly quiet. Lady Malcomb was with him a few days since. She is about to quit this Rock; 'tis really a hideous spot.

The part allotted for Napoleon is undoubtedly the healthiest, but the most dreary—the disagreement between him and the Governor and the additional restrictions keep him to the house or nearly so. He is a most extraordinary man, and really has shown great fortitude—there is a sort of secrecy attempted to be kept up, however, that is morally impossible—and such suspicion of anything that concerns Buonaparte that it is perfect misery— however it must have an end.

The only recompense I have to offer you for the trouble I give you is a small part of Napoleon's hair, if it is worth the acceptance of Lady Anne. Sartini, who does me the honour to notice me, cuts Napoleon's hair always, and when he left gave me the enclosed. I wish they would give me half the allowance of the Supreme Head here and take away all the Staff. I'd be answerable for Napoleon.

Most faithfully yours,

J. POPPLETON.

Wm. Gregory, Esq., &c., &c., Castle, Dublin.

INDEX

Note: Names in the text are spelled as in the 1898 edition of this book, but for the purposes of the index, the correct or more commonly used spellings are used here. A peer, whose title changed during his lifetime, is normally entered under that by which he was normally known during the period covered by this book; for example, the 2nd Marquess of Anglesey only succeeded to the title in 1854, and appears in this index as the Earl of Uxbridge. There is occasionally some lack of uniformity amongst reference books regarding dates of birth, so I have taken the dates from those works I believe to be the most trustworthy. A list of works used appears at the end of the index.

COLIN SMYTHE

219

PRINCIPAL REFERENCE WORKS USED

Boylan, Henry, *A Dictionary of Irish Biography*, Dublin, Gill & Macmillan, 1978.

Burke, Sir Bernard, *A Genealogical History of the Dormant, Abeyant, Forfeited, and Extinct Peerages of the British Empire* (commonly called *Burke's Dormant and Extinct Peerages*), 1883, reprinted Baltimore, Genealogical Publishing Co., 1978.

Burke's Irish Family Records, London, Burke's Peerage, 1976.

Burke's Peerage, Baronetage & Knightage, London, Burke's Peerage, 1938.

Chaplin, Arnold, *A St. Helena Who's Who*, London, Arthur L. Humphreys, 1919.

Cokayne, G. E. (editor), *The Complete Peerage*, 1887–98, new edition, revised and much enlarged by Vicary Gibbs, H. A. Doubleday, Duncan Warren, Lord Howard de Walden and Geoffrey H. White, London, St. Catherine Press, 1910–59, 13 vols., reprinted 1981.

Crone, J. S., *Concise Dictionary of Irish Biography*, Dublin, Talbot Press, 1928, revised 1937.

Dictionary of National Biography (Compact Edition), Oxford University Press, 1975.

Haydn, Joseph, *Haydn's Book of Dignities*, 1894, reprinted Baltimore, Genealogical Publishing Co., 1970.

Hickey, D. H., & J. E. Doherty, *A Dictionary of Irish History since 1800*, Dublin, Gill & Macmillan, 1980, and Totowa (N.J.), Barnes & Noble Books, 1981.

Judd IV, Gerritt P., *Members of Parliament 1734–1832*, Yale University Press, 1955.

Pine, L. G., *New Extinct Peerage 1884–1971*, London, Heraldry Today, 1972.

Powicke, Sir F. Maurice, & E. P. Fryde, *Handbook of British Chronology*, London, Royal Historical Society, 1961.

Stenton, M. (editor), *Who's Who of British Members of Parliament*, Vol. I., 1832–1885, Hassocks (Sussex), Harvester Press, & Atlantic Highlands (N.J.), Humanities Press, 1976.

Thomas, Joseph, *Lippincott's Pronouncing Dictionary of Biography & Mythology*, Philadelphia & London, Lippincott & Co., 1915.

Vincent, Benjamin, *Haydn's Dictionary of Dates*, London, Ward Lock, 1910.

Walker, B. M., *Parliamentary Election Results in Ireland 1801–1922*, Dublin, Royal Irish Academy, 1978.

Webb, Alfred, *A Compendium of Irish Biography*, 1878, reprinted New York, Lemma Publishing Corp., 1970.

ERRATA AND ADDENDA

p. 51   8 lines up   for Castsle, read Castle

p. 74   4 lines up   correct as 1898 edition, but probably should be covered-in for covered him

p. 91   14 lines up   correct as 1898 edition, but Ebrington should read Elrington

p. 101   line 27   for liberities read liberties

p. 107   line 10   for aagin read again

p. 117   line 13   close quotation marks after *lux*

p. 127   line 17   correct as 1898 edition, but Townsand should read Townsend

p. 177   line 14   for Gergory, read Gregory

p. 204   3 lines up   for tic doulourteux, read tic douloureux

INDEX

243

p. 226 FLYN, Mr. in text, but must be FINN, William Francis (1789-1862, M.P. for Co. Kilkenny 1832-37, married O'Connell's sister Alicia in 1812)

FREMANTLE, Sir William Henry, insert after dates, resident secretary for Ireland 1789-1800, M.P. for Enniskillen 1806-06, Harwich 1806-07, Saltash 1807-08, Tain burghs 1808-12, Buckingham borough 1812-27, supporter of Catholic Emancipation, Kt. 1827), 120

GORT, for Verecker, read Vereker. The exact place of his engagement with the French was at Collooney, Co. Sligo, not Killala

p. 227 GOULBURN, Henry, for Secretary for Ireland, read Chief Secretary for Ireland

GREY, Charles Grey, for Charles Grey, 2nd Earl, read Charles, 2nd Earl, and for 107 read 108

p. 228 HOBHOUSE, for Secretary for Ireland 1832-33, read Chief Secretary for Ireland 1833

p. 229 INSURRECTION Acts, insert (54 Geo. III, c. 180, and 3 Geo. IV, c. 1)

IRISH Church Temporalities Act, insert (3 & 4 Will. IV, c. 37)

p. 231 LITTLEHALES, Sir Edward, was military under-secretary for Ireland. Delete query entry about Joseph Littledale

LLOYD, Dr. insert Bartholemew (1772-1837, Professor of Mathematics, Natural and Experimental Philosophy, and Greek at T.C.D., Provost 1831-37)

LOUIS XVIII delete entry

MAHON, Nicholas, insert (c. 1746-1841, Dublin woollen merchant, active in Catholic Emancipation movement, and a delegate to the Catholic Convention of 1792)

MAHON, Charles James Patrick, read, The O'Gorman Mahon

p. 232 read MANNERS-Sutton, Charles

MANSELL, Dr. for 165, read 168

MANDERS, Alderman, insert (probably Richard Manders, Lord Mayor of Dublin 1801-02)

MORGAN, Lady, read *O'Donnell*, 8

MORLEY, Mr., insert John (1838-1923, Chief Secretary for Ireland 1886, 1892-95, cr. Viscount Morley of Blackburn 1908)

for MOUNT CASHEL, read MOUNTCASHELL

for MOUNT EARL, read MOUNT-EARL

p. 233 O'CONNOR, Arthur, insert after date, a prominent United Irishman, and after Philipstown 1791-95, imprisoned in 1798, freed and went to France 1802, in 1804 appointed General of Division in French Army, strongly opposed to O'Connell and his policies.

O'CONNOR, Mrs. A. for Condorset, read Condorcet

p. 234 PEACE Preservation Act, correctly, Peel's police measure of 1814 (54 Geo. III, c. 131), and add page refs. 41, 89-90

p. 235 PIGOTT, correctly Richard Pigott (?1828-89, journalist and forger of the 'Parnell' letters investigated by Special Commission 1888-90)

REBELLION of 1789, read 1798

p. 236 REFORM Bill for 1831 read 1832 and add page refs. 178-79, 200-02

RIOTOUS Assemblies Act, delete entry

RUSSELL, Lord John, for 31 read 32

p. 237 SHAW, Mr. almost certainly Frederick Shaw (1799-1876, M.P. for Dublin City 1830-31, 1832, Dublin University 1832-48, succeeded as 3rd Bart. in 1869)

SMITH, Sir (William) Sydney, far more likely the reference must be to Rev. Sydney Smith (1771-1845, cr. a Canon of St. Paul's Cathedral 1831, renowned for his wit, much involved in Catholic Emancipation and church reform)

p. 238 SMYTH, Robert, correct entry to read (1777-186?, High Sheriff of Co. Westmeath 1823, M.P. for Co. Westmeath 1824-26)

STANLEY OF ALDERLEY, correctly Edward Geoffrey Smith Stanley (1799-1869 Chief Secretary for Ireland 1830-33, 14th Earl of Derby from 1851, called Lord Stanley, when his father succeeded to the Earldom in 1834, M.P. for Stockbridge 1822-26, Preston 1826-30, Windsor 1831-32, North Lancashire 1832-44, when summoned to the House of Lords for his father's barony. Prime Minister 1852, 1858 and 1866)

p. 240 TALLEYRAND, for PERIGOLD, read PERIGORD

WARBURTON, Major, insert George, and Inspector General of Constabulary for Connacht 1825

WELLINGTON, insert comma after title

WILCOX, Mr. see WILLCOCKS

p. 241 WILLCOCKS, Major, insert page references 65, 66 and Christian name Richard

WILSON, Mr. insert Edward (a magistrate)

WOLFE, Col. insert (probably John Wolfe of Forenaghts, Co. Kildare 1745-1816, High Sheriff Co. Kildare 1779, Freeman of Dublin 1775, Colonel Kildare Militia, and M.P. for Kildare)

WYNN, Mr. insert Charles Watkin Williams Wynn (1775-1850, M.P. for Montgomeryshire 1799-1850, President of the Board of Control 1822-28)

WYNNE, Owen, for burgh, read borough

YOUNG, Arthur, insert, author of *A Tour in Ireland* (1780)

p. 241 The reprint of G. E. Cokayne's *Complete Peerage* will appear in 1982.

p. 242 Gerritt P. Judd IV's *Members of Parliament 1734-1832* was reprinted by the Shoe String Press (Hamden, Conn.) in 1972.

I am most grateful to Richard Hawkins of the New History of Ireland project organised under the auspices of the Royal Irish Academy for most of the above information.

COLIN SMYTHE.